The United States
and the Americas

THE AMERICAN ASSEMBLY was established by Dwight D. Eisenhower at Columbia University in 1950. Each year it holds at least two nonpartisan meetings that give rise to authoritative books that illuminate issues of United States policy.

An affiliate of Columbia, the Assembly is a national, educational institution incorporated in the state of New York.

The Assembly seeks to provide information, stimulate discussion, and evoke independent conclusions on matters of vital public interest.

CONTRIBUTORS

MARIO BAEZA, TCW/Latin America Partners, L.L.C.

NANCY BIRDSALL, Inter-American Development Bank

JORGE I. DOMÍNGUEZ, Harvard University

ALBERT FISHLOW, Council on Foreign Relations

GARY C. HUFBAUER, Council on Foreign Relations

JAMES JONES, Former U.S. ambassador to Mexico

BARBARA R. KOTSCHWAR, Organization of American Studies

ABRAHAM F. LOWENTHAL, Pacific Council on International Policy

NORA LUSTIG, Inter-American Development Bank

LESLEY O'CONNELL, Inter-American Development Bank

SUSAN KAUFMAN PURCELL, Americas Society

JEFFREY J. SCHOTT, Institute for International Economics

PETER H. SMITH, University of California, San Diego

SIDNEY WEINTRAUB, Center for Strategic and International
  Studies

THE AMERICAN ASSEMBLY

Columbia University

The United States and the Americas

A Twenty-First Century View

Albert Fishlow and James Jones

Editors

W. W. Norton & Company

New York • London

This book is composed in Baskerville
Composition and manufacturing by The Haddon Craftsmen, Inc.

Library of Congress Cataloging-in-Publication Data
The United States and the Americas : a 21st century view / Albert
  Fishlow and James Jones, editors.
        p.   cm.
    Includes bibliographical references and index.
    ISBN 0-393-97447-2 (pbk.)
      1. Latin America—Relations—United States—Forecasting.
    2. United States—Relations—Latin America—Forecasting.
    I. Fishlow, Albert.   II. Jones, James.
    F1418.U654   1999
    303.48'27308—dc21   98-56622
                                                              CIP

W. W. Norton & Company, Inc., 500 Fifth Avenue, New York, N.Y. 10110
http://www.wwnorton.com

W. W. Norton & Company Ltd., 10 Coptic Street, London WC1A 1PU

1 2 3 4 5 6 7 8 9 0

Contents

Preface

This volume was prepared as background reading for an American Assembly on the Future of the Western Hemisphere and U.S. National Interests held at the end of May 1998. This was a particularly opportune time. President Clinton had just returned from his third visit to Latin America as president, to attend the second Summit of the Americas held in Santiago, Chile. Although the United States did not have fast-track authority, the process of regional integration did appear to be moving forward. Further, the region was demonstrating its new maturity and commitment to continuing reform. Despite the Asian financial crisis, Latin America was still making impressive progress. In addition, new hemispheric problems were being addressed, including those most vital to the United States, such as drug trafficking, illegal immigration, and corruption. Perhaps most relevantly for many in this country, U.S. trade with Latin America was increasing faster than with any other region of the world.

There had not been a similar concentration of attention on the Americas since the 1960s. Nonetheless, the United States appeared to lack a coherent strategy for the region. Moreover, there was little or no public consensus on what that policy should be. It is odd that such a policy vacuum concerning the Americas endures while the region is receiving so much attention and while the real American stakes and economic interests in the hemisphere appear to be growing dramatically.

This unusual combination of conflicting circumstances afforded a timely challenge, and an opportunity, on which The American Assembly sought to build in holding the initial Assembly in 1998, as part of a much larger and continuing effort.

The overall cochairs for this series are **Carla Hills,** chair and CEO of Hills & Company and former U.S. special trade representative and secretary of the Department of Housing and Urban Development, and **Paul A. Volcker,** most recently chair of James D. Wolfensohn, Inc. and a member of The American Assembly's board.

The editors of this volume are **Dr. Albert Fishlow,** who is the Paul A. Volcker senior fellow for international economics at the Council on Foreign Relations, and **James Jones,** formerly the U.S. ambassador to Mexico.

The project leadership brought together the very distinguished authors of the various papers in this volume, which places tomorrow's critical questions within the context of historical perspective. Their names and biographies are set out within the volume.

The American Assembly meeting for which this volume was commissioned was part of a four-phase project, that included the following elements:

Phase I was high-level consultations carried out by the project leadership with leaders from throughout the hemisphere who reviewed early drafts of some of these papers and helped in the formulation of the policy questions that were discussed in Phase II.

Phase II was The American Assembly at Arden House in May of 1998 at which a broadly representative group of U.S. national leaders convened to prepare a statement concerning U.S. national interests. That statement and list of participants are included in this book. This volume was sent to all participants some weeks prior to the Assembly.

The chapters in this volume benefited from a critique by a working group organized by the Council on Foreign Relations, after which they were revised by their author(s). The Assembly expresses its appreciation to the Council for this valuable collaboration.

Phase III of this project will be a truly *American* Assembly, a gathering in 1999 of high-level representatives from all of the major countries and regions of the hemisphere, at which participants will seek to prepare a statement of shared vision for what the future of the hemisphere ought to be in about twenty-five years. This hemisphere-wide Assembly—and also Phase IV—will be cochaired by **Carla Hills** and **Paul Volcker,** together with **Enrique Iglesias,** president of the Inter-American Development Bank, **Cesar Gaviria,** secretary general of the Organization of American States, and **Jose Antonio Ocampo,** executive secretary of the U.N. Economic Commission for Latin America in the Caribbean. We are in the process of identifying cosponsoring institutions in each of the hemisphere countries and regions whose leaders will form an advisory group, under the leadership of our cochairs, to design this Assembly as well as the Phase IV programs.

Phase IV will be a series of regional American Assemblies—replicas of the 1998 Arden House event—but organized and held locally by local organizations throughout the hemisphere. For example, we anticipate American Assemblies in the United States to be held in the West, Southwest, Southeast, Northeast, and Midwest. Similarly we are identifying the organizations that will be our partners and local hosts for Assemblies in each of the largest countries in the hemisphere and also for one to be held in the Caribbean and one in Central America.

The American Assembly is grateful to those organizations and individuals who by their generous contributions made this program possible:

- The Tinker Foundation
- The William & Flora Hewlett Foundation
- David Rockefeller.

We also appreciate the contribution by the Alex C. Walker Educational & Charitable Foundation.

As in all publications of The American Assembly, the views expressed are those of the individuals writing each chapter, and do not necessarily reflect the views of the Assembly, nor of any of the organizations and individuals listed above or listed as participants in any Assembly activity.

The American Assembly believes that this volume is being published at a singularly appropriate moment. A national dialogue on the growing stake of the United States in the hemisphere is not being advanced as effectively as it might, perhaps due to the lack of a coherent policy that is understood and agreed to by a majority of American citizens. It is our hope that this volume, and the various future programs in this series, will help to stimulate a national dialogue in the United States that can lead to more positive results, including a shared hemispheric vision that is in all of our national interests.

Daniel A. Sharp
President and CEO
The American Assembly

The United States
and the Americas

1

The Western Hemisphere Relation: Quo Vadis?

ALBERT FISHLOW

Introduction

In this chapter, I seek to do three things. First, I set out the changing pattern of trade and foreign investment between the United States and Latin America over the course of a century. Second, I focus especially on the policies of the recent past, emphasizing the efforts of the United States to lead in the establishment of a free trade agreement incorporating the Western Hemisphere as a whole. Third, by way of conclusion, I review the range of current issues pending, now that the Santiago Summit has been held.

The story of the past is relevant in its continuing demonstration of the rising and waning power of hemispheric emphasis. Redis-

ALBERT FISHLOW is Paul A. Volcker senior fellow for international economics at the Council on Foreign Relations. For many years he was a professor of economics at the University of California, Berkeley, serving as department chair and the first dean of International and Area Studies. In 1975–76 Professor Fishlow served as the deputy assistant secretary of state for Inter-American Affairs, and he has published extensively and actively served on many groups associated with inter-American affairs.

covery of Latin America by the United States always comes as a policy novelty. But so, too, comes the reality of a policy stage for the United States that inevitably is broader. Hence the constant pressures of regionalism and globalism, even in early days, before such characterizations became common.

The 1990s are no different. Regionalism was reinvented by President Bush in an effort to elicit a response from Europe and Japan to push forward the Uruguay Round of multilateral trade negotiations, much postponed from its original target date. But surprisingly, Mexico read Bush's speech and acted upon it, thereby making NAFTA into a reality even while multilateral negotiations went forward. President Clinton took the further initiative of supporting its ratification during the 1992 campaign, thereby disappointing several Democrats, led by Richard Gephardt, less persuaded of the virtue of expanding trade with poorer neighbors. The subsequent Miami Summit elaborated the possibility of hemispheric trade. But the expiration of "fast-track" at the end of 1993, and failure to secure extension, has again reopened the question.

What to do about U.S. policy toward the hemisphere has again become a highly relevant subject. I venture some brief suggestions about future policy in the conclusion.

Early History

The "Western Hemisphere Idea" has been an ultimate basis for U.S. policy toward Latin America for more than a century. From its beginnings in the 1880s, there have been two bases for such a view, two bases that recur with constancy. On one side there was the recognition that historical consequence "imposes upon us a different relation to those peoples than that which we hold to other nations." Both of the halves of the continent, after all, had managed independence far before the great majority of modern countries. And on the other, economics had arisen as a motivation: this was the moment when the United States emerged as the principal industrial power of the world, and yet its engagement with its neighbors, beginning rapid expansion, was much smaller than the European presence.

Congress approved a Pan-American Conference in Washington in 1889–90 to discuss the creation of a regional customs union. Latin America was opposed, and so the matter ended then. But the question of U.S. engagement in the emerging economy of the region persisted, through foreign investment, concentrated in Mexico; acquisition of Cuba in the war with Spain in 1898; and the assertion of a much more active foreign policy in the Roosevelt era. Indeed, by 1904, formally for the first time, the Roosevelt Corollary to the Monroe Doctrine established a unilateral responsibility for the United States in the region as a whole in these words:

> In the Western Hemisphere the adherence of the United States to the Monroe Doctrine may force the United States, however reluctantly, in flagrant cases of wrongdoing or impotence, to the exercise of an international police power.

This was already reality, as the United States progressively increased its economic position.

By 1914 the United States already held the largest foreign investment stake in the Caribbean and Mexico, although it lagged far behind the British presence in the region as a whole. By 1930 U.S. investment abroad aggregated $15 billion, of which a third was in Latin America; but note that almost half of direct investment was concentrated in the region.

There was a corresponding realignment of trade flows. Between 1913 and 1929 the percentage of Latin American imports supplied from the U.S. increased from 24 to 39 percent. Nor was this a result of dominance in the nearby countries: excluding Cuba and Mexico, the gain went from 19 to 34 percent. On the other side of the accounts, there was a corresponding, but smaller, expansion. The share of Latin American exports to the United States grew from 30 to 34 percent; excluding Mexico and Cuba, the gain was a greater proportional increase from 16 to 26 percent.

However, the greater U.S. growth, and its continuing diversification, provided an early indication of asymmetry. Latin American imports did not increase their market share, remaining at 25 percent and increasing slightly from 16 to 20 percent when Cuba and Mexico are excluded. The importance of the Latin American market to U.S. producers did not multiply either. It rose from 14 to 19 percent of total U.S. exports, and from 10 to 14 percent when Cuba and Mexico are excluded.

Over the same interval, as U.S. economic presence became more significant, the United States first indulged in a series of regular interventions in the region in Mexico and the Caribbean. This evolving hegemony provoked an internal debate about the extent of imperialism. Outside, Pan-Americanism became for the Latin American countries in the period after World War I an attempt to defend against increasing U.S. power. A formal effort, supported by thirteen of the Latin American states in 1928 at the Havana Pan-America Conference, to prohibit military intervention within the hemisphere, failed. It provoked a debate "so productive of ill feeling and bad language that the minutes of the meeting had to be re-written." This determination to find a way to bind the rapidly evolving United States has become a virtual principle of Latin American policy within the subsequent twentieth century.

U.S. policies eased thereafter, during the Great Depression and World War II. The Good Neighbor Policy of the Roosevelt administration was precisely that. It involved more than U.S. acceptance of the principle of nonintervention in the Montevideo meeting in 1933. The Platt Amendment limiting Cuba was removed in 1934. U.S. Marines were withdrawn from Haiti, and control over the National Bank was terminated. Responses to expropriations of U.S. petroleum interests in Bolivia and Mexico in the late 1930s were more sympathetic than simple assertion of inviolable property rights. Equally, the hemisphere became the object of Cordell Hull's reciprocal trade program. Not irrelevantly, that was partially in response to increasing German and Japanese competition. The Export-Import Bank, set up in 1934, focused especially on Latin American trade during the 1930s, although its total disbursements were quite small, and principally directed to Cuba and Brazil.

Overall, economic interdependence was a yet unenunciated doctrine at this time. The Good Neighbor Policy was a political tool, not an instrument to deal with economic aspirations. And the economies of the region, in fact, thrived under the import substitution regime that was the product of lowered exports, lack of access to capital goods, and high levels of domestic protection. The war extended that period of lack of competitive imports, but this time with growing exports and accumulating reserves. Not surprisingly, the paramount U.S. interest was assuring access to a continuing supply of raw materials at low prices. A more compelling version was stated by Nelson Rockefeller in 1940:

> If the United States is to maintain its security and its political and economic hemisphere position, it must take economic measures at once to secure economic prosperity in Central and South America; and to establish this prosperity in the frame of hemisphere economic cooperation and dependence.

World War II intensified economic interdependence, but in a special way. More Latin American exports found their way to the United States, but fewer U.S. exports went to the region than immediately before the war. Reserves accumulated within Latin America. Import substitution was now enforced by virtue of lack of supply rather than lack of purchasing power. This experience was supposedly temporary. At war's end, Latin America looked forward to the shared fruits of peace and the benefits of continued greater economic engagement.

Post–World War II Frustrations and the Alliance for Progress

They were soon disappointed. At the time of greatly increased assistance to Europe under the Marshall Plan, the secretary of state answered pleas for a counterpart regional effort—to go along with the new emphasis upon mutual hemispheric defense—by asserting that Latin American economic development required "a type of collaboration in which a much greater role falls to private citizens and groups than is the case in a program designed to aid European countries to recover from the destruction of the war." This was the message that would be repeated countless times over. In the late 1940s and early 1950s, reality corresponded to the rhetoric. U.S. priorities were elsewhere. The importance of the hemisphere was seemingly only security, with economic concerns of secondary significance.

The Economic Commission of Latin America (ECLA), whose creation fifty years ago was opposed by the United States, soon became the basis of a distinct vision of economic change that was profoundly different. It emphasized deliberate import substitution industrialization and a prominent public sector role. It argued for dismantling the structure of primary export dependence on which previous development had depended. It accepted inflation as the modest cost of such a transformation. Such a strategy, internally generated, became a substitute for the conventional affirmation of free markets and freer trade enunciated by the United States. No wonder that in 1954 Arthur Whitaker proclaimed the euthanasia of the Western Hemisphere idea: "The revolution against the Western Hemisphere idea has been discussed at length because the revisionists' victory over it was definitive. Subsequent developments have made it increasingly unlikely that the issue will be reopened."

Yet it was, and shortly thereafter. The triumph of Castro in Cuba provided the fuel for the major effort, the Alliance for Progress, that sparked a dramatic reassertion of joint commitment to rapid hemispheric economic development. The United States not merely enunciated a special relationship with the countries of the region, but also accepted a special responsibility. Long-term and continuing economic assistance was to underwrite political democratization and structural reform in Latin America. No less than a peaceful revolution was envisioned.

The Alliance had its successes. The flow of public resources from the United States doubled between 1961 and 1965. Internal reform of taxation and expenditure systems did occur. Attention was directed to the highly unequal distribution of landholding, although very little was accomplished. Growth rates did experience a gain in the 1960s relative to the 1950s. But relative to the ambitious initial targets, the Alliance was a disappointment.

I cite three fundamental contradictions in that program. First was its assertion of regionalism within a world of increasing globalism. A second was lack of consensus between the United States and Latin America on the role of the public sector as leader of the process of economic development. A third was the presumption of effective leadership by the new democratic governments that arose at the end of the 1950s. Let me take these up in turn.

Latin America, because it failed to enter the international market with the enthusiasm and energy of the Asian tigers, declined almost continuously between 1960 and 1975 both as a source of supply and as a market for the United States. In the former year, 19 percent of U.S. exports went to Latin America, and in the latter, 16; 27 percent of imports came from Latin America in 1960, and only 17 percent in 1975. The story for Latin America was no different: exports to the United States declined from 40 to 35 percent; imports fell from 40 to 31 percent. In 1975 the trade pattern was not dissimilar to what it was in 1914. What was true of trade held for foreign investment: in 1950 Latin America accounted for 38 percent of U.S. engagement abroad; in 1975 the figure was 18 percent. The margin at that time was still the largest of all the developing areas, but that too would change over time.

The reality was that the world was diversifying considerably over the very period that the Alliance was established. Moreover, the Alliance was at its most successful in generating public credits. Yet the level of development of the major Latin American economies and the declining role of import substitution made increased exports central to their development process. And there, instead of providing stimulus, the Alliance—and subsequently President Johnson's pledge of support for increased intraregional trade—moved in the wrong direction. Regional integration was seen as import substitution at the regional level, and it was wrongly stressed. Despite elaborate plans for integrating automobile production through component parts coming from all the countries, the scheme came to nothing. Intraregional trade among the countries, through LAFTA and the Central American Common Market, meant little.

There were two distinctive features of the logic of the model of import substitution extended from the national to the international level. First was the prospect of assuring the market for exports that was deemed lacking in the outside world. This was to be guaranteed by the principle of reciprocity: intraregional imports and exports would have to be in approximate balance. "Otherwise [integration] would simply mean that foreign exchange which had been formerly used to pay for imports from the rest of the world would be transferred to other Latin American countries." The second key requirement was the expectation of large efficiency gains from economies of scale. This would soon compensate for the initial losses associated with trade diversion to higher cost sources of supply. Industrialization could then proceed as the major source of economic expansion.

The logical basis for expanded intraregional trade in Latin America thus differed from the static calculations of trade creation and trade diversion common in the discussion of the organization of the European Common Market. It was rooted instead in avoidance of the foreign exchange constraint to growth that dominated attention to the Latin American situation. From 1962 to 1966 there was a large gain in intraregional trade, but precious little was in fact accomplished. Regional imports did not substitute for third-party imports in large volume. That meant that regional exports were not fully incremental. On the other side, potential imports of manufactured products were competitive with local production and were therefore successfully resisted by national producers.

The failure of integration ultimately derived from the fact that Latin America was not a cohesive economic region. There was no logic in sacrificing autonomy in favor of a coordinated plan when local interest groups resisted the granting of concessions and sought only advantages. The scheme as a whole gave undue weight to the benefits of central planning and much less to the virtues of effective macroeconomics. It condoned the commitment to exports of primary products by paying too little attention to overvalued exchange rates and excessive tariffs. In Latin American implementation, intraregional trade and extraregional commitment were substitutes rather than the complements they proved in the European Treaty of Rome.

A second fundamental problem was the apparent emphasis placed upon public sector leadership. New Ministries of Planning and long-term plans were required throughout Latin America as a condition of U.S. aid. The Alliance Charter made scant mention of private investment. Indeed, it explicitly stated that the greater part of the needed $20 billion in external resources should come from public funds. But such a role inevitably soon meant conflict with the United States. In 1962, at the first inter-American meeting held to evaluate the progress of the Alliance, Secretary of the Treasury Douglas Dillon commented:

> There is one area in which during the past year we have not only made no progress but where we have suffered a serious setback. Private investment, both domestic and foreign, has suffered damaging blows and has lost confidence. . . . The plain fact of the matter is that private enterprise has not always been made to feel that it is truly a part of the Alliance.

In 1962 the Congress passed the Hickenlooper Amendment to protect the property of U.S. citizens in expropriation disputes then brewing in Brazil. The intent was clear. There was a continuing strong preference in U.S. business circles to enunciate that the government did not provide support to countries whose policies failed to encourage private enterprise. This was more fundamental than payment of adequate and effective compensation in the event of expropriation. It had to do with the primacy of capitalism as the only way of conducting policy. And that was inconsistent with the initial notion of support for peaceful revolution.

In the third instance, Latin America was itself about to undergo significant internal political change, not populist, but of a military character. First Brazil was racked by military intervention. Then came the Dominican Republic, where U.S. intervention was actively necessary. Argentina fell back into military control, and then Peru. What had been a continent pursuing democratic change and incorporating the poor and uneducated rapidly became a set of governments committed to slowing down that process by assuring the maintenance of law and order.

The Alliance thus was launched at a difficult moment. Instead of continuing advance toward shared goals, the countries of the region soon were divided. In such a world, U.S. foreign policy rapidly altered from commitment to far-reaching social change that had been part of the Alliance conception to assuring the continuity of responsible governance. It was the right, and not the left, to which the remains of the Alliance soon were responsive. That was hardly surprising in the Vietnam era that was beginning to dominate the U.S. posture abroad.

Rediscovering Latin America

The United States lost interest in Latin America during the 1970s. Growth continued in the region, aided by expanding debt at low interest rates and corresponding import surpluses. American engagement was limited. Venezuela assumed temporary significance at the moment of the oil price rise and the beginning of North-South discussions that led to no significant product. President Carter's engagement with the region was defined, on one side, by his strong support for human rights, a stand fully appreciated only later when civilian leadership in Latin America resumed. On the other, he attempted to place Latin America within a more global framework: the regionalism inherent in the Alliance gave way to a globalism more attuned to economic realities. There was little the OAS, ECLA, or the Inter-American Development Bank could do in a world of much expanded private loans and continued, but slow, Latin American penetration of new markets. The Panama Canal treaty providing for eventual Panamanian control and the fall of Nicaragua to the Sandinistas received inordinate public attention; both are now of modest significance in any recounting of hemispheric strategy.

The 1980s were worse for U.S. policy. Two particular issues dominated, and in both it is difficult to detect a positive role for foreign policy. One was Central America. President Reagan made aggressive policy against the Sandinistas into his regional commitment. Rather than the modest public funding for economic assistance that had been declining, there was now aggressive support for the Contra opposition in Nicaragua. I simply note a Latin American view of the matter—and one that is not atypical—that is somewhat bewildered:

> The strategic globalism of the Reagan administration has given place to a novel policy in the history of hemispheric relations. . . . [T]here exists an almost complete identity between the policy toward Central America in the present North American administration and its policy toward

Latin America. In a continent of more than 350 million inhabitants the North American attention and interest have concentrated in a microcosm formed by five countries that do not surpass some 20 millions. . . .

Ironically, the surprising Chamorro victory in the 1990 Nicaraguan election finally brought that episode of engagement to an end, as did the subsequent negotiated settlements in El Salvador and Guatemala. What additionally had assisted was the dramatic end of the cold war in 1989. Central America was no longer a wedge of Communist influence that had finally moved onshore, and was threatening the southern border of the United States. It remained primarily a region of poverty and great inequality, as it had been.

The second area of importance was economic. Latin American dependence upon debt as a solution to the first oil shock in 1973 turned from a brilliant solution in the 1970s, with its negative real interest rates, into a disaster with the second oil shock in 1979. That gave rise to a new and painful U.S. strategy of high interest rates and recession that soon had direct implications for the countries of the region. By the early 1980s countries were slowing down, but continuing to borrow. Then came the fateful Friday the thirteenth in August 1982 when Mexico announced it no longer could meet its interest obligations.

That set in motion a set of reactions that was to last almost until the end of the decade. That process can be rapidly summarized. First, there was a phase of drastic balance of payments correction between 1982 and 1984. This reflected a period of strong reduction in the value of Latin American imports: between 1981 and 1984 these fell by some 45 percent. Indeed, so rapid was the decline that *World Financial Markets* at the end of 1984 could speak of a "lasting resolution of the LDC debt problem." Such a resolution was inevitable given the initial exposed position of the international banks and the joint emphasis of the IMF and the Federal Reserve Board upon saving them: Latin American debt was about half the total developing country obligation.

But instead of getting better, the economic difficulties grew worse. The second phase, associated with worsening international prices and declining export earnings, exposed a fundamental reality: banks were not inclined to lend more, but rather were committed to reducing their exposure abroad, and especially in the region. Latin America was forced to deal with the crisis through much more fundamental realignment than had been imagined.

Phase 3 of the readjustment began with the announcement of the Baker Plan in 1985, which was a tripartite strategy of reliance on banks, international institutions, and country adjustment. But this formal official recognition of the gravity of the economic ills faced by almost all the Latin American countries—Chile had moved independently to refinance its debt, and Colombia did not declare default—evoked little response from the banks. They remained on the sideline, unprepared to make greater concessions. Nothing happened except continuing lack of growth and debt rescheduling until the 1988 decision of Citibank to write down its outstanding debt.

The following year the final stage, the Brady Plan, became effective, and Mexican debt was settled at a price of about 65 cents on the dollar, with the option of more favorable returns for those banks willing to commit more. Other large countries soon settled at comparable discounts—Brazil only in the 1990s—with smaller ones like Bolivia and Costa Rica receiving greater gain. The various relief packages did not reduce outstanding debt that much. Indeed the IMF estimates that only about 8 percent of total obligations were canceled, and that was after accumulated interest had been added. But the reality was that declines in interest rates, recovery in the world economy and hence in export growth, and lack of domestic expansion had combined to reduce the burden of debt service payments in the early 1990s.

What is impressive is the limited role the U.S. State Department, and the foreign policy apparatus as a whole, played in this whole process. The Treasury and the Federal Reserve Board became the real players. This confirmed the wisdom of the Carter emphasis upon globalism rather than regionalism as the basis of economic relationship with Latin America. Ironically, the reverse was soon to prove true in the new emphasis that was soon to be given to establishing a Free Trade Area of the Americas (FTAA).

Enterprise of the Americas

At the beginning of the 1990s, there emerged a new and different basis to expansion of intraregional trade within the hemisphere. In the first instance, it was now inclusive of active United States participation, unlike the Johnson policy of 1967. In the second, it was coterminous with a dramatic reduction of the high levels of protection that earlier had defined the development strategy of Latin America. Such a change was associated with a corresponding new commitment to internal macroeconomic stability and low rates of inflation. And in the third, trade expansion was allied with a process of privatization and receptivity to foreign investment.

Let me now elaborate on these central points.

On June 27, 1990, President Bush announced his Enterprise for the Americas Initiative, formally opening the possibility of a free trade agreement ranging from the Yukon to the straits of Patagonia. This opportunity, like its much earlier (1982) predecessor, the Caribbean Basin Initiative, rested on three bases: investment promotion, aid accompanied by debt reduction, and the elimination of trade barriers. But the centerpiece of the new initiative, and its greatest departure from past policy, was its trade provisions.

First, Bush offered closer cooperation with the Latin American countries in the Uruguay Round, including the promise to seek deeper tariff cuts in products of special relevance. Second, Bush announced that "the United States stands ready to enter into free trade agreements with other markets in Latin America and the Caribbean, particularly with groups of countries that have associated for purposes of trade liberalization." Finally, given that such a step was likely to be too dramatic for some countries to consider, Bush also offered the negotiation of bilateral "framework" agreements that would permit more incremental negotiations covering particular issues of relevance.

By the end of 1990, seven countries had negotiated bilateral framework agreements with the United States—Bolivia, Chile, Colombia, Costa Rica, Ecuador, Honduras, and Mexico. Subsequently, an agreement was concluded in 1991 that added a first regional grouping, the Mercosur, involving four countries as a unit—Argentina, Brazil, Paraguay, and Uruguay. But real attention was focused in the first instance on free trade with Mexico. Agreement to move ahead was signaled in September 1990 when Bush notified Congress of his intention to negotiate a free trade agreement with Mexico.

This turn to regionalism in United States trade policy was somewhat accidental, the result of two independent circumstances. First, it was part of a U.S. effort to push the Uruguay Round of GATT negotiations to a satisfactory conclusion. There is little reason to believe that a major new advance focusing exclusively on the hemisphere was an expected result of Bush's new Enterprise of the Americas Initiative. Second, Mexico's early willingness to move ahead was more a product of fear that new freedom in Eastern Europe would deter needed American investment than belief in the virtues of integration.

On its side, Mexico's decision to press for closer association with the United States was motivated by three factors. First, despite the fact that trade between the two countries was relatively free— especially after Mexico began to liberalize trade in 1985—an accumulation of adverse U.S. decisions affecting bilateral exchange occurred in the 1980s. Second, an agreement would serve to lock in a variety of wide ranging economic reforms that Carlos Salinas wanted to continue and consolidate. Integration meant permanence for a more liberal Mexican economic model. But there was also a third motive: to influence positively the perceptions and expectations of the private sector, both foreign and domestic. Mexico needed to expand investment if it was to grow.

Those same factors were operative for other countries in the region at the time. This has added up to a fundamentally different basis for regional trade in the 1990s. Now it is associated with increased foreign investment and prospects for future growth. The gains are predicated upon the possibility of assured access to the United States market. I emphasize this dynamic effect. For given the already substantial reduction in tariff and nontariff limitations throughout the hemisphere, the static advantages of greater trade are a trivial percentage of national income. These derive from one-time increased trade created by lower barriers. But it is to the future, and continuing expansion, that one must look. Exactly because Latin America offers the prospect of much lower costs, and because of its substantially lower income, it stands to be the largest gainer from growing trade. It is a win-win situation, but those at the bottom are more proportionally benefited. That is the bottom-line reality that has stimulated Latin American interest in the possibility of creating trade linkages with the United States.

Negotiations for Mexican entry into the existent trade agreement between Canada and the United States formally commenced in the fall of 1991. They were concluded less than one year later, in August 1992. The agreement is massive, consisting of thousands of pages. There are a preamble and twenty-two chapters, apart from the language on phasing of tariff reductions. But its underlying message is simple and direct: "North America will have something approaching free trade in goods, including agricultural commodities, after a transition period of 10 years, but up to 15 years in some sectors and, in a few cases even longer." The further changes, subsequent to President Clinton's election in the fall of 1992, added special features in the environmental and labor area required to assure congressional ratification in 1993. The treaty went into effect on January 1, 1994.

The Outcome of the Miami Summit

Once NAFTA went into operation, and record increases in trade levels were immediately accomplished, it was natural that the question of its expansion to other countries in the hemisphere would soon arise. The specific mechanism chosen was a meeting of heads of all the American states, except Cuba, in Miami at the end of the year. Foreign policy with Latin America took on a greater economic significance than at any time since the Alliance for Progress.

The obvious and central, but not exclusive, part of the agenda was hemisphere-wide free trade. Indeed, there were twenty-three initiatives in all signed at Miami, of which FTAA was merely one. But in terms of Latin American interest, it was the most important. This was a situation promising practical gains. All the countries committed themselves to achieve an agreement on hemispheric free trade by 2005. And there was immediate follow-up.

The first Western Hemisphere Trade Ministerial was held in Denver in June 1995. Seven Working Groups were launched dealing with the central features of any continental trade scheme: Market Access; Customs Procedures and Rules of Origin; Investment; Standards and Technical Barriers to Trade; Sanitary and Phytosanitary Measures; Subsidies, Antidumping and Countervailing Duties; and Small Economies. A second meeting was held in March 1996 in Cartagena, with four more Working Groups established: Government Procurement; Intellectual Property; Services; and Competition Policy. And a twelfth group on Dispute Settlement was created at the Ministerial in Belo Horizonte in May 1997.

At the same time, the level of hemispheric interaction has much increased. Regular meetings of various ministers have occurred, searching for other areas of cooperation, and there is a degree of engagement not matched since the creation of the Alliance for Progress almost forty years ago. There are good economic reasons for interest on both sides. The great increase in trade that accompanied NAFTA is one; and so too is the expansion in foreign direct investment, not only from the United States but Europe and Japan, that increasingly occurred after the "tequila" shock had affected Mexico in late 1994. That event showed still another advantage of moving closer to the United States: the $50 billion package created by the United States provided financial assistance that underwrote rapid Mexican economic recovery at the end of 1995 and up to the present.

On the other side, three principal costs confront the countries of the region. First, engagement in close trade alliance automatically sets limits to national macroeconomic policy. Renunciation of the use of trade and exchange rate instruments limits the ability to operate independently. It is no accident that virtually all countries in the region have moved rapidly to lower inflation rates comparable to U.S. values. Or that Argentina has adopted a gold standard to fix exchange rates. Or that Mexico, post-1994, immediately adopted a strategy of adjustment to restore fiscal balance. These adaptations become a necessary component of policy. Such policy limitations are seen by adherents of integration as a major advantage rather than cost. For they assure a continuity that had been lacking for many years.

Second, benefits from a closer association may not be distributed evenly: it is the likely attraction to future investments that will be decisive for individual members. Indeed, it is precisely such a reality that serves as a disciplinary device limiting national economic autonomy. There is no assurance that all countries will derive significant benefits. Indeed, unlike the previous Latin American emphasis upon domestic markets, it is now the possibility of effective export that counts. That translates into a new concern with competitiveness and continuing technological progress.

Third, protection levels in Latin America will have to change more radically in order to conform to lower United States values. Despite the substantial reduction in tariff levels since the end of the 1980s, now lowered to an order of 15 percent, the regional level is still much higher than the 4 percent in the United States. That exposes participants to a larger share of U.S. trade in Latin American imports than the reverse. Much greater adjustment is likely to be necessary. That raises the issue of whether there will be additional sources of finance to help meet the burden. And it explains the reluctance of domestic industrial sectors to enter into such free trade. They are afraid of the potential consequences.

Such potential costs within Latin American countries explain much of the hesitation some have shown in moving forward. Preliminary calculations at a regional level support this emphasis on dynamics and adaptability as the crucial factors determining future success. One study shows a one-time increase of Latin American imports to the United States of less than 10 percent if all trade restrictions were removed. The implicit maximum gain in Latin American income would then be less than 2 percent. Further, the only two large gainers would be Mexico and Brazil. Note as well that the positive effect achieved by the United States is of an order of magnitude smaller: in the range of only .1 percent. That is precisely consistent with two realities. Trade flows from the region to the United States are a lesser percentage of U.S. income than the reverse; and the United States is already a comparatively open market.

One obvious response to such data is the conclusion that "in view of the limited potential of the FTA approach, Latin American countries might do better by assigning relatively greater importance to multilateral liberalization efforts." Recall, however, that Latin American participation in world exports has declined by two-thirds since 1950. The appeal of a regional trade option is its hope of defining and disciplining a new economic strategy that can reverse that unfortunate history. Multilateralism as a motivating force has not provided the positive stimulus to Latin America that has operated elsewhere. But that regional option is not necessarily limited to the United States. The countries of the European Community are another option, and a very real one. And Mexico and Chile are part of APEC, the Asian grouping.

A central part in framing a Latin American response will be played by the countries of the Mercosur, and, in particular, Brazil. These countries stand apart from the others in the region by reason of the success of their efforts at integration. The Treaty of Asuncion dates back to 1991; a common external tariff came into being on January 1, 1995. Subsequently, Chile and Bolivia have become associate members, with the Andean countries already in an advanced stage of negotiations. Inclusion of the latter would mean a South American free trade agreement to go along with NAFTA.

What differentiates Mercosur is the strong political purpose of association. Its initial creation owes itself to the rise of civilian government in the 1980s in Argentina and Brazil, and to the range of various agreements undertaken in such areas as nuclear research, military cooperation, etc. At the same time, both leading countries committed themselves to elimination of inflation and reduction of external protection, promoting closer, and novel, economic links between them. Trade has expanded quite rapidly in the 1990s, with Brazil becoming the principal market for Argentine exports, and the region mounting in significance for Brazilian sales abroad, particularly of manufactured goods. And now, in the midst of the foreign exchange crisis, President Carlos Menem has lent his total support to Brazil.

Since the first Denver meeting, and even before, in negotiating a target date of 2005 instead of 2000 for hemispheric free trade,

Brazil has defined a view of hemispheric integration different from some of its Latin American neighbors. It has preferred a slower pace of negotiation, that only in the final stages would permit the questions of market access, services, intellectual property rights, and competition policy to be considered. It earlier would emphasize agreement on harmonization, agricultural subsidies, technical norms, etc. The United States has taken virtually the opposite view, preferring to begin the discussion with these subjects, and moving on to the others, of less significance, later.

Brazil has also insisted upon a negotiation between established groups, like Mercosur, rather than between individual countries; the United States has only seemed to move toward such a position quite slowly. In the Belo Horizonte meeting of 1997, a compromise was reached: the FTAA was committed to co-exist with bilateral and subregional agreements to the extent that the rights and obligations of those agreements are not covered or go beyond the rights and obligations of FTAA. Brazil saw this as a victory; Charlene Barshevsky, Trade Representative of the United States, thought differently. President Clinton's recent trip, where he publicly hailed Mercosur, was seen by some to advance the Brazilian conception. Ultimately, the compromise adopted in Santiago was to make the United States and Brazil cochairs of the integration effort in the final period, 2003–2005. This concession to reality, in the absence of U.S. fast-track, leaves the question of hemispheric integration in the hands of the two countries necessary to its success.

Conclusion

The Santiago Summit brought to a close a very successful period of U.S. relations with Latin America and the Caribbean. Indeed, there are few paralleis even for comparison.

There were discussions about the continuing success of democracy and extension of human rights in the hemisphere. It was a happy moment. In every country, with the exception of Cuba, the electoral process predominates. This is a far cry from the situation some fifteen years ago. The agonies of dictatorships and explicit U.S. intervention in Central America are barely recalled. This made it possible to advance in areas still lacking: assurance of a free press; efforts to train judges and to bring the system of justice up to acceptable standards; an emphasis upon decentralization and the strengthening of local governmental institutions.

Under the same broad category of preserving and strengthening democracy, justice and human rights and the continued problems of drug production and use were given importance. So too was attention directed to rising crime and corruption. Unspoken, however, was the issue of illegal immigration—just as it was excluded in the NAFTA treaty—that so affects the continuing range of U.S. relations with Mexico, Central America, and the Caribbean. And the environmental issue was noted with brief comment, but subordinated to multilateral responsibility of the United Nations.

Education became a much larger issue, as it should. Given the longstanding lag in regional primary and secondary advance, and the continuing large public cost of higher education, Latin America and the Caribbean have fallen behind other regions. While the question moved to first priority, in the end it is much more a domestic rather than an international issue. How much will be spent and how it is to be raised and allocated are fundamental issues that will be determined in future years. External assistance is less significant than internal consensus. Income maldistribution, for which the region unhappily is known, and a matter not unrelated to inadequate schooling, also received deserved attention. But again, despite increased resources made available from the Inter-American Development Bank, the World Bank, and AID for microenterprise, for improved safety nets, etc., the necessity for improvement depends upon domestic decision.

What will happen to the dream of a Free Trade Area of the Americas? This is quite differently a truly joint undertaking. The United States is in the midst of dealing with the sudden Asian crisis, a new and unexpected development. Is the reassertion of other areas of global responsibility about to put an end to the temporary regional emphasis that Latin America enjoyed? As we have seen, it would not be the first time that this has happened.

But such a cyclical policy has potential costs even greater than in the past. If the twenty-first century, originally seen as the Asian century, sees an economic revival of Latin America, as it should, will that region's new commitment to more open trade lead it to lesser interest in linkage to the United States? Will a recovery of Japan and a more unified European Union offer the appealing prospect of greater independence? Will the United States once again fail to pursue its natural advantage in the hemisphere?

The several chapters that follow explore these same issues, seeking to define U.S. national interests and opportunities. Everyone is aware that a second stage of reforms in the region is vital to the continuing vitality of democracy and to a process of renewed economic expansion. The overall implications for future U.S. policies are covered in a final chapter.

2

Economic and Political Constants/Changes in Latin America

MARIO BAEZA
SIDNEY WEINTRAUB

L atin America, from an investment and economic point of view, has been somewhat of an enigma to the U.S. financial community. It has been a region characterized by multiple lending booms and busts; wide shifts between export led growth models and import substitution models; periods of deep anticolonialist sentiment juxtaposed against the need for foreign capital flows to finance economic growth; and periods of intense and often frantic

MARIO BAEZA is chair and chief executive officer of TCW/Latin America Partners, L.L.C., and a managing director of Trust Company of the West. Previously Mr. Baeza was president of Wasserstein Perella International Limited and chair and chief executive officer of the firm's Latin America division, a partner at Debevoise & Plimpton where he founded and headed the firm's Latin American Group, and a visiting professor of law at Stanford University and Harvard University. He serves on the boards of corporations and nonprofit groups, including the Council on Foreign Relations and the U.S. Cuba Trade and Economic Council, Inc.

SIDNEY WEINTRAUB holds the William E. Simon chair in political economy at the Center for Strategic and International Studies and is Dean Rusk professor emeritus at the Lyndon B. Johnson School of Public Affairs at the competition among U.S. and European financial institutions to control the lucrative business of underwriting or syndicating Latin American sovereign debt.

From the point of investment flows through U.S. financial institutions, developments in Latin America did not result from a coherent strategy aimed, for example, at priming markets for U.S. exports or developing supplier inputs for U.S. products (as has been the case with Japan's financing and investment in Southeast Asia). Rather, the U.S. financial community has tended to view Latin America opportunistically—whenever domestic uses of capital were limited or constrained, the U.S. financial community turned to Latin America as the place to earn higher returns and increase or sustain profitability.

Latin American countries, on the other hand, have had to ride the various currents of the ebb and flow of the U.S. financial community's interest in the region, which every twenty or thirty years shifted from an early interest in competing with the British, Dutch, and German banks and investors (which were the early dominant providers of capital to the region), to a turning away as we focused on World War I, to a resurgence of interest after the war and through most of the 1920s, to the turning away during the depression years, to a resurgence of interest after our preoccupation with rebuilding Europe after World War II had ended, to the lending boom of the 1970s that led to the debt crises of the 1980s. The pattern continues to the present. By 1990 when the bloom had come off the rose of leveraged buyouts and U.S. real estate, the U.S. financial community again turned to Latin America.

This section of the chapter explores the events that led up to the debt crisis of the 1980s and the consequence of that crisis, which is commonly referred to as the "lost decade." It then explores the structural changes and reforms that have been adopted under the aegis of the IFC programs and the subsequent reemergence of Latin America as an important destination of global capital flows.

University of Texas, Austin. Dr. Weintraub was a member of the U.S. foreign service from 1949 to 1975, and has been a senior fellow at the Brookings Institution. His most recent book is *NAFTA at Three: A Progress Report*.

Finally, it examines briefly the challenges that remain, as well as the short- and long-term risks to the continuation of capital flows to the region. With respect to the latter issue, an attempt is made to understand Latin America in the new international context of development, including brief contrasts and comparisons with Southeast Asia.

Prelude to the Debt Crises of 1982

Although theories abound as to the various causes of the Latin American debt crisis, there is general consensus around the view that the crisis was precipitated by the 1970s lending boom, coupled with the poor management of that capital by Latin American governments, and was triggered by a severe downturn in the world macroeconomy.

For the U.S. banking system, the 1970s was a period of heavy lending to Latin American governments. The reasons for this lending boom have little to do with Latin America (other than it could use the money) but much more to do with the fact it was a period in which U.S. financial markets were becoming increasingly efficient, permitting major corporations to became less reliant on banks to raise capital. Instead, large corporations and municipalities began to issue short-term commercial paper directly to the ultimate purchasers of that debt to finance their working capital and other needs. At the same time, deposits were eroding as customers bought the commercial paper directly from corporations and relied less on banks as intermediaries to generate investment returns. Banks countered by issuing their own form of commercial paper called CDs to raise capital as opposed to relying as heavily on bank deposits. The banks in turn lent this money to developing countries where the demand for capital was high and they could earn high returns. During the first oil shock (1973–74), participating banks not only absorbed much of the excess liquidity brought on by petrodollars, but used this liquidity to make loans to Latin American countries that faced staggering balance-of-payment problems caused by the oil shock. A second lending boom after 1979 was associated with the second major oil shock. The prevailing view at the time was that "governments don't go bankrupt."

Eventually, intense competition among major banks to make loans to Latin American countries became so intense that margins on the loans plummeted, although profitability was maintained by sheer volume. By the end of 1985 Latin America owed foreign creditors $368 billion or 54 percent of the region's GDP and more than $1,000 for every man, woman, and child in Latin America. Seventy-five percent of this debt was owed to commercial banks worldwide, of which $82 billion was held by U.S. banks. Of this $82 billion, $53 billion was held by money center banks whose total capital at the time was $42 billion. This is what is known as overlending.

On the Latin American side, the governments borrowed eagerly but generally made poor use of the proceeds. To begin with, through most of the 1970s exchange rates were kept artificially high. Strong currencies were used as the mechanism to hold down inflation without causing a recession. During the period 1977–81, for example, it is estimated that Argentina's currency was overvalued by 80 percent, Brazil's by 31 percent, Chile's by 57 percent, and Mexico's by 38 percent. The problem is that an overvalued currency leads to trade deficits and capital flight, which in turn creates the need for more borrowing. Trade deficits were especially pernicious since it is through trade surpluses (current account surpluses) that the foreign debt was to be serviced. The real killer, however, was the fact that over half of the amounts borrowed were being used by central banks to finance capital flight. For example, between 1976–82, Argentina capital flight is estimated at $22.4 billion. By 1982 Argentina had total foreign debt outstanding of approximately $44 billion. Aside from financing trade deficits and capital flight, the proceeds from these borrowings were used to finance large budget deficits, much of it going to support money-losing, poorly run state owned monopolies, with a dose for corruption thrown in.

If the combination of overlending and poor management of the funds wasn't sufficient to trigger a crisis, the downturn in the world economy was. By 1981 there was a tightening of U.S. monetary policy. World interest rates doubled from their 1979 levels. There was a worldwide economic slowdown resulting in a plummeting of commodity prices on which many Latin American countries depended for their hard currency earnings. The lack of an adequate export base from which to repay foreign borrowings, in the absence of new borrowings, led to the debt crises initiated by Mexico in 1982 when it announced it would have to default on its sovereign debt. Eventually all Latin American countries, except for Colombia, would go into default on their debt—a virtual repeat of earlier debt crises.

Consequences of the Debt Crisis

When Latin American countries awakened from the shock of the debt crisis, they encountered a very different world. To begin with, commercial banks, which had been actively soliciting mandates to syndicate ever-increasing amounts of debt, overnight halted all lending to the region. Suddenly, Latin American debtors who had become accustomed to rolling over interest payments and borrowing further to finance current account imbalances had to scramble to meet payroll for government employees and ongoing projects. This was accomplished by printing more money. Overvalued currencies gave way to massive devaluation. This, in turn, led to hyperinflation. During the period 1982–87, Mexico had an average annual inflation rate of 92 percent, Brazil 184 percent, and Argentina 329 percent.

The other shoe dropped on the private sector. If their sovereign government was technically bankrupt, so technically was every corporation within that country. This follows the rating agencies' standard practice of not allowing a local company to have a better credit rating than its host country. Interest rates on local currency debt skyrocketed to over 100 percent, trade lines were revoked, and a depression ensued; much of the private sector was bankrupted in the process.

And so, Latin America, which had financed most of its growth through bank borrowings over the previous ten years, now found itself without a lender of last resort. The great U.S. financial institutions, chastened by the losses in the portfolio, appealed to the U.S. government and multilateral institutions for help and then turned their attention to the domestic front where leveraged buyouts and hostile takeover became the path to high margin lending and renewed profitability.

Most Latin American countries responded at first by circling the wagons and retreating further into their statist model. Preserving jobs and keeping up employment became the key policy prescription as one Latin American government after another took over its failing banking systems, propped up or took over failing enterprises, and subsidized private sector initiatives. At one point, the Mexican government not only controlled all of the banks (save one, Citibank) and insurance companies but also owned and operated discotheques, nightclubs, and laundromats. With almost no access to capital, countries attempted to become islands unto themselves gaining whatever hard currency they could from the exports of raw materials (oil, copper, etc.) and low value-added products. The result was that for most of the balance of the 1980s Latin American economies were systematically decapitalized. This, in turn, translated into almost no investment in physical infrastructure (telephones, electricity, ports, railroads, roads) or human infrastructure (education, health and welfare, etc.). Not surprisingly, in the period 1982–87 there was a drop in real wages.

The End of the Statist Model

Latin American countries might still be muddling through their statist policies if it were not for their inability to attract capital with the concomitant effects of lack of investment in infrastructure, reduction of global competitiveness, and an inability to generate sufficient export revenues. This reality, together with other world changes such as the fall of the Berlin Wall and the collapse of the Soviet Union, reinforced the view that the statist model does not work. In short order, one Latin American country after another followed the U.S./IFC prescription and announced the adoption of programs that decisively cut back the role of government in private sector activities, slashed tariffs, substantially reduced trade barriers, and welcomed back and encouraged direct foreign investment in private sector and public enterprises. The cornerstone of this new approach was the privatization of state owned companies, which had the dual effect of stimulating massive capital inflows (much of it returning capital flight money) and removing from the government's budget money-losing enterprises. It also paved the way for foreign capital to finance the investment in technology and equipment required for improving Latin America's infrastructure. Collaterally, it also did much to reduce corruption, which was endemic in a system where government permits and permissions were required to do almost anything.

Adherence to these structural reforms, which included control of budget deficits, led ultimately to the re-emergence of Latin America from the debt crises, as virtually all Latin American countries were able to restructure their bank loans through the Brady Bond program. Brady Bonds served as a way to convert nonliquid bank loans into tradable bonds based on the acceptance by the holder of a discount and/or an extension of the payoff term. Brady Bonds carried a U.S. government guarantee as to the payment of principal at maturity.

Now for the Hard Part

Much of the high-profile privatizations have been completed in Mexico, Peru, and Argentina and are underway in Brazil. With the key structural reforms in place, now the hard part begins. The key to Latin America's ultimate success and stability will be its ability to attract forms of long-term capital other than debt. This is quickly happening throughout the region as direct foreign investment is on the rise, and equity investments, rather than loans, are helping to meet the region's capital shortage.

As Mexico found out in 1994 when it found itself too heavily reliant on short-term borrowing to finance trade and budget deficits caused, in the case of the trade deficit, by an overvalued currency, mistakes of the past can and will be repeated in Latin America. Such has been its history.

Direct investment, as opposed to loans, is also important because foreign direct investors often transfer technology and know-how, which allow Latin American firms to become more efficient and globally competitive. This has secondary and tertiary effects in terms of the education and training of workers to be participants in the global economy. This is how the Asian firms were able to develop so quickly into powerful exporters—either they formed a part of a global production unit (as in cars or computers) where massive investments in R&D and technology were being made in other parts of the world or they were able to develop economies of scale and scope by having the right mix of long-term equity capital and less-expensive labor from which to compete.

If Latin American countries are to succeed with their new export led growth model they will have to find a way to invest more in their people's education and to find a fairer distribution of wealth throughout society. Again, in contrast to Asia, where strong growth rates have been coupled with an increase in equity in the distribution of wealth, in Latin America strong growth has generally led to greater disparity in income and wealth. This must be addressed.

Finally, Latin American countries will have to learn to deal increasingly with external shocks that may come in the form of Asia's meltdown, a Mexican peso crisis, or a sudden drop in capital flows reflecting changes in the monetary policy of the United States. These countries will also have to continue to deal with vexing issues of corruption and poverty, which threaten the attractiveness of their countries to foreign investment and continuously raise the specter of political instability.

For years, Latin America has been an enigma to the U.S. financial community. Just when things seem to get on track, it blows up. On the other hand, it tends to blow up for the same reasons, having its roots in a propensity to overlend to governments that do not use the proceeds productively. It's as if every new generation of bankers rediscovers Latin America and ends up making the same mistakes. Given the new international context of development and the shifting emphasis to direct foreign investment perhaps this pattern can at last be broken.

Economic Opening

Persons who do not follow Latin American developments closely tend to look at the region based on a set of stereotypes that are at least fifteen years out of date. These are that the region is made up of countries that are unstable politically, authoritarian in nature, and closed economically through high protection against imports and resistance to foreign investment. The extent of the changes that have occurred since the early 1980s has not yet been fully absorbed by the general public or even by the Congress of the United States. This section deals with the economic changes since the emergence of the debt crisis in 1982 and is followed by a discussion of the political opening.

The New Model

The development model in Latin America and the Caribbean changed following the sad experience of the "lost decade" of the 1980s. Formerly closed markets began to open, at first unilaterally and then through negotiations. The most salient manifestations of the negotiations are the network of integration arrangements in the hemisphere, from NAFTA in the north to Mercosur in the south. The high point of this process, at least of the new aspiration, came at the Miami Summit in December 1994 when there was agreement to conclude negotiations for a Free Trade Area of the Americas (FTAA) by the year 2005.

Despite the substantial progress made in reducing trade barriers, the hemisphere is by no means open. Import tariffs, which on the whole are in their teens, are still relatively high by the standards of industrial countries. (The Inter-American Development Bank gives the region's average tariff as 13 percent now compared with 45 percent before the model change.) In most countries nontariff barriers of considerable consequence exist, dealing with agricultural imports, government procurement, protection of intellectual property, and limits on providing financial services. The catch phrase of the 1990s is "open integration," but the discrimination against outsiders can be substantial. However, the contrast between the paradigm that dominated the region after World War II—really, from the Great Depression of the 1930s—and that which now prevails is remarkable. Export pessimism has given way in most countries to export led growth. All countries of the hemisphere are now members of the World Trade Organization, whereas many deliberately remained outside the General Agreement on Tariffs and Trade (GATT) earlier. The preoccupation today is not how to stifle foreign investment, but how to attract it. There can be legitimate complaints about specific actions of particular governments in restricting imports or in providing blatant preference to nationals in project bidding, but this type of restriction, which was the norm earlier, is no longer the general practice.

The new model was sorely tested in the aftermath of the Mexican financial collapse at the end of 1994 and 1995, when the tequila effect had some impact across the hemisphere, more severe in some countries than others. Yet the new model was not jettisoned. It was confirmed in Mexico, where the economic effect was greatest, and in Argentina, where the most severe secondary repercussions took place.

There is by no means uniformity across countries. Chile was the first to open, and its economic accomplishments, following the crisis there in 1982, have inspired emulation elsewhere in the hemisphere. Mexico followed and began to open its market to imports after the debt crisis of 1982. Mexico's entry into free trade with Canada and the United States had much reverberation throughout the hemisphere. Brazil was more slow to open in the belief that its large industrial base still provided scope for further economic growth through import substitution, but the difference is vast between what prevailed before the 1980s and what exists now. Argentina is a staunch supporter of Mercosur because it has enabled the country to augment its manufactured exports to the other member countries, especially Brazil. Chile seeks admission into NAFTA, but also concluded that it made little economic sense to face discrimination in the Mercosur market.

The new model has not been without its problems. Unemployment remains unacceptably high in Argentina. The use of macroeconomic tightening to deal with the Mexican crisis in 1995 inflicted severe hardship on most of the population, and there has been a backlash against "neoliberalism"—really, against the free play of the market. Venezuela, in the years after Rafael Caldera became president in February 1992, sought to revert to the older model in some respects, but then conceded this was failing and returned to what is now mainstream practice elsewhere in the hemisphere. There undoubtedly will be many instances of protectionism in the future under the new openness, but it is safe to say that the status quo ante is dead.

Trade and Investment Consequences

Table 1 shows the changes in Latin American and Caribbean trade since 1990. The growth in imports and exports has been reasonably steady, but by no means spectacular. The dollar figures are in nominal terms, and real growth was therefore lower. It is hard to say how much lower without looking at the trade-inflation relationship country by country, and examining whether exports were priced in national currencies (thereby making national inflation rates a relevant deflator), or in dollars and other currencies (which requires using other deflators). Still, Latin American and Caribbean trade growth was higher than the growth in world trade generally and, according to the WTO, the region's trade increased from 4 to 5 percent of world trade between 1990 and 1996.

TABLE 1 Latin America and the Caribbean: Total Exports and Imports (millions of dollars and percentages)

	1990	1991	1992	1993	1994	1995	1996e
Global Exports	137,781	136,242	145,504	155,644	181,573	218,989	242,758
% growth	10.5%	−1.1%	6.8%	7.0%	16.7%	20.6%	10.9%
Global Imports	110,235	128,880	157,007	174,272	205,546	226,317	250,306
% growth	11.9%	16.9%	21.8%	11.0%	17.9%	10.1%	10.6%

Sources: IDB and IMF

The economic integration arrangements in the hemisphere have had considerable influence on trading patterns. According to the IDB, intraregional exports grew by 18 percent a year between 1990 and 1996, double the rate of extraregional exports, and the proportion of total intraregional exports over this time period rose from 12 to 18 percent. Intraregional imports also grew by 18 percent a year between 1990 and 1996, but extraregional imports grew by almost as much, by 14 percent a year. Intraregional imports over this time period grew from 15 to 18 percent of total imports.

The proportions of intragroup to total exports of the various subregional groupings grew from 1990 to 1995 as follow (based on IDB data): Mercosur, from 8.9 to 20.4 percent; Andean Community, 4.2 to 12 percent; and the Central American Common Market (CACM), 16.2 to 21.2 percent. (Intra-NAFTA exports grew from 42.4 to 46.3 percent over this same period[1]; and in 1995 intra-CARICOM exports were 13 percent of total exports, but much of this can be explained by oil exports from Trinidad and Tobago.)

In each of the three cases, Mercosur, the Andean Community, and CACM, the biggest intragroup export increase was in manufactures; and this, in essence, was at the heart of the integration motivation. Consequently, the subregional integration effort has a solid foundation of practical results, which was not the case for the earlier integration efforts during the import substitution period. There is little evidence that this growth in intragroup trade has had any substantial trade diversion effect.

It is important to keep in mind the differences of export markets of the various groups of countries. The countries farther north, those in Central America, the Caribbean, and northern South America (especially Venezuela and Colombia), rely heavily on the U.S. market, whereas those farther south do not. For the four Mercosur countries, only 16 percent of merchandise exports in 1995 went to the United States and Canada. For the Andean countries, the proportion was 42 percent; and for the CACM countries, 37 percent. The proposed FTAA, therefore, has much more resonance in the northern part of the hemisphere, where assured access to the U.S. market is critical, than in the south, for which access to the U.S. market, while important, is less vital.

Foreign investors have reacted largely positively to the new, more open economic model in Latin America and the Caribbean. Table 2 provides data on foreign direct investment in the region from 1990 through 1996. The growth over this time was impressive. The slight decline in 1995 can be explained by the drop in investment that year to Mexico, whose economy was going through the nation's worse year since the Great Depression of the 1930s.

TABLE 2 Latin America and the Caribbean: Foreign Direct Investment (net inflows, in billions of U.S. dollars)

	1990	1991	1992	1993	1994	1995	1996e
Latin America	8.1	12.5	12.7	14.1	24.2	22.9	25.9
Argentina	1.8	2.4	2.6	3.5	0.6	1.3	2
Brazil	1	1.1	2.1	1.3	3.1	4.9	5.5
Chile	0.6	0.5	0.7	0.8	1.8	1.7	2.2
Mexico	2.5	4.7	4.4	4.4	11	7	6.4

Source: World Bank

The region also has been attractive to foreign portfolio investors. Total capital inflows to the region (according to the Economic Commission for Latin America and the Caribbean) exceeded $50 billion in 1996, about half long-term direct investment and the other half net portfolio investment. As with direct investment, portfolio investment into Mexico, which dropped sharply in 1995 because of economic depression there, has since resumed. In fact, of $41 billion of gross international bond issues of countries in the region in 1996, Mexico floated almost $17 billion, more than any other single country.

The region's balance-of-payments position has been relatively healthy in recent years. The region's merchandise trade has been more or less in balance and its current account deficit in the range of $30–40 billion, almost all covered by capital inflows.

Significance of Economic Opening

For many years prior to the 1990s, the salience of Latin America and the Caribbean (LAC) in world trade declined consistently. The old development model and its accompanying export pessimism marginalized LAC's role in world trade, except for primary commodities. The region was therefore insulated from external factors, but not completely because primary product earnings fluctuated, sometimes quite wildly.

The model shift, with its stress on exports (not export pessimism any longer but export essentiality) did more to promote industrialization than did import substitution, even though its very rationale was to develop viable manufacturing activities. Perhaps the only country to develop a viable industrial sector from the earlier model was Brazil, thanks in large part to its large internal market. The development of a vibrant industrial sector is probably best illustrated by Mexico, where exports of manufactures increased from less than 40 percent of the total in the mid-1980s to almost 85 percent now (data are from the Bank of Mexico). The opposite side of this development is the decline in the proportion of petroleum and other mineral exports from more than 50 percent of the total in the mid-1980s to about 11 percent today.

This transformation from looking inward to participating more fully in the world economy has put a premium on national economic policies and how favorably, or unfavorably, they are viewed by outside observers. The economic meltdown in Mexico at the end of 1994 and in 1995 was a consequence of lack of confidence in the conduct of financial policy in Mexico. This lack of confidence reverberated throughout the LAC region, but ultimately settled down into analysis of each country's economic fundamentals. Exchange rates are much more significant today when markets are relatively open, and success in exporting higher value-added manufactured products is essential to meeting development goals, than they were earlier when imports were restricted and exports of raw materials were valued largely in dollars and other foreign currencies.

What we see today is that the LAC region has joined the world economy, with all the benefits and responsibilities that go with this. By the same token, the world—the investors and traders—has learned to pay attention to the LAC region much more than they did before. It is this combination—looking outward by the region, and looking inward at the region by the rest of the world—that is perhaps the most important economic development of the past fifteen to twenty years.

Democracy and Economic Opening

Perhaps the most encouraging aspect of the changes in Latin America in the 1980s and 1990s is that democratic opening accompanied the new economic model. In some cases, the democratic opening came first, as in Argentina and Brazil, and in others the economic changes came first, as in Chile and Mexico. But there has been a remarkable merging of the two in each of these countries, as well as in others.

There is considerable literature on the connections between economic and political opening, whether glasnost must necessarily be followed by perestroika, and vice versa. In Mexico, the firm belief of Carlos Salinas, when he was president, was that economic opening had to come first, otherwise the vested interests in the status quo would frustrate the economic reforms. In Argentina, this philosophic debate on sequencing had only modest relevance, when President Raúl Alfonsín was elected in the wake of the military fiasco in the Malvinas/Falklands and the collapse of the military government. In each case, however, the second transformation followed the first in the immediately succeeding administration—political opening came to Mexico under Ernesto Zedillo after he became president in 1994, and economic opening came to Argentina after Carlos Menem was elected president in 1989.

The intention here is not to dwell on an academic discussion that transcends developments in the Western Hemisphere, but a few words of opinion on this theme of interaction between economic and political opening might be in order, at least as the combination has played out in Latin America. A shift to greater reliance on markets as opposed to central government direction has the effect in the region of decentralizing decision making from a few insiders to a dispersed group of actors. This very fact set in motion a desire for greater power in choosing the people who make the policy decisions at the center. The process of moving from economic opening to political democracy can be rapid, as it was in Mexico once the economic transformation began in earnest, or somewhat longer, as it was in Chile after the Pinochet golpe in 1973. In Latin America, where a Western culture prevails, pressure for the political accompaniment to economic liberalism is inexorable, in our view. It is no accident, we believe, that all democracies are market economies, even though all market economies are not immediately transformed into democracies.

The reverse sequence, from democracy to market dominance, has much the same logic. If the population is permitted to choose its leaders, the society as a whole will eventually also wish to make more of the economic decisions that affect daily lives, and this surely leads to greater reliance on markets. This, in any event, is demonstrable in Latin America.

Whatever one's views on this thesis of the inevitability of convergence of economic and political opening, this has been the pattern in Latin America, where the convergence came quite quickly once the changes began. The emergence of democratic regimes in the region was substantial during the 1980s, a time of considerable economic hardship when many analysts predicted that precisely the reverse would take place, that is, a growth of authoritarianism to deal with the economic situation. Salinas was proved wrong; economic reforms were possible in a politically open context, as was demonstrated in Argentina and Brazil. Alfonsín turned out to be wrong in that political opening was not enough, that its economic counterpart also was needed.

Just as it would be unwise to overstate the degree to which most Latin American countries have opened their economies, it would be unwise to declare victory and label the hemisphere as democratic in the way that exists in the more developed countries of North America and Western Europe. Elections are now conducted in a reasonably democratic manner, but even here there are flaws. Access to funds, media attention, and government largesse during electoral campaigns are still highly unequal. In at least three countries, Argentina, Brazil, and Peru, constitutions were changed to permit re-election of incumbent presidents, whereas one would expect these changes to be made in favor of future presidents in truly democratic situations.

But the electoral situation in the hemisphere is light years more democratic than it was fifteen to twenty years ago. There is now opposition dominance in at least one house of the legislature in Mexico and Argentina. Elections in Brazil are a free-for-all. Augusto Pinochet gave up the presidency in Chile after he lost a plebiscite. The list of examples could be extended.

Democracy, however, means more than open elections. There is little confidence in judicial systems throughout the hemisphere. Human rights are still widely abused. The media are more open than ever before, but examples abound of efforts to stifle criticism—in Peru and Panama most recently. Journalists are still murdered promiscuously in Mexico. The influence of narcotic traffickers still counts for much in Bolivia, Colombia, and Mexico, just to name three countries. Corruption is rampant in country after country.

These deficiencies are recognized, but altering the situation is slow slogging. In the multilateral process growing out of the Summit of the Americas in Miami in December 1994, the LAC countries took the lead to address some of these issues, such as the existence of corruption and money laundering. It is most improbable they would have acted this way before the democratic changes of the 1980s and since. The countries of the hemisphere have also indicated their approval of a protocol of nonrecognition of governments that come to power by nondemocratic means. This surely would not have been the case twenty years ago, when many of the leaders had come to power themselves precisely this way.

Perhaps the deepest flaw in the combined political-economic structure is the prevalence of poverty and high inequality. Latin America has been a "champion" among the regions on this score, surely among emerging or middle-income countries. This situation cannot be blamed on the current economic model or the existing political structure because it emerged long before the changes of the last two decades. However, the situation has not improved under the new model, except for the reduction of poverty that has accompanied the solid and sustained economic growth in Chile.

The U.S. Interest

The U.S. interest in Latin America and the Caribbean during the cold war was driven by the East-West contest. Alongside official mouthings in favor of democracy, the actual programs were designed to prevent defections to the Communist camp. Sometimes this emphasis had a positive policy outcome, as in the creation of the Alliance for Progress, whose anti-Communist origins mirrored those that led earlier to the launching of the Marshall Plan in Europe. At other times, East-West emphasis led to bloodshed, as in the wars in Central America.

The end of the cold war permitted U.S. practice and ideology to come together in the political sphere. The broad U.S. emphases in the LAC region now are to promote greater democracy and market economies, precisely what is happening. There is now more identity of interests between the United States and other countries of the hemisphere than in decades, perhaps than ever before.

During the 1980s, before the Soviet Union collapsed but after the Latin American economic model began to change, there was much talking past each other by the United States and other countries of the region. Latin American leaders wanted to emphasize economics; the United States wanted to focus on their anti-Communist credentials. Democracy in the region was defined by the United States as being anti-Communist.

Perhaps the single action that most brought out how much the Latin American view of economic policy had changed was the reaction to the call by President George Bush in June 1990 for free trade from Alaska to Tierra del Fuego. This was greeted enthusiastically in Latin America. Had the same proposal been made a few years earlier, when Latin America looked inward economically, the idea of free trade in the Americas surely would have been rejected out of hand as a maneuver of economic imperialism. Much of the earlier enthusiasm has waned because of evident U.S. hesitancy in carrying out the initial proposal, but the idea of hemispheric free trade remains very much alive, as witness the preparations to launch negotiations to this end after the meeting of hemispheric leaders in Santiago, Chile, in April 1998.

Latin America has become a growing market for U.S. products and an important destination for U.S. direct and portfolio investment. The market dominated model that now exists in the region dovetails perfectly with the U.S. economic philosophy. The emergence of democratic regimes is precisely what the United States preaches in its foreign policy. Market economics, however imperfect, combined with political democracy, admittedly still in its infancy—who could ask for anything more?

However, the seriousness of the United States will be measured in the region by U.S. willingness to engage in free trade negotiations, to do what the United States said it wanted. Latin America is moving ahead on its own subregional arrangements regardless of the U.S. action. But a plethora of subregional and bilateral discriminatory economic arrangements, particularly without U.S. participation, is not the same as a hemispheric-wide trade agreement that includes the United States.

Policy Conclusions

Latin America, or more completely Latin America and the Caribbean, is a geographic reality but a substantive abstraction. U.S. policy with respect to Mexico is dominated not only by the relative importance of the country, but by its proximity and the large Mexican-origin population in the United States. Proximity, historical relationship, and the domestic U.S. population of Cuban Americans also determine U.S. policy toward Cuba. Brazil demands attention by U.S. policy makers because of its economic salience in South America and its sheer size, yet its distance from the United States results in less consistent emphasis than is devoted to Mexico. Chile, for reasons not always evident, attracts more attention from the United States than one would expect from its relative economic weight, but still not enough for the Congress to honor repeated executive branch commitments for negotiations for access to NAFTA.

The differences between countries are evident, yet it is just as appropriate to talk of U.S. policy toward Latin America and the Caribbean as it is of policy toward any other region. The policies of the countries of the region have a certain similarity—import substitution transforming into more open economies, shifts from authoritarian to more democratic regimes, large social and income inequalities, cultural affinities (at least among Latin Americans and among English-speaking Caribbeans).

Apart from the differences between countries, hemisphere-wide U.S. policy is complicated by dramatic shifts in the region's own economic and political policies. During the past fifteen to twenty years, these changes have been from rigid import substitution to vigorous efforts at export expansion; resistance to foreign direct investment to its ardent solicitation; and in the political field, from authoritarianism to more democratic regimes; and from an ideological mistrust of U.S. intentions to greater pragmatism. There are no assurances that the current paradigms are durable, as witness the stirrings against "neoliberalism" and the guerilla activities in Mexico, Central America, and Colombia.

The greater policy impediment is the inconstancy of U.S. attention. Central America dominated U.S. policy during the 1980s, but has since fallen off the radar screen. The United States proposed a Free Trade Area of the Americas but has been unable to deliver anything concrete since the Miami Summit of December 1994. Because there are no vital U.S. security interests in Latin America and the Caribbean other than to deny meaningful influence in the region to potentially hostile extraregional actors, policy attention is diminished when these threats are absent. Hence the episodic nature of U.S. policy activity—intense when a security threat is perceived, negligible when it is not.

Because this pattern has persisted for so long, it must be accepted as a fact of life, at least for now. It is in this context that the following policy recommendations are made.

1. Because of the current economic model in the region, there is now an opportunity to secure even more open markets and consistency of policy to attract U.S. and other direct investment necessary to make the current Latin American economic model viable in exchange for greater assurance of long-term access to the U.S. market for the region's goods and services. If the opportunity to secure hemispheric free trade is now squandered, it may be lost indefinitely. Obtaining fast-track trade authority should thus be a central feature of U.S. policy.

2. U.S. ability to engage Latin America on political and social issues—democracy and all its paraphernalia, including better systems of justice, combating corruption, improving human rights, raising educational opportunities—is maximized if the United States does not behave as though it is indifferent to the region's economic development aspirations. If the United States is not prepared to launch hemispheric free trade negotiations, most of its other pronouncements on crucial political and social issues will ring empty. The price of admission to political and social influence in the hemisphere is a willingness to negotiate for hemispheric free trade and, in Central America and the Caribbean, to provide a greater degree of trade parity with Mexico.

3. The United States must deal with resentments created by some of its noneconomic policies, particularly those that are ineffective in any event. Perhaps the most significant of these is the annual drug certification process. Even if countries are eventually certified, the degrading debate surrounding the proceedings surely alienates all Mexicans, even those seeking close cooperation with the United States. The U.S. Congress should terminate the annual certification procedure and insist that the executive use diplomatic pressure in its place.

4. In the same vein, the embargo against Cuba finds no resonance in the rest of the hemisphere. One way to proceed is to take modest, unilateral steps to ease the embargo, such as permitting more food and pharmaceutical sales, as suggested in a bill proposed by Senators Warner and Dodd, among others, and easing tourism restrictions. The timing for this may now be propitious in light of the effervescence created by the visit of the pope in January 1998. The Helms-Burton legislation, with its use of secondary boycotts, is opposed not only by the European Union as being contrary to U.S. obligations in the World Trade Organization, but by Canada and Mexico as well, under both the WTO and NAFTA. The Congress, as well as easing the embargo against Cuba, should eliminate the extraterritorial features of current policy.

5. As this is written, there is some question as to whether the Congress will provide additional commitments for the IMF in its role as lender of last resort. The issue today is East Asia, but could well be Latin America in the future, as it was in the past. This issue

should be kept alive by the administration because the need will not disappear. Securing these funds undoubtedly will require some adjustments in IMF procedures, particularly less secrecy in its operations.

Note

[1]The proportion of Canadian and Mexican exports going to the United States was high, in the 60 to 70 percent range, even before NAFTA. Moreover, 1995 was a bad year for Mexico, and U.S. exports there declined, only to pick up again in 1996 and 1997.

3

U.S. Interests in Free Trade in the Americas

GARY C. HUFBAUER
JEFFREY J. SCHOTT
BARBARA R. KOTSCHWAR

Introduction

In April 1998 the leaders of the thirty-four democratic nations in the Western Hemisphere reconvened in Santiago, Chile, and launched negotiations on a Free Trade Area of the Americas (FTAA). As they did in the Miami Declaration following the Summit of the Americas in December 1994, the leaders committed to make significant progress in the talks by 2000 and to complete the FTAA negotiations by 2005. To be sure, free trade in the region

GARY C. HUFBAUER is vice president and director of studies at the Council on Foreign Relations, where he holds the Maurice R. Greenberg chair. Previously, he was the Reginald Jones senior fellow at the Institute for International Economics and the Marcus Wallenberg professor of international financial diplomacy at Georgetown University. From 1977–80 Dr. Hufbauer served in the Treasury Department as deputy assistant secretary, responsible for trade and investment during the Tokyo Round and director of the International Tax Staff.

will only be achieved several years thereafter, depending on the transition terms negotiated in the agreement.

Seven years is a long time for trade negotiations, even if the Uruguay Round took that long due to a prolonged impasse on agricultural reforms. The Summit leaders clearly have built in some slack time in the process to allow countries to consolidate their domestic and subregional reforms, to develop hemisphere-wide consensus in areas where national positions are widely divergent, and to build domestic political support for the prospective agreement.

From the onset, however, the FTAA talks face serious obstacles that seem to justify a cautious timetable and that could well hamper negotiations for the rest of this decade: namely, fallout from the Asian financial crisis and the lack of U.S. fast-track trade negotiating authority. Each problem deserves a brief mention.

First, contagion from the Asian financial crisis has already infected the region, damping trade and reducing near-term growth prospects. The crisis has further depressed already weak commodity markets, reducing export earnings and prompting compensating budget cuts and tax increases in several Latin American countries; sharp currency depreciations have resulted in fiercer competition in North American markets from East Asian suppliers; and surging interest rates on emerging market debt will

---

JEFFREY J. SCHOTT is a senior fellow at the Institute for International Economics, where he specializes in the field of agriculture. He was a senior associate at the Carnegie Endowment for International Peace from 1982–83 and worked in the area of international economics at the U.S. Treasury from 1974–82. Dr. Schott has written numerous books on international economics and U.S. trade policy.

BARBARA R. KOTSCHWAR is a senior trade specialist at the Trade Unit of the Organization of American Studies, where she is responsible for analyzing regional integration trends in the Western Hemisphere and for providing technical and analytical support to the Free Trade Area of the Americas process, in particular to the Working Group and Advisory Group on Smaller Economies. Previously, she worked on trade issues at the Institute for International Economics.

reduce capital inflows to Latin America below the strong levels of recent years. The cumulative impact of these developments over the near term will be slower growth, higher unemployment, and stronger resistance to trade liberalization throughout the hemisphere.

Second, doubts have resurfaced about the U.S. commitment to the FTAA due to the impasse over fast-track legislation. Although President Clinton pledged in his State of the Union address on January 27, 1998, to push for the renewal of the trade negotiating authority, prospects for action in 1998 seemed negligible given the severe constraints of the congressional calendar and the priority given to legislation to fund U.S. commitments to the IMF to replenish reserves depleted by the Asian rescue programs. If past experience is a guide, policy drift in 1998 could lead to benign neglect in 1999.

To be sure, the United States can and will proceed with FTAA negotiations without fast-track authority. However, U.S. negotiators will be sharply constrained in what they talk about and will be reticent to offer proposals that require significant changes in U.S. practices, policies, and trade barriers. Other countries will respond in kind, and the FTAA talks will dwell on mundane matters and technical issues.

The United States can and should do better, given the important economic and political interests at stake. This chapter reviews U.S. trade and investment in the region, and then turns to the key U.S. interests in successful FTAA negotiations.

U.S. Trade and Investment in the Americas

Latin America already is an important market for U.S. companies and has become increasingly attractive for direct investment as economic reforms have taken root. The region (including Mexico) now accounts for about 19 percent of total U.S. merchandise exports and 16 percent of U.S. imports (see tables 1 and 2).[1] U.S.-Mexico trade accounts for more than half of those totals, even though Mexico produces only about a quarter of regional output.

U.S. exporters enjoy a growing but underdeveloped market for their goods in South America, and have been rapidly expanding their presence in those markets. Total U.S. trade (exports and imports) with the region, excluding Mexico, has nearly doubled since 1991, and the United States has enjoyed a small trade surplus with the region each year.

As seen in Table 1, U.S. exports to Latin America (excluding Mexico) grew 13 percent annually from 1991 to 1997. This growth rate was substantially higher than the growth of U.S. exports to Europe and Asia. As a consequence, U.S. exports to Latin America (including Mexico) now account for 19 percent of total U.S. exports, against 15 percent in 1991.

TABLE 1 U.S. Merchandise Exports
(in millions of U.S. dollars)

	1991	1992	1993	1994	1995	1996	1997	Annual growth rate 1991–1997
Argentina	2	3.2	3.8	4.5	4.2	4.5	5.8	19%
Brazil	6.1	5.8	6.1	8.1	11.4	12.7	15.9	17%
Chile	1.8	2.5	2.6	2.8	3.6	4.1	4.1	16%
Mexico	33.3	40.6	41.6	50.8	46.3	56.8	71.4	13%
Latin America (excluding Mexico)	30.2	35.2	36.8	41.7	50	52.6	63	13%
Latin America (including Mexico)	63.4	75.8	78.4	92.5	96.3	109.4	134.4	13%
Europe	123.5	122.6	119.8	123.5	140.6	148.8	163.1	5%
Asia	130.6	138.3	146.7	161	197.4	207.3	213.8	9%
Total U.S. Exports	421.7	448.2	465.1	512.6	584.7	625.1	688.9	9%
Latin America/ Total U.S. Exports (%)	15	16.9	16.9	18	16.5	17.5	19	

Source: U.S. Department of Commerce, *Commerce News* and website.

U.S. investment in Latin America has also grown sharply. Over the period 1993–96, U.S. foreign direct investment (FDI) in the region (including Mexico) increased by more than 40 percent, measured on a historic-cost basis, to a cumulative $144 billion in 1996, representing 18 percent of total U.S. FDI abroad (see table 3).[2] More than half of U.S. FDI in Latin America is in the financial services sector; investments in manufacturing account for only 28 percent of the U.S. total. However, U.S. FDI in industrial sectors has grown markedly in recent years. Privatization of state owned enterprises has contributed to this trend, particularly in Brazil where U.S. FDI has increased by about 55 percent during the period 1993–96.

TABLE 2. U.S. Merchandise Imports
(in millions of U.S. dollars)

	1991	1992	1993	1994	1995	1996	1997	Annual growth rate 1991–1997
Argentina	1.3	1.3	1.2	1.7	1.8	2.3	2.2	9%
Brazil	6.7	7.6	7.5	8.7	8.8	8.8	9.6	6%
Chile	1.3	1.4	1.5	1.8	1.9	2.3	2.3	10%
Mexico	31.1	35.2	39.9	49.5	61.7	74.3	85.8	9%
Latin America (excluding Mexico)	31.3	33.5	34.5	38.5	42.4	49.5	53.7	9%
Latin America (including Mexico)	62.5	68.7	74.4	88	104.6	123.8	139.5	14%
Europe	104.1	112.7	119.1	136.4	152.4	164.6	181.4	10%
Asia	210.2	233.1	256.4	291.3	321.6	326.6	354.6	10%
Total U.S. Imports	488.4	532.7	580.7	663.3	743.4	791.4	870.7	10%
Latin America/ Total U.S. Imports (%)	12.8	12.9	12.8	13.3	14	15.4	16.1	

Sources: U.S. Department of Commerce, *Commerce News* and website.

An FTAA would help reinforce these broad trends by providing substantial new liberalization by Latin American countries in return for guarantees of continued good access to the U.S. market and the removal over a long transition period of a few notable U.S. barriers in textiles and agriculture (comparable to what was done

TABLE 3. U.S. Foreign Direct Investment in Selected Countries on a
Historical-Cost Basis, 1990–1996
(millions of U.S. dollars)

	1990	1991	1992	1993	1994	1995	1996
Argentina							
Total	2,531	2,831	3,327	4,442	5,436	7,496	8,060
of which Manufacturing	1,336	1,176	1,334	1,732	2,056	3,233	3,703
of which Financial Services	505	663	972	1,373	1,583	1,796	2,054
Brazil							
Total	14,384	14,997	16,313	16,772	18,400	23,706	26,166
of which Manufacturing	11,494	11,626	12,274	12,491	12,478	18,362	19,346
of which Financial Services	1,946	2,265	2,837	2,976	3,237	3,492	4,183
Chile							
Total	1,896	2,069	2,544	2,749	4,601	5,878	6,745
of which Manufacturing	226	89	178	233	368	547	591
of which Financial Services	1,233	1,233	1,420	1,511	2,053	2,285	2,611
Mexico							
Total	10,313	12,501	13,730	15,221	16,169	15,980	18,747
of which Manufacturing	7,784	8,978	9,546	9,235	9,822	9,843	11,408
of which Financial Services	619	670	795	2,106	2,198	2,562	3,307
Offshore Financial Centers*							
Total	30,886	33,071	41,186	46,191	54,283	58,014	64,641
of which Manufacturing	234	233	185	227	438	238	395
of which Financial Services	28,258	29,929	38,123	42,994	49,427	53,238	59,060
Latin America and other Western Hemisphere							
Total	71,413	77,677	91,307	100,482	115,093	128,252	144,209
of which Manufacturing	23,655	24,618	26,710	27,333	29,266	36,883	40,611
of which Financial Services	36,452	39,016	48,683	54,979	62,796	66,414	74,813
Total World							
Total	430,521	467,844	502,063	564,283	640,320	717,554	796,494
of which Manufacturing	170,164	179,230	186,285	192,244	211,431	250,253	272,564
of which Financial Services	130,327	141,835	161,839	201,758	239,868	256,867	289,717

Source: U.S. Department of Commerce, *Survey of Current Business,* August 1994, August 1995, September 1996, September 1997.
*Bermuda, Panama, Netherlands Antilles, and UK Caribbean Islands.

in the NAFTA). Whether some specific barriers will be exempted
from the FTAA liberalization commitments and the length of the
phaseout periods for remaining trade barriers will undoubtedly be
left hanging until the end of the talks.

U.S. Interests and Objectives

The United States has two broad reasons for pressing ahead with the FTAA. First, the FTAA is the linchpin of the broad array of political, economic, and social initiatives that the United States is pursuing with its hemispheric neighbors. Failure to move forward on the trade agenda will thus weaken U.S. initiatives in other important areas. Second, the FTAA is an integral part of overall U.S. trade strategy. An FTAA would complement efforts in bilateral, regional, and multilateral forums to expand U.S. trade and production, and boost the productivity and income of U.S. workers.

FTAA As Part of the Broader U.S. Agenda

Closer trade relations have important spillover effects on overall U.S. relations with the region. Trade pacts act as a magnet for attracting support among hemispheric neighbors for other important political and foreign policy goals: its antidrug efforts, its immigration concerns, its emphasis on better environmental and labor conditions, and its efforts to engender simultaneous gains in market oriented policies and democratic practices.

In fact, a survey of U.S. relations with South America reveals a list of important areas where the United States is acting as demandeur: better functioning democracy, better worker rights and better enforcement of those rights, more equality and better treatment of the poor, greater attention to the environment, particularly tropical forests, stricter enforcement of antinarcotic policies, sharply reduced corruption, and others. To be sure, achievement of these goals would improve the lives of important but neglected segments of South America. However, each of the goals gets the U.S. government deeper into the business of telling other governments how to order their affairs, and this tutelage is more often resented than appreciated.

The most important carrot the U.S. government can hold out for broad cooperation on the social agenda is trade and investment talks. Practically speaking, U.S. bilateral aid is dwindling, and the multilateral development banks have seen their heyday. By contrast, given the right legal and institutional framework, there is enormous scope for trade and investment growth between the United States and South America. This prospect is an important magnet for conducting fruitful talks on the social agenda.

The linkage between the FTAA process and economic and political reforms was well illustrated by the Mexican response to the 1994–95 crisis—namely, greater liberalization rather than the retreat behind protectionist walls that characterized Mexico's response to the 1982 crisis. The linkage was also illustrated by contested Mexican elections in 1998, which demonstrated the salutary effect of economic integration on political reform. Conversely, if the United States slithers away from the FTAA process, there could well be a "three times at the altar" backlash in Latin America.

Recall that Roosevelt's Good Neighbor Policy was inspired by the rise of the Axis powers in Europe. By the end of the Second World War, however, the United States paid significantly less attention to Latin America.

Likewise, the Alliance for Progress was largely inspired by the fear of Communist incursions: the fear that Moscow, via Havana, would extend its reach well into Central and South America. As these fears diminished, the Alliance withered.

In a similar fashion, the Brady Plan, the Enterprise for the Americas Initiative, and the FTAA grew out of the debt crisis of the 1980s, and fears that default and protection would be the Latin American answer to severe economic hardships.

If the United States now drops the ball on the FTAA process—a process launched by the Bush administration and wholeheartedly embraced by the Clinton administration—it seems possible that South America will coalesce around Brazilian economic and political initiatives, with an admixture of European influence. This outcome need not be inimical to broad U.S. interests, but it is unlikely that South American capitals would then pay as much attention to U.S. concerns, especially when it comes to the nuances of policy debate and the social agenda.

Furthermore, lack of progress on the FTAA would both increase the risk of policy reversal in Latin America and of self-contained regional pacts. The dangers of policy reversal are obvious. Inward looking populism is a recurrent theme in Latin America, and a few years of market economics do not erase the memory of decades dominated by leaders like Peron and Allende. In addition, the absence of worthwhile FTAA talks could reinforce the discrimination inbred in existing regional pacts by reducing prospects for broader trade liberalization that would ultimately dilute the value of regional trade preferences.

By contrast, the FTAA would erase preferential relationships that have diverted the exports of some Latin countries. Caribbean countries and Colombia in particular depend on the U.S. market for their textile and agricultural exports. These nations pose special policy challenges to the United States by sending immigrants and drugs to the U.S. market. An FTAA could expand opportunities for legitimate economic activities and perhaps ameliorate these problems.

Finally, the FTAA through its newly created Committee of Government Representatives can serve as a testing ground for addressing civil society themes that have been superimposed on the trade agenda. Since labor and environmental concerns are both important in U.S. domestic politics, work in this committee could begin to address tensions that have recently bedeviled trade negotiations.

FTAA As Part of U.S. Global Trade Strategy

The second reason for the United States to pursue the FTAA is to advance its overall strategy of demolishing barriers, particularly opaque behind-the-border barriers. The rationale for this strategy is straightforward.

Evidence shows that U.S. firms that export typically pay higher wages, and offer steadier employment, than firms that do not export. It seems logical to conclude that an expansion of the U.S. export sector will enlarge the number of steady, good-paying jobs. Similarly, firms that are able to spread their huge R&D and other investment costs over global markets are better able to fund cutting-edge technologies and production facilities (Microsoft and Boeing illustrate the point). These are the central economic arguments behind the U.S. demolition of trade and investment barriers on a global basis.

To a certain extent, this is already happening, as NAFTA rules and disciplines, many of which set useful precedents for the Uruguay Round agreements, have been "exported" to non-NAFTA countries by means of the bilateral free trade pacts negotiated by Mexico with a number of Latin American countries and by Canada's free trade agreement with Chile. All of Mexico's post-NAFTA negotiations—the G-3 agreement between Mexico, Colombia, and Venezuela as well as bilateral free trade agreements with Bolivia and Costa Rica—incorporate rules and disciplines that would accommodate the extension of the pact to the other NAFTA partners. Mexico's current negotiations with the other Central American republics are also taking this approach, and Mexico has renegotiated its 1992 FTA with Chile to bring it into line with NAFTA-like norms.

Within the Western Hemisphere, eight countries—the three NAFTA countries plus Bolivia, Chile, Colombia, Costa Rica, and Venezuela—have accepted NAFTA-style rules and disciplines in a number of important areas. Perhaps most important, all eight of these countries have adopted NAFTA norms for foreign investment, which greatly exceed those in the WTO TRIMs Agreement. These pacts require national treatment and most-favored-nation treatment, and generally prohibit performance requirements for both goods and services as a condition for establishment, acquisition, expansion, management, conduct, or operation of a covered investment.

The FTAA will further advance the U.S. agenda in at least two key ways.

First, the FTAA will avert discrimination against U.S. exporters when other countries, especially Brazil but possibly the European Union, enter into FTAs with South and Central American countries without U.S. participation. Most countries in the hemisphere continue to pursue bilateral and regional free trade pacts without the United States. In most instances, the new agreements are designed as way stations to an eventual FTAA, but the tariff preferences are accorded only to member countries, and thus discriminate against U.S. based exporters.

One example of this is the Canada-Chile FTA, which was signed in December 1996 and entered into force in June 1997. This agreement liberalized 75 percent of trade between the two countries at its inception, and aims to eliminate all barriers to trade within six years. The agreement includes origin rules that are liberal relative to those in the NAFTA—for example, 35 percent local content as compared to the 60 percent required in the auto sector by NAFTA—and also provides for the phase out of the use of antidumping duties against imports from either partner within six years.

What this means for the United States is that U.S. firms now have less favorable access to the Chilean market than do companies based in Canada, whose goods no longer face the 11 percent Chilean tariff. In some cases, U.S. sales have been lost to Canadian competitors; in others, U.S. firms have had to source their exports from plants in Latin America or Canada to secure the tariff preferences, at the expense of U.S. production and employment.[3]

Other bilateral and regional arrangements concluded in the Western Hemisphere also create disadvantages for U.S. firms. For example, U.S. fruit producers may face losses from Chile's free access to the markets of Canada, the Mercosur, Colombia, Venezuela, and Mexico. An example cited by Deputy USTR Jeffrey Lang is that Chilean fresh fruit producers pay a 2 percent duty when exporting to Venezuela whereas U.S. producers face a 15 percent tariff.

In sum, while the spirit of attacking trade barriers is very much alive in Latin America, without an FTAA, U.S. firms may not escape significant barriers to access to those markets and discrimination compared to other regional suppliers. Moreover, the mosaic of trade agreements within Latin America is hardly complete.

Second, the FTAA will provide an insurance policy against new protectionist impulses in this region by locking in domestic reforms through international obligations, and thus substantially raising the cost of policy reversals. This means more secure U.S. access to the rapidly growing markets in Latin America. While Latin America and the Caribbean represent relatively small markets for current U.S. exports (in the aggregate, we ship more to Mexico than to the rest of the hemisphere combined), the market could grow briskly—perhaps 10 percent per year over the next decade.

While the Latin American market is not large, it is currently the most dynamic market in the world for U.S. exports. In 1997 U.S. exports to the region grew by 18 percent—a rate twice that of U.S. exports to the rest of the world—reaching $129 billion. Since the Miami Summit, U.S. exports to Latin America and the Caribbean (excluding Mexico) have increased by 46 percent, while exports to the rest of the world have grown by only about 31 percent.

It's worth noting that these gains for the United States will come at relatively low "cost," when costs are measured in the mercantilist arithmetic that says larger imports are a bad thing. The reason is that average U.S. barriers now measure about 3 percent in tariff-equivalent terms, whereas average Latin American barriers still range from 10 to 20 percent in tariff-equivalent terms. In other words, while GATT/WTO agreements have removed most of the "water" in the tariff schedules of Latin America, much of the "muscle" remains, both in tariff and nontariff barriers. The FTAA will cut away this "muscle" for the comparatively low "price," again using mercantilist arithmetic, of cutting away U.S. barriers to products such as sugar, orange juice, apparel, footwear, and the like. As in the NAFTA, reforms in these politically sensitive product sectors are likely to be phased in over a lengthy transition period.

Rebuttal of U.S. Critics of the FTAA

Against these strong reasons for U.S. pursuit of the FTAA, there are two major negative arguments.

The **first negative argument** is essentially the cry of the "No More NAFTAs" school. This argument is an admixture of specific complaints about Mexican failings and more general complaints about the global economy. The specific complaints revolve around the Mexican crisis of 1994–95, the overselling of NAFTA (particularly in terms of arithmetic over new jobs), the continuing Mexican role as a major source and transshipment country for drugs, and, to a lesser extent, Mexican difficulties with Chiapas rebels and similar dissidents. The more general complaints can be summarized in the sharp contrast between the glowing prosperity on Wall Street over the past decade and the meager performance of the average wage packet.

The **second negative argument** is the advocacy, by Jagdish Bhagwati notably, of a WTO-only approach, and his skepticism about the trade-diverting and bloc-creating aspects of an FTAA or other regional agreements. These critics argue that an FTAA would divert attention and negotiating resources away from new global initiatives in the WTO. They thus argue that the FTAA would represent the end of the road of trade liberalization, not the inspiration for new WTO initiatives.

The "No More NAFTAs" Criticism

In U.S. political debate, the most telling argument against an FTAA initiative is the NAFTA experience. The pros and cons of NAFTA are familiar to all observers of trade politics and can be briefly summarized.

- Prior to NAFTA, U.S. tariffs on Mexican imports were generally low (under 5 percent on average), but some important or potentially important imports were subject to stiff nontariff barriers—notably fruits and vegetables, sugar, and textiles and apparel. Mexican tariffs on U.S. exports were significantly higher, averaging above 10 percent, and many important U.S. exports were subject to severe nontariff barriers—notably autos and parts, and a range of consumer goods. NAFTA calls for the progressive elimination of tariff and nontariff barriers. After four years, this central feature of NAFTA has caused relatively little backlash. Meanwhile, trade among NAFTA partners has expanded faster than historical norms, and in 1997 accounted for nearly 50 percent of their total merchandise trade with the world ($490 billion out of $1,006 billion).
- Prior to NAFTA, Mexico maintained an array of investment restrictions. These were significantly liberalized by the agreement, and in the wake of the 1994–95 peso crisis, Mexico accel-

erated the required pace of liberalization, especially in the financial sector. By accepting NAFTA, by sticking to its terms in economic hardship, and more generally by embracing the rule of law in dealing with foreign investors, Mexico greatly enhanced its investment climate. The result was a healthy and continuing inflow of foreign investment—in spite of the peso crisis and subsequent sharp recession. U.S. direct investment in Mexico has averaged about $3 billion per year over the last several years (out of total direct investment flows into Mexico of about $7 billion per year), and the U.S. direct investment stock (at historical value) reached $19 billion in 1996. The investment dimensions of NAFTA have proven far more controversial than the trade dimensions, for three reasons: (1) "good news is bad news"—the decision by firms to locate plants in Mexico seems to imply a decision not to locate in the United States; (2) many U.S. workers view the possibility of plant relocation into Mexico as an adverse bargaining tool in their own wage negotiations; (3) strong investment protections in the NAFTA text are unfavorably contrasted with weak labor and environmental protections.

- NAFTA proponents and opponents read the causes of the Mexican peso crisis of 1994–95 in very different lights. Proponents trace the causes to bad economics: an overvalued exchange rate, exceptionally large current account deficits, deceptive fiscal accounts, an excessive buildup of short-term dollar liabilities (especially Tesobonos), and a very unsteady hand when the crisis struck. But Mexico's macroeconomic policies were not part of the NAFTA bargain. Jealous of its sovereignty, Mexico was not inclined to listen to lectures from the U.S. Treasury or the International Monetary Fund in 1993 and 1994.

- NAFTA opponents read history through a political lens. In their view, the U.S. embrace of Mexico—extended by Washington, Wall Street, and Main Street—that accompanied the ratification of NAFTA practically forced President Salinas to juggle the books in 1993, and facilitated his pursuit of misguided policies in 1994. To quote the Economic Policy Institute: "The peso crisis is also intricately linked with the politics of NAFTA. The artifi-

cially high peso held down inflation in Mexico, helped to win
votes in the U.S. Congress for passage of NAFTA in 1993, and
improved the electoral prospects of Mexican Presidential candidate Ernesto Zedillo in 1994."

• NAFTA proponents and opponents have different takes on the
aftermath of the peso crisis. Proponents cite the Treasury/IMF
rescue package (a nominal total of $50 billion, of which less
than $30 billion was actually utilized) as evidence of newfound
political ties between Washington and Mexico City. They find in
the quick Mexican recovery—about eighteen months against
four years after the 1982 crisis—the payoff of a flexible, market
oriented economy, capped by the NAFTA accord.

• NAFTA opponents emphasize the adverse U.S. trade balance
with Mexico. In 1996 the U.S. bilateral deficit reached $16.2 bil-
lion, contrasted with a small surplus in 1993. The arithmetic of
U.S. jobs associated with swings in the trade balance is, in their
view, decidedly negative: about 250,000 fewer jobs in 1996 than
in 1993, with the losses concentrated in manufacturing employment. Moreover, they find in the close political association
between the United States and Mexico fertile ground for "moral
hazard": both Wall Street and Mexico City expect the U.S.
Treasury to ride to the rescue when debt collapse is imminent;
hence neither lender nor borrower properly assesses the risk of
bad loans and bad policies.

• Finally, and most tellingly, NAFTA opponents cite an array of
disappointed expectations. Illegal immigration from Mexico
continues at high levels, with border apprehensions about 1 million persons annually; environmental progress is slow, and des-
perate conditions characterize the Rio Grande river and border
cities; labor practices in Mexico haven't changed much in three
years, and with peso devaluation, real wages are often much
lower. As for illegal drugs, to quote the Economic Policy Institute: "NAFTA weakened border inspection of U.S. trade. A
tragic side effect was to increase the transshipment of illegal
drugs. Transshipment of illegal drugs through Mexico has
increased greatly. 80% of the cocaine now entering the U.S.
comes through Mexico."

By 1997 the "No More NAFTAs" camp had captured a good deal of political ground. A *Business Week*/Harris Poll of American opinion, reported in September 1997, showed that 36 percent of the respondents opposed NAFTA; that 34 percent thought the United States was harmed by NAFTA; that 56 percent believed expanded trade decreases the number of U.S. jobs; that 40 percent thought that expanded trade leads to lower wages; and that 54 percent opposed renewal of fast-track authority. These poll numbers, coupled with the last-minute, less-than-overwhelming White House push, easily explain fast-track's failure in the November 1997 straw vote.

We have little sympathy for the arguments put forward by the "No More NAFTAs" school. But we do concede that their arguments, underlined by the Mexican peso crisis, have altered the terms of political debate within the United States. We draw two lessons from this experience.

First, full employment is not enough. By that we mean that full employment in the United States, by itself, is not enough to ensure broad based support for free trade in general or fast-track legislation in particular. In addition to full employment, the United States needs a resumption of rising real wages, particularly for the bottom half of the labor force, before most Americans will again associate free trade with rising living standards. Of course a sustained rise in real wages depends on many factors besides the trade policies of the United States. Worker training and skills are particularly important. Pessimists should read the recent book by Bob Davis and David Wessel, *Prosperity*. These authors paint a picture of rising real wages for the American middle class over the next two decades, based on better training and effective use of information technology. Diffusion of information technology broadly among firms and workers is critical for a resumption of productivity growth—say to the level of 1.5 percent per worker per year. But even this optimistic prognosis carries implications: either free traders must accept the counsel of patience, waiting until background circumstances improve, or they must rely on strong presidential leadership to overcome popular skepticism.

Second, we endorse the slogan "No More NAFTAs," but with a

twist. The basic political flaw in NAFTA was that once it was over-attacked, it had to be oversold. NAFTA never had the potential for luring droves of U.S. corporations or sucking millions of American jobs into Mexico. Indeed, in 1996 U.S. direct investment in Mexico was less than one-half of 1 percent of nonresidential investment in the United States. Conversely, NAFTA could never transform Mexico into an economy with the prosperity of Texas, relatively free of corruption and drugs, with high labor and environmental standards. Those are tasks for two generations of Mexicans, not a single trade and investment agreement. Nor could NAFTA create hundreds of thousands of new U.S. jobs and significantly higher wages in the United States. Those gains essentially depend on good macroeconomics, a flexible labor force, better worker skills, and effective use of information technology. Yet in the political over-selling of NAFTA, critical for its enactment, themes were sounded that created overblown expectations—a perfect setup for NAFTA opponents. Thus when we say "No More NAFTAs," we mean no more free trade agreements that convey the aura of economic and political transformation abroad, and markedly more prosperity at home. This simple prescription has practical consequences.

The FTAA should not attempt to be comprehensive, covering huge swaths of economic and political life. The more ground that is covered, the greater the need for overselling, and the larger the space for disappointment, failed implementation, and recrimination.

We advocate "think small." The FTAA should focus primarily on removing tariff and nontariff barriers that interrupt trade at the border. Most investment issues can be left to the good sense of countries as they preen their images in the never-ending beauty contest to attract foreign investment—although an investment pact could be included in the FTAA package since the Western Hemisphere nations seem to be more "like-minded" on this topic than the OECD members. Most labor and environmental issues should be discussed outside the FTAA talks, but within the broader context of hemispheric relations. Most competition issues can be left for another day. FTAA members must retain responsibility for their own macroeconomic policies—monetary, fiscal, and exchange rate arrangements.

By history and geography, the United States is "married" to Canada and Mexico. The NAFTA accord recognized and extended unions created long before by common metropolitan areas, migration, investment, and culture. In these circumstances, a comprehensive agreement was appropriate. And, under the right circumstances, NAFTA might be extended to the Caribbean area and Central America, small countries that have strong links to the United States.

U.S. links with South America are far less extensive. Correspondingly, there is less call for a comprehensive agreement that irritates sensitive nerves and demands enormous political capital. In structuring the FTAA, the slogan "No More NAFTAs" makes sense. The FTAA goal should be to construct a simple free trade area: shallow integration, not economic union. The social agenda deserves continued attention, but it should not be viewed as a precondition for the FTAA. "Positive context" should be the watchword, not "economic sanctions."

The "WTO-Only" Criticism

The second negative argument against U.S. participation in the FTAA relates to concerns that the FTAA, and all regional pacts for that matter, are inherently discriminatory and thus promote trade diversion (even if they are subsequently shown to be on balance trade-creating). Moreover, the proliferation of different customs procedures and content requirements in these pacts can create substantial entry barriers to third-country suppliers. Accordingly, critics argue that FTAs are decidedly inferior to multilateral trade pacts, and indeed divert attention and resources away from the conduct of global negotiations.

We have no disagreement on the desirability of WTO negotiations: global trade deals clearly provide "more bang for the buck." We also share concerns about the tools of discrimination built into many FTAs, including most notably the NAFTA rules of origin. But, historically, such pacts have proven to be "building blocks" rather than "stumbling blocks" to multilateral trade reforms (to cite the apt distinction coined by Jagdish Bhagwati and popularized by Robert Z. Lawrence), and if properly constructed can continue to do so—and thus help participating countries prepare for new WTO negotiations that will overlap the FTAA talks at the start of the twenty-first century.

Latin America is not that big, when scaled against world economic magnitudes, but the FTAA can help demonstrate both to North and South Americans that countries at widely disparate per capita income levels can all benefit from freer trade and investment. Just as U.S.-Canada FTA and NAFTA served as templates for the framework agreements on services and intellectual property in the Uruguay Round, the FTAA can push the next global round of trade negotiations to accelerate the removal of tariffs and to tackle additional behind-the-border barriers.

While the FTAA has not yet taken form, there are several agreed-upon principles, set out in the San Jose ministerial declaration. The most important are that the FTAA will be consistent with the WTO, and that the FTAA will be a single undertaking. This means that all of the countries that sign the FTAA will adhere to all its obligations, and all agreements must have as their floor the WTO obligations.

To be sure, the demands of parallel regional and multilateral trade talks, with hundreds of negotiating sessions each year, seem daunting to small economies with limited staff and financial resources. But these talks would be complementary: the FTAA would require deeper liberalization applicable to a small group of countries (albeit those comprising the bulk of the trade for many of them); the WTO would demand less in terms of reform but apply the results to a broader range of countries.

Conclusions

What are the chances that the United States can achieve its laudable trade and foreign policy objectives in the hemisphere through the creation of the Free Trade Area of the Americas?

The Santiago Summit got the process off to a good start. The leaders formally launched the negotiations, established nine Working Groups to address the broad agenda of trade issues, and agreed on administrative procedures to manage the cumbersome process of engaging thirty-four countries in detailed trade negotiations. On the latter point, the leaders made two particularly important decisions: to hold another summit hosted by Canada in 2001 or 2002 and to assign the United States and Brazil as cochairs of the final two years of the FTAA negotiations, giving the leading economies in North and South America key responsibility for completing the deal. One could not have expected a better result out of Santiago, even if President Clinton had arrived with fast-track authority in his pocket.

So far, so good. But if the United States is to make substantive progress in the talks over the next few years, President Clinton will need to have fast-track authority well before the final stages of the talks in the early twenty-first century. The reason is straightforward: without fast-track, U.S. negotiators will be reticent to offer to reduce the few remaining, but important, barriers, protecting the U.S. market, particularly in sectors such as agriculture and apparel. Our hemispheric partners already have good access to the U.S. market in most areas, and will be hesitant to offer to reduce *their* key trade barriers, jealously guarded by their own domestic lobbies, if their governments are not assured of something in return from the United States.

Thus the FTAA negotiations risk prolonged drift, much like the Uruguay Round talks before the resolution of the U.S.-European impasse on agriculture, if the United States cannot claim its traditional role of demandeur in trade talks because of the lack of fast-track. Meanwhile, the United States and our hemisphere partners will be distracted by other regional and multilateral initiatives proceeding in parallel with the FTAA talks. The Mercosur countries will focus attention on the consolidation of their customs union and on new trade talks with the European Union. All thirty-four FTAA participants will be engaged in new WTO negotiations that are likely to be in full swing by the end of the decade. And domestic politics in the United States might refocus U.S. initiatives on domestic responses to globalization rather than new international initiatives. In brief, the FTAA process could be afflicted by a serious case of "attention deficit disorder."

This pessimistic scenario might be reversed by the third summit meeting in Canada in 2001 or 2002, which could become the "Resurrection Summit" for hemispheric trade relations. But the United

States would be better off "getting religion" in time to start the new millennium with a strong and active commitment to hemispheric trade.

Notes

[1]By comparison, sales to the U.S. market represent about half of all merchandise exports by Latin American and Caribbean countries.

[2]These data include investments in offshore financial centers, which account for 40 percent of U.S. FDI in Latin America and the Caribbean.

[3]For example, in 1997 the Canadian telecommunications firm Northern Telecom won a contract worth close to $200 million, partly because of tariff relief.

4

The United States and the Social Challenge in Latin America: The New Agenda Needs New Instruments

NANCY BIRDSALL
NORA LUSTIG
LESLEY O'CONNELL

Introduction: Why Social Progress in Latin America Is Relevant to the United States

A chapter on social equity in Latin America may not at first blush seem germane to a study of U.S. national interests in the Western Hemisphere. Unlike trade and national security, the problems of income inequality, poverty, and inadequate access to education and health in Latin America are not evident U.S. foreign policy concerns.

In this introduction we suggest why these so-called social issues should be a critical concern for U.S. foreign policy toward Latin America; in two subsequent sections we describe the social equity

NANCY BIRDSALL is executive vice president of the Inter-American Development Bank. She previously held various policy and management positions at the World Bank, where most recently she served as director of the Policy Research Department. She has been a senior advisor to the Rockefeller Foundation and has served on several committees of the National Academy of Sciences. Dr. Birdsall is also a member of the board of directors of the Population Council and the Social Science Research Council.

challenge in Latin America, and discuss how that challenge can be addressed using U.S. foreign policy instruments.

In the immediate aftermath of World War II, the United States through the Marshall Plan in Europe and massive assistance to Japan and other countries of East Asia supported open markets and open political systems. During the cold war these seemed the best guarantors of prosperity in those regions and thus the ideal bulwarks against the spread of communism. Not only implicit but central to U.S. support for open markets and open politics in Europe and Japan was support for what we will call in this chapter "sound and shared prosperity": economic and political systems that were based on transparent rules and on equal (i.e., broadly shared) economic opportunities.

The postwar foreign policy recipe did not need to specify "sound and shared" explicitly. It did not need to specify "sound" because in these settings the judicial and financial institutions that underlie property rights and reasonably sound banking and financial systems had existed in the prewar period; they did not have to be created from scratch. (Of course, financial systems were also much less liberalized and much less vulnerable to volatile international flows of capital in the immediate postwar period than they are everywhere today—as the financial crisis in Asia in 1997 has suggested.)

Even more to the point for this chapter, U.S. postwar assistance to reconstruction in Europe and Japan did not need to specify

NORA LUSTIG is the senior advisor and chief of the Poverty and Inequality Advisory Unit at the Inter-American Development Bank. From 1989–93 she was a visiting fellow and from 1993–97 a senior fellow in the Foreign Policy Studies Program at the Brookings Institution. Previously, Dr. Lustig was a professor of economics at El Colegio de México in Mexico City. She has served as a consultant for the Mexican government, the IDB, and the World Bank and has worked for the U.N. Economic Commission for Latin America.

LESLEY O'CONNELL is a consultant at the Inter-American Development Bank and an assistant to the executive vice president. Her research interests include policy responses to poverty and inequality in Latin America and labor market research in the region. The authors are grateful to Norma Garcia and Jose Antonio Mejia for their assistance.

"shared" prosperity because the ingredients for building economies based on widespread opportunities were essentially in place. In postwar Western Europe and Japan, social indicators such as education enrollment and income distribution reveal that in these regions a relatively large middle class already existed. For example, secondary enrollment rates in postwar United Kingdom, Germany, and Japan exceeded 70 percent. In contrast, only a few of the larger countries in Latin America today have reached this level of enrollment.[1]

A second critical indicator is income distribution. Looking at France, Germany, the United Kingdom, the United States, and Canada just after World War II, the median among the countries of the share of income of the richest 10 percent of earners was about 30 percent. Today, the median of the share of income of the richest 10 percent in the larger Latin American countries is about 40 percent.[2] In the long run, the relatively low income of a large share of potential consumers in Latin America could reduce the potential market for U.S. exports, and inhibit the kind of market integration that has fueled postwar prosperity among the OECD countries.[3]

Moreover, there are greater concerns than economic interests to justify U.S. attention to shared prosperity in its southern neighbors. In the post–cold war era, U.S. military hegemony is mediated by the less manageable forces of a global financial market and such new global challenges as greenhouse gas emissions, rapidly disseminated infectious disease, and the irrelevance of national borders to migratory movements and narco-trafficking. U.S. foreign policy toward Latin America is increasingly about issues outside the domain of the traditional strategic and military spheres; trade and investment regimes, immigration, and the war on drugs dominate the U.S. foreign policy agenda for this hemisphere.[4]

These global threats today can best be addressed, as was the case with the threat of communism, by support for healthy and sustainable growth in the rest of the world. The challenge is more immediate in Latin America, if only for its geographic proximity. It is also more manageable than elsewhere, because most countries of this hemisphere are politically committed to open markets and to the strengthening of democratic processes. But it is in a special sense also more challenging—because in Latin America the ingredients are not in place to ensure that prosperity, the key to healthy economic and political relations for the U.S., is adequately shared and thus sustainable.

So the message of this chapter is the following: it is not enough to support in general terms economic growth, open markets, and democracy in Latin America. The problem is that economic growth rates in Latin America are unsteady around a low average, and are sustained on a narrow base of middle and upper class contributors and beneficiaries. Growth is still relatively low and too narrow to deliver the benefits of better trade, safer investment, and less emigration of people and narcotics that are critical objectives of U.S. foreign policy in the hemisphere. The key to more sustained expansion is growth that is more inclusive, more shared, and built on a foundation of more sound judicial and financial systems—in short more like the postwar growth enjoyed in Japan and Western Europe.

The Morning After: Social Gaps and Inequality in Latin America

The region has been described as suffering from "morning after" problems (quoting Bernard Aronson in "The Morning After in Latin America," the *Washington Post*, October 12, 1997, c9). After a decade of dramatic economic reforms, countries are waking up with a headache—the need to do still more and deeper reforms to lock in the benefits of the last decade's efforts. Over the past decade, countries have implemented tough fiscal and monetary programs that have brought inflation from four-digit annual rates to single digits in most countries. Markets are as open as in any region of the world, with nontariff barriers eliminated and tariff rates down from 40 percent a decade ago to less than 15 percent today. Once highly centralized governments are being dismantled, with extensive privatization in some countries taking the state out of microeconomic decision making, and local elections and revenue sharing making once highly centralized political systems more accountable and responsive to voters as well as consumers.

These stabilization and structural reforms have started to pay off. During the 1990s most countries have enjoyed positive economic growth, fueled by higher rates of investments and consumption, and by greatly increased access to global capital markets. Mexico and Argentina recovered rapidly from the peso crisis of late 1994 and 1995, in marked comparison to what happened in the 1980s, when the 1982 debt crisis led Latin America into a decade of negative growth. Studies by the Inter-American Development Bank (IDB) economists suggest that the reforms of the last decade account for two percentage points of the region's average of 4 percent annual growth.[5]

But poverty and inequality in Latin America—both of which increased during the 1980s—have proven to be intractable in the face of reform. Latin America remains one of the most unequal regions in the world and one with the largest gap in human capital development controlling for the region's per capita income. (See Tables 1 and 2 on poverty and inequality in Latin America.) Latin America has a Gini coefficient—a typical measure of income inequality—that is approximately fifteen points above the average for the rest of the world. It is estimated that in 1995 the wealthiest 20 percent of the population was receiving close to 60 percent of the income, close to sixteen times that of the poorest 20 percent of the people. This share of income ratio (of the wealthiest 20 percent to the poorest 20 percent) compares to 10 to 1 in the United States, 8 to 1 in Asia, and approximately 5 to 1 in Western Europe. This high inequality is a symptom of poverty. The income of the poorest 40 percent of the population is probably some 20 percent lower than it would be with a typical pattern of income distribution. And the number of poor people, which currently stands at between 140 and 150 million individuals with daily earnings of less than $U.S.2, could be a third lower than it is.[6]

Reflecting and reinforcing these statistics on poverty and inequality is a series of more visible problems. Unemployment has increased inexorably throughout the 1990s,[7] despite growth—a sign that the pattern of growth continues to be based on capital-intensive sectors and processes, not altogether surprising given the relatively high cost of labor relative to labor productivity in the region. Low growth combined with a low elasticity of employment to growth (evidenced by rapid increases in productivity in the

TABLE 1: Poverty incidence estimates for Latin America and the Caribbean

Country/source	1979	1980	1981	1982	1983	1984
ONLY METROPOLITAN AREAS						
Argentina (Greater Buenos Aires)	4.4					
(poverty line local current currency)	239,028					
Paraguay (Metropolitan Asunción)				50.8*	54.5*	46.5*
(poverty line local current currency)					12,208	14,734
ONLY URBAN AREAS						
Bolivia (urban)						
(poverty line local current currency)						
NATIONAL						
Bahamas						
Londoño/Székely	3.3					
Pov. line is $2 PPP 1985 per capita per month						
Brazil	31.2	28.2	28.7	21.7	33.1	
Pov. line is $2 PPP 1985 per capita per month						
Chile						
Colombia						
Pov. line is $2 PPP 1985 per capita per month						
Costa Rica						
(poverty line local current currency)						
El Salvador						
(poverty line local current currency)						
México					28.5	
(poverty line local current currency)					9,007	

Notes: (*) Income not adjusted for possible underreporting.
All poverty lines are reported in per capita per month local current currency, unless stated otherwise.

Sources:
Argentina: Altimir, Oscar, and Luis Beccaria (1997) "Efectos de los cambios macroeconomicos y de las reformas sobre la pobreza urbana en la Argentina,"
Paper prepared for the project "Politicas Macroeconómicas y Pobreza en América Latina y el Caribe" sponsored by IDB, UNDP and ECLAC.
Bahamas: Londoño, Juan Luis and Miguel Székely (1997), "Persistent Poverty and Excess Inequality: Latin America During 1970–1995," OCE Working Paper Series #358.
Bolivia: Vos, Rob, Haeduck Lee and José Antonio Mejia (1997) "Structural Adjustment and Poverty in Bolivia," Indes Working Paper #I-3. Inter-American Development Bank.
Brazil: Londoño, Juan Luis and Miguel Székely (1997), "Persistent Poverty and Excess Inequality: Latin America During 1970–1995," OCE Working Paper Series #358.
Chile: Anriquez, Gustavo, Kevin Cowan and José De Gregorio (1997) "Poverty and Macroeconomic Policies: Chile 1987–94,"
Paper prepared for the project "Politicas Macroeconómicas y Pobreza en América Latina y el Caribe" sponsored by IDB, UNDP and ECLAC.

1985	1986	1987	1988	1989	1990	1991	1992	1993	1994	1995	1996
9.6					13.8			13.0		20.2	
68.5					1,106,455			146.4	155.8		
47.4*	42.1*	38.6*	32.7*	31.5*	31.3*	29.2*	27.6*	22.3*	21.8*	20.8*	
9,449	22,817	27,784	34,604	47,906	60,199	76,785	90,508	103,306	124,438	140,183	153,906
			71*				57*		59*		
			133				220		271		
	4.6		5.8	6.8		8.1	8.9	8.9			
31.5	25.7	33.3		45.4	46.3		42.7	45.4		43.5	
	45.1			38.6		32.6		28.4			
		23.1			19.6	19.1	17.4	16.5	15.2		
21.2	21.2	19.6	18.8	22.8	20.0	15.7	14.6	14.5	15.5		
1,739	2,101	2,448	2,914	3,751	4,570	5,016	5,919	7,015	7,988		
						41.0	41.0	40.0	34.0		
						271	327	368	400		
			32.6				31.3		31.8		
			158,584				316,245		378		

Colombia: Mejía, José Antonio and Rob Vos (1997) "Poverty in Latin America and the Caribbean. An Inventory, 1980–95," Working Paper Series I-4, INDES. Inter-American Development Bank.
Costa Rica: Sauma, Pablo and Leonardo Garnier (1997) "Efecto de las politicas macroeconómicas y sociales sobre la pobreza en Costa Rica,"
Paper prepared for the project "Politicas Macroeconómicas y Pobreza en América Latina y el Caribe" sponsored by IDB, UNDP and ECLAC.
El Salvador: Mejía, José Antonio and Rob Vos (1997) "Poverty in Latin America and the Caribbean. An Inventory, 1980–95," Working Paper Series I-4, INDES. Inter-American Development Bank.
Mexico: Lustig, Nora C. and Miguel Székely (1997) "México: Evolución económica, pobreza y desigualdad," Paper prepared for the project "Politicas Macroeconómicas y Pobreza en América Latina y el Caribe" sponsored by IDB, UNDP and ECLAC.
Paraguay: Morley, Samuel and Rob Vos (1997) "Poverty and Dualistic Growth in Paraguay," Paper prepared for the project "Politicas Macroeconómicas y Pobreza en América Latina y el Caribe" sponsored by IDB, UNDP and ECLAC.

TABLE 2: Gini coefficient estimates for Latin America and the Caribbean.

Country	1979	1980	1981	1982	1983	1984	1985
ONLY METROPOLITAN AREAS							
Argentina (Greater Buenos Aires)	...	0.332	...	...	...	...	...
Paraguay (Metropolitan Asuncion)	...	...	...	...	0.473	0.463	0.47⊂
ONLY URBAN AREAS							
Bolivia (urban)	...	...	...	...	...	...	...
Ecuador (urban)	...	...	...	...	...	...	...
NATIONAL							
Brazil	0.602	0.571	0.550	0.543	0.591	...	0.60⊙
Chile	...	0.531	...	...	...	...	...
Colombia	...	...	...	...	...	...	...
Costa Rica	0.480	...	...	...	...	...	...
El Salvador	...	...	...	...	...	...	...
Honduras	...	...	...	...	...	...	...
Jamaica	...	...	...	...	...	...	...
México	...	...	...	...	...	0.429	...
Perú	...	...	...	...	...	...	...
Venezuela	0.384	0.447	0.443	0.445	0.449	0.593	0.4�⊂

Sources:
Argentina: Altimir, Oscar and Luis Beccaria (1997) "Efectos de los cambios macroeconomicos y de las reformas sobre la pobreza urbana en la Argentina,"
Paper prepared for the project "Politicas Macroeconómicas y Pobreza en América Latina y el Caribe" sponsored by IDB, UNDP and ECLAC.
Bolivia: Mejía, José Antonio and Rob Vos (1997) "Poverty in Latin America and the Caribbean. An Inventory, 1980–95," Working Paper Series I-4, INDES. Inter-American Development Bank.
Brazil: Londoño, Juan Luis and Miguel Székely (1997), "Persistent Poverty and Excess Inequality: Latin America During 1970–1995," OCE Working Paper Series #358.
Chile: Londoño, Juan Luis and Miguel Székely (1997), "Persistent Poverty and Excess Inequality: Latin America During 1970–1995," OCE Working Paper Series #358.
Colombia: Mejía, José Antonio and Rob Vos (1997) "Poverty in Latin America and the Caribbean. An Inventory, 1980–95," Working Paper Series I-4, INDES. Inter-American Development Bank.
Costa Rica: Mejía, José Antonio and Rob Vos (1997) "Poverty in Latin America and the Caribbean. An Inventory, 1980–95," Working Paper Series I-4, INDEX. Inter-American Development Bank.
Ecuador: Larrea, Carlos (1995) "Structural Adjustment, Income Distribution and Employment in Ecuador," Mimeo, Centre for International Studies, University of Toronto.
El Salvador: Mejía, José Antonio and Rob Vos (1997) "Poverty in Latin America and the Caribbean. An Inventory, 1980–95," Working Paper Series I-4, INDES. Inter-American Development Bank.

1986	1987	1988	1989	1990	1991	1992	1993	1994	1995	1996
0.344	...	...	...	...	0.358	...	...	0.362	...	0.384
0.489	0.449	0.463	0.483	0.398	0.445	0.454	0.472	0.480	0.503	...
0.514	...	...	0.515	...	...	...	0.520	...	0.537	...
...	...	...	0.420	0.440	0.510	0.480	0.490	...	...	...
0.563	0.580	...	0.607	0.611	...	0.594	0.617	...	0.614	...
...	...	...	0.590	0.585	0.580	0.575	0.570	0.565	...	...
...	...	...	...	...	...	...	0.610	0.580	0.571	...
...	...	...	0.460	0.459	0.472	0.463	0.465	0.478	0.464	0.469
...	...	...	...	...	...	0.531	0.523	0.530	0.500	...
.55 (urb)	...	...	0.591	0.579	...	0.552	...	0.553	0.562	0.535
...	...	0.431	0.433	0.418	0.411	0.382	0.379	...	...	...
...	...	...	0.469	...	...	0.475	...	0.477	...	...
0.430	...	...	...	...	...	...	...	0.449	...	...
0.474	0.469	0.474	0.461	0.459	0.457	0.446	0.449	0.498	0.471	...

Honduras: Mejía, José Antonio and Rob Vos (1997) "Poverty in Latin America and the Caribbean. An Inventory, 1980–95," Working Paper Series I-4, INDES. Inter-American Development Bank.
Jamaica: Londoño, Juan Luis and Miguel Székely (1997), "Persistent Poverty and Excess Inequality: Latin America During 1970–1995," OCE Working Paper Series #358.
Mexico: Lustig, Nora C. and Miguel Székely (1997) "México: Evolución económica, pobreza y desigualdad," Paper prepared for the project "Politicas Macroeconómicas y Pobreza en América Latina y el Caribe" sponsored by IDB, UNDP and ECLAC.
Paraguay: Mejía, José Antonio and Rob Vos (1997) "Poverty in Latin America and the Caribbean. An Inventory, 1980–95," Working Paper Series I-4, INDES. Inter-American Development Bank.
Peru: Londoño, Juan Luis and Miguel Székely (1997), "Persistent Poverty and Excess Inequality: Latin America During 1970–1995," OCE Working Paper Series #358.
Venezuela: Londoño, Juan Luis and Miguel Székely (1997), "Persistent Poverty and Excess Inequality: Latin America During 1970–1995," OCE Working Paper Series #358.

1990s) has meant that the one-time employment losses associated with the privatization process and downsizing of public employment have not been compensated by sufficient private sector job creation. High levels of violence and criminality make the lives of the urban poor even more miserable—murder rates are higher in Latin American cities than in any other region. Corruption in public life, especially where linked to drug trafficking, threatens the political fabric in many countries. Though public spending on education and health has increased by as much as 20 percent in the 1990s, most of the increase has gone to higher salaries for teachers and health workers, and the shortfalls in investment in public social services and infrastructure of the 1980s have not been made up.

With significant political and social capital already exhausted during the last decade of economic reform, these social problems are trying the patience of the middle class and of the voters; they make the region vulnerable politically to any financial or economic shock, and they provide fodder to a resurgence of populist attacks on the open market policies that have brought a return to modest growth. Perhaps more importantly, the sharp inequities and persistent social exclusion pose a continuous threat to democratic institutions and social peace.

What are the ingredients of a successful attack on these social problems? In the rest of this section, we outline two: raising the "sound," sustainable growth rate in the region through labor, tax, judicial, financial, and other so-called second generation reforms; and moving toward "shared" or more inclusive growth by complementing the second generation reforms with a big push in education. (In fact, as should become clear, "sound" and "shared" growth are highly interdependent.)

Raising the Rate of Sound Growth

Available estimates by the IDB suggest that without deepening and extending current reforms the region's sustainable rate of annual growth is no more than 4 percent. There are at least two problems. First is the vulnerability of current growth to external financial shocks as well as to internal political changes because of still-weak banking and financial sectors and because in several countries the structural reforms to pension and civil service systems needed for fiscal stability are not in place. The stabilization and reforms completed by many countries in the early 1990s produced a better framework for growth but also led to spending and credit booms in excess of what local economies could absorb. High growth rates in the region in the mid-1990s were partly influenced by this temporary overabundance of spending and credit. Such financial booms led to financial, external, and fiscal vulnerabilities. In some countries, banks became overextended and took on excessive risk. External debt increased at an unsustainable rate, while the real exchange rate appreciated and exports lost competitiveness.

Efforts to strengthen financial systems in the aftermath of the 1994–95 Mexican peso crisis helped inoculate Latin America from the first-round effects of the 1997 Asian flu. But the region is still vulnerable. The maintenance of macroeconomic stability is difficult where financial systems are weak or poorly regulated, or when fiscal institutions do not allow room for maneuver during critical periods, as Brazil's recourse to tight monetary policy and high interest rates in late 1997 showed. Much remains to be done to strengthen the banking sector and to deepen domestic capital markets in the region.

Second, the reform process has been incomplete, ironically limiting the growth benefits of the considerable success of stabilization programs and trade liberalization. Privatization efforts in many countries are still in their early stages, and their benefits are threatened because of weak regulatory systems and institutional difficulty in enforcing the market rules of the game. In Mexico, for example, poorly done banking privatization was one of the factors behind the Mexican peso crisis, and the banking sector's rescue program is costing Mexican taxpayers a substantial amount. Likewise for the privatized toll roads, which became financially unviable, forcing the government to put up public monies for a rescue package of considerable amount. Only a half dozen countries have addressed the fiscal burden of underfunded pension systems. Reform of labor market systems also has moved slowly.

These largely institutional reforms are more politically demanding and more technically complex than the first generation reforms—fiscal, monetary, and exchange rate adjustments and trade liberalization, which can be accomplished by a small technical cadre that has political backing. Institutional reforms require more political and social consensus to initiate and to sustain. Yet they are absolutely necessary to guarantee the benefits of first generation reforms.

Inclusive Growth—Closing the Education Gap

Without sustained growth, efforts to reduce poverty and improve living standards will not show any significant results. But even with sustained growth, the pace of poverty reduction will be too slow unless current inequality in the distribution of income improves. For example, at yearly growth rates of 3 percent per capita, it could take between 60 and 200 years, depending on the country, to completely eradicate poverty as measured by the proportion of individuals living below U.S.$2 per day.[8] Hence, making the growth process more inclusive is crucial. Only with broad based, inclusive growth will the base of stakeholders in the reform process increase, facilitating the consensus building necessary for the deepening of democracy and sustained governability in the region.

The key to inclusive growth is ensuring the current poor acquire education. In its 1997 *Economic and Social Progress Report,* the IDB identified the lag in education as the greatest obstacle to future growth in the region. It estimates that if the workforce had one more year of schooling than is expected from current trends over the next decade, the weighted average growth rate would rise by 1.5 percentage points annually, an effect equal to approximately half the permanent effect of all structural reforms to date. To remove this obstacle to growth, the countries of the region must improve the levels and quality of schooling as well as the distribution of human capital.

Weak Human Capital Accumulation. Controlling for its per capita income, Latin America's performance in human capital accumulation is weak compared to other regions. This is particularly true for education: average schooling attainment is two years below what would be expected given its per capita income, a record barely better than that of sub-Saharan Africa and well below that of South and East Asia. At the beginning of the 1990s workers had an average of 5.2 years of education, nearly a third less than would be expected for countries with the region's level of development. More than a third of the children entering primary school were not finishing, over twice the rate of other regions in the world.

The education gap, moreover, has increased over the last three decades. At the start of the 1970s, Latin America had a low level of education, lower than the countries of Europe and Southeast Asia with comparable income levels but not different from the rest of the developing world, once adjusted on a per capita basis. Since then, education in Latin America (led by Brazil, Mexico, Venezuela, and Central America) has grown at a positive but slow rate, well below the growth achieved by the Asian countries and the rest of the developing world. In 1980 the region's work force lagged behind the average for the developing world in number of years of education by an average of one year. By the mid-1990s, this figure had doubled. Compared to East and Southeast Asia, Latin America's shortfall in education increased from less than one year in 1970 to about four years in 1995 (see Figure 1).[9]

Unequal Human Capital Distribution. Compared to East Asia and the industrialized countries, Latin America has high inequality of human capital.[10] (Its inequality of land, another critical productive asset, is the highest of any region—Figures 2a and 2b.) Thus the low rate of overall accumulation—an average of healthy increases in the number of years of school completed for a small number and limited increases for the great majority—is due in part to the unequal nature of the accumulation. The inequality of education in Latin America has remained virtually unchanged in the last twenty-five years compared to marked improvement in East Asia (see Figure 3).

What has been the effect of low and unequal human capital accumulation on the growth rate in Latin America over the last

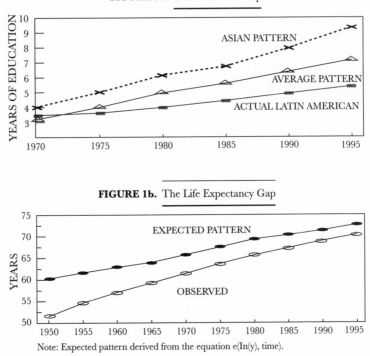

FIGURE 1a. The Education Gap

ASIAN PATTERN

AVERAGE PATTERN

ACTUAL LATIN AMERICAN

YEARS OF EDUCATION

1970   1975   1980   1985   1990   1995

FIGURE 1b. The Life Expectancy Gap

EXPECTED PATTERN

OBSERVED

YEARS

1950   1955   1960   1965   1970   1975   1980   1985   1990   1995

Note: Expected pattern derived from the equation e(In(y), time).

Source: Inter-American Development Bank (1996).

three decades? A now conventional result of econometric studies is that a higher level of education at the beginning of a period is good for growth. Recent analyses indicate that taking into account the level of education, it is also likely that the distribution of education separately affects growth; greater inequality in the distribution of education across adults is associated across countries with lower growth.[11]

Moreover, an unequal distribution of education interacting with higher returns to higher levels of education helps sustain higher income inequality. In Latin America, a relatively small pro-

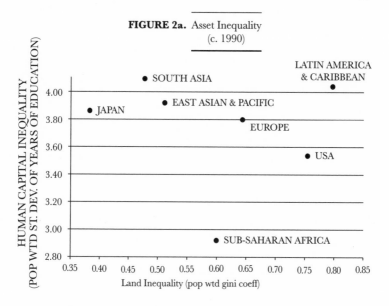

FIGURE 2a. Asset Inequality
(c. 1990)

portion of the population has completed secondary or higher education. These relatively few skilled workers earn a substantial wage premium due to their limited supply, thus contributing to overall high income inequality. The Latin American experience stands in marked contrast to that of East Asia, where education policy has produced a large supply of skilled workers, eroding any substantial premium they might have earned above the wages of the unskilled.

Measures to Improve Human Capital. What can be done to increase the average schooling and improve the distribution of educational attainment in Latin America? The problem is not primarily one of low public commitment to health and education; as a percentage of GDP, expenditures are similar to other developing regions, at 6.6 percent (see Table 3). The problem instead has had two parts. First, Latin America has not benefitted from the higher absolute expenditures per child (to use education as an example) that East Asia managed. As the economies of those regions grew faster in

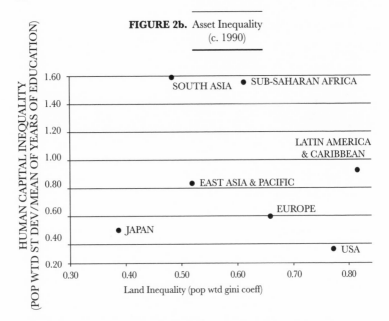

FIGURE 2b. Asset Inequality
(c. 1990)

Note: In figure 2a, the measure of human capital inequality is the standard deviation of education of the population aged 25 years and over. In figure 2b, the measure of human capital inequality is the coefficient of variation, i.e., the standard deviation divided by the mean; this measure controls for the effect of any changes in the average level of education on the distribution. Note that Latin America's high inequality of human capital (figure 2a) declines relative to other regions when the standard deviation of adults' education is divided by the mean of adults' education. Latin America's relatively high level of education compared to other developing regions is not enough to offset its high standard deviation, given its mean, compared to East Asia and the developed regions.
Sources: Human capital inequality was calculated using Barro-Lee's (1933) education attainment data. Land ginis are from Deininger and Squire (personal correspondence).

the 1970s and 1980s and as the number of school-age children fell with a decline in fertility, the same effort in GDP terms was higher in absolute terms.[12] Secondly, public expenditures on education in Latin America have been relatively heavily concentrated at the university level (between 30 and 40 percent of the total, compared to 10 to 30 percent in other regions), reducing per child expenditures at primary and secondary level (and nominally limiting the number and reducing the pool of successful candidates eligible for university training). This allocation has been only one symptom of the inefficient use of public expenditures and the unequal inci-

FIGURE 3. Inequality of Human Capital: A Regional Comparison

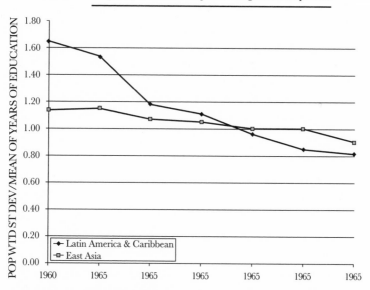

Note: East Asia includes Hong Kong, Indonesia, Republic of Korea, Malaysia, Singapore, Taiwan, and Thailand. Human capital inequality is measured here by the mean-adjusted standard deviation of years of education.
Sources: Human capital inequality was calculated using Barro-Lee's (1933) education attainment data.

TABLE 3. Social Expenditure in the 1990s (% of GDP)

| | | Public Expenditure | | Private Expenditure |
	Total	Education	Health	Health
Latin America	6.6	3.6	3.0	3.1
Other Developing Countries	6.4	4.2	2.2	1.9
All Developing Countries	6.5	4.1	2.4	2.2
Worldwide	9.9	5.1	4.8	3.2

Source: Inter-American Development Bank (1996).

dence of public spending—that is, the relatively low proportion of public spending that has benefitted the poor.

Public spending on education has increased in the 1990s, but the region's educational institutions suffered near collapse in the 1980s, and are now in urgent need of systemic reform. The issue is less one of expanded coverage than of fundamental changes in organizing and financing to allow competition and create accountability to consumers. It is not the purpose of this paper to set out the nature of the necessary reforms; this is addressed extensively elsewhere. What is critical is that the challenge be seen not merely as one of more schools, more books, or better teachers, but one of institutional reform and changes in incentives to make educational systems responsive to parents and communities, and accountable—which often means decentralizing national systems, and giving much more autonomy at the school level to school directors and parents.

This reform process is not easy. For example, designing and imposing a top-down reform without the support of mid-level bureaucrats and teachers' unions will not work. Moreover, improving educational standards requires multiple efforts, in such areas as health and nutrition for children, as well as financial measures directed to reducing the high dropout rates of the poor—such as scholarships for poor families with school-age children. By the mid-1990s, however, it was already evident that the governments of the region were prepared to address more systematically financial and organizational challenges in the social sectors—in part because first generation reforms had created a more stable macro-economic environment. The number and scope of reform efforts has been growing, and the priority of education for the region was enshrined in the 1998 Santiago Summit Plan of Action.

The United States: Supporting Sound and Shared Growth in Latin America

Just as Latin America is experiencing the "morning after" a decade of reforms, the United States in this post–cold war world is redefining its relationship with the region. The traditional rubric of military and strategic alliances that governed hemispheric relations in the past has been displaced by a more complex network of concerns and actors driven by regionalization, globalization, and democratization. U.S. interest in promoting the economic, social, and political development of the region has advanced from the monolithic goal of stemming communism to a multidimensional agenda to advance a range of concerns. Principal of these is cultivating new markets for U.S. trade and investment. Supporting democracy and broad based development in the region also provides the underpinnings for regional peace and a climate of cooperation in coping with common problems. Greater and more inclusive prosperity enables countries to become more effective partners of the United States in controlling global drug and crime cartels, maintaining a healthy environment, and preventing the spread of infectious diseases. In addition, shared prosperity in Mexico and Central America reduces the pressures to migrate to the United States.

The context in which the United States interacts with Latin America has also changed dramatically. International trade has largely replaced foreign aid; private capital flows dwarf multilateral lending; and societies are increasingly integrated as advances in telecommunication and transportation systems thin borders. The United States must employ new instruments to achieve its increasingly complex agenda. It can accomplish this at three levels: (1) bilaterally, through open markets and targeted aid; (2) multilaterally, in effective partnership with the countries in the hemisphere; and (3) plurilaterally, as hemispheric relations among civil society and private actors expand.

Bilaterally—From Aid to Trade

With the dwindling of aid following the end of the cold war and the liberalization of commercial and financial markets, U.S. leverage in the region has shifted along with the region's development strategy—from aid to trade.

Targeting Aid. Although bilateral aid to Latin America is an important instrument for furthering sound policies, it is no longer the main vehicle by which the U.S. can influence policy making in the region. Official aid has lost some of its sway for two reasons. First, aid is drying up. USAID managed resources dropped from $1.5 billion in 1985 to $400 million in 1997. Second, it constitutes a drop in the bucket compared to private capital flows; most Latin American countries have access to private capital markets and no longer look to official development assistance as their main source of funds.[13]

Despite its reduced volume, bilateral aid continues to be a useful tool for the United States to support specific, highly focused initiatives critical to the success of the second generation reforms discussed above. A good example is the support that USAID provides for innovative programs of reform of basic education, where small amounts can catalyze significant change. A second example is USAID's support to citizens' groups to build capacity for effective public scrutiny of governments, including via active citizen participation at municipal and community levels.

Although targeted aid continues to play an important role, the single best vehicle for promotion by the United States of "sound and shared" prosperity in the region is through the opening of markets and the expansion of trade and investment flows. This strategy is also in the U.S. economic interest.

Expanding Trade. As Latin America has prospered, so has the United States. With the recovery of the region from the debt crisis in the mid-1980s, bilateral trade has increased manyfold: U.S. exports to Latin America and the Caribbean more than tripled from $31 billion in 1985 to $95 billion in 1995, supporting 2 million U.S. jobs in that year alone. The region is the fastest growing and largest market for U.S. exports of goods and services. In 1996 it consumed 39 percent of U.S. exports compared to 30 percent by Asia and 23 percent by Europe. Moreover, Latin America spends an estimated 40 cents of every dollar earned from its exports on U.S. products. The U.S. supplies over two-fifths of the region's imports. In no other part of the world is the United States so competitively positioned. But this position is being challenged by Europe and Asia.[14]

Practically all the countries in Latin America are betting on an open market growth strategy. In the last decade, programs of trade liberalization have spread throughout the region. These programs have eliminated restrictions and permits for imports, reduced and unified tariffs, and unified exchange rates. Tariffs have been reduced from 41.6 percent in the pre-reform years to 13.7 percent in 1995, and maximum tariffs have been cut from an average of 83.7 percent to 41 percent. More than two dozen bilateral and regional trade agreements have been signed, and in 1994, at the Summit of the Americas in Miami, the countries of the region committed themselves to the creation of a hemispheric free trade area (FTAA).

However, the continuation of open market growth strategies in large part depends on their success in encouraging shared growth. In the short run, trade liberalization in Latin America has been associated with increased unemployment and wage inequality and has raised concerns about poverty and employment stability.[15] But studies suggest that liberalization is also promoting shared growth by increasing the real income of the poorest population while decreasing that of the wealthiest.[16] These distributive effects may derive from the stimulation of labor-intensive exports (since that is the most abundant factor in developing countries), thereby generating employment, and from the elimination of the rents importers and protected industries were receiving. The poorest also may benefit from decreases in consumer prices caused by increased competition.

(Similarly, the social inequities in Latin America are eroding U.S. support for free trade. A recent indicator was the U.S. failure to adopt fast-track negotiating authority. The obstacles to securing fast-track reflect the American public's concern that the employment and social conditions in the region will adversely affect them. The American people are not willing to buy goods made by children or exploited prisoners or extremely low-paid workers. However, tackling interregional social and environmental shortcomings through trade agreements can undermine free trade initiatives as labor and environmental issues can give rise to protectionism. As discussed below, the U.S. needs to directly address these issues through other channels, including official forums, such as the working committees created through the 1994 Summit of the

Americas, the multilateral institutions, and the ILO and other UN agencies, as well as through nongovernmental and private initiatives.)

Promoting shared growth in Latin America requires increasing the region's access to U.S. markets. Increasing trade opportunities with the U.S. is important because for many countries the United States is their largest market. This is particularly true for some of the region's poorest countries. For example, the Central American and Caribbean countries need improved access to U.S. markets because of their loss of markets and of investments to Mexico due to NAFTA.

U.S. trade policy in agriculture is of particular relevance to promoting shared growth in the region. The agricultural sector accounts for a significant portion of the exports of most Latin American and Caribbean countries and is an important source of employment and income for the rural poor. However, U.S. agricultural policies restrict agricultural imports while subsidizing exports. A system of target prices, deficiency payments, and price support through nonrecourse loans encourages excess production of cotton, grains, sugars, and oilseeds.[17] Though some developing countries benefit from the existing U.S. programs through lower food prices and in some cases out-in-out grants, the programs undercut the position of indigenous producers in developing countries, affecting their long-term food security as well and jeopardizing economic development. This effect is compounded by U.S. restrictions on agricultural imports. The U.S. maintains an import quota on raw sugar that depresses the world market price of sugar. Some Latin American and Caribbean countries with access to the U.S. market benefit from import quota rents because they sell at the higher U.S. price. (Latin America and the Caribbean supplied over 65 percent of total U.S. sugar imports during the 1995–96 period.) But the remaining producers face depressed international demand and prices.

Increasingly barriers to trade take the form of consumer and environmental protections. Most important of these to Latin America and the Caribbean are the phytosanitary regulations and marketing orders (designating that the grade, quality, size, or maturity regulation of imports meet the requirements of domestic orders). The United States also protects the textiles and clothing industry, another industry with an employment impact on the poor. The United States was the only member of the World Trade Organization to have imposed new quotas under the Agreement on Textiles and Clothing safeguard procedures. It established safeguard quotas toward Colombia, Costa Rica, the Dominican Republic, El Salvador, Guatemala, Honduras, and Jamaica. The United States also maintains antidumping and countervailing duties on a number of products. These "trade remedy actions" are often kept in place for many years and serve as barriers to trade. Examples of products affected by these trade policies are outlined in Table 4.

TABLE 4

Quota Limits on Textiles	Countervailing Duties (as of 2/96)	Antidumping Duties (as of 2/96)	Standards and Regulations	EEP Awards to LAC Countries
Brazil	Argentina - wool, leather	Brazil - orange juice	Phytosanitary regulations- avocados, tomatoes	Brazil - barley malt
Colombia	Brazil - castor oil, cotton yarn	Chile - carnations	Marketing order regulations- avocados, dates, grapefruit, table grapes, kiwi fruit, limes, olives, onions, oranges, prunes, raisins, tomatoes, and walnuts	Caribbean - barley malt
Costa Rica	Chile - carnations	Mexico - fresh cut flowers		Cent. America - wheat
Dom. Republic	Peru - chrysanthemums			Colombia - barley malt
El Salvador				Honduras - wheat
Guatemala				Nicaragua - wheat
Honduras				Venezuela - barley malt
Jamaica			Marine Mammal Protection Act- yellow fin tuna	Trinidad and Tobago - wheat

Source: Barriers to U.S.–Latin American Trade, 1996, ECLAC (1996).

Since 1990 most countries of the region have unilaterally begun liberalizing their agricultural markets, introducing tariffs to replace absolute barriers, eliminating quota restrictions, reducing the role of state trading agencies, and removing export taxes. These reforms continued even in the face of the declining profitability of the sector due to the appreciation of their currencies and the international decline in key agricultural products. Unfortunately, the strain on profitability has increased domestic pressure for protection and reduces the potential impact of increased agricultural production on employment and wages. Continued efforts by the U.S. to open its agricultural markets would be consistent with an emphasis on inclusive growth in the region, and are critical to continued liberalization in this sector.

Multilaterally—as Partners in the Hemisphere

As U.S. influence in Latin America through bilateral ties has been weakened by the decline in aid and the region's increasing integration in global commercial and capital markets, U.S. participation in multilateral organizations (the International Monetary Fund, the World Bank, the Inter-American Development Bank, the Organization of American States, the Pan American Health Organization, and other agencies of the UN system) has become an increasingly important vehicle for U.S. foreign policy. This is especially true of the IMF and the multilateral development banks given their command over financial resources and given the centrality of economic relations in the overall foreign policy relationship of the United States in the last several decades.

The United States is the largest single shareholder of the IDB (more than 30 percent of shares and more than 60 percent of usable callable capital) and a major shareholder of the World Bank (17 percent of shares) and of the IMF (18 percent). It has exercised substantial influence on these organizations through its influence in the selection of their leadership (including the president of the World Bank, the executive vice president of the IDB, and the senior deputy managing director of the IMF) and its participation in the definition of their institutional priorities. Indeed these international financial institutions provide an increasingly active forum for the discussion and design of economic policy, an increasingly central ingredient of U.S. foreign policy.

Starting in the early 1990s, the United States put social development in the forefront of the policy discussions in these institutions. This shift in emphasis followed the dramatic macroeconomic and trade reform of the 1980s in Latin America and reflected the consensus that policies to encourage "sound and shared" prosperity were needed.[18]

U.S. leadership explains in part why reducing poverty and social inequities has become the centerpiece of the IDB and the World Bank's mandates. In the case of the IDB, now the region's main source of multilateral financing, the United States led the successful effort to increase the IDB's capital (from $60 billion to $100 billion) in 1994. A key mandate associated with that capital replenishment was the U.S. proposal that 50 percent of the IDB's new lending operations and 40 percent of their dollar value go to programs and projects addressing problems of poverty and social equity. (In the 1990s the IDB and the World Bank have each approved new loans of between $5 billion and $7 billion annually.) More generally, the 1994 replenishment mandate supported "sound growth" by emphasizing economic reform and prescribing institutional reforms that enable markets to function better: programs to modernize the state, improve fiscal administration, make the judiciary more independent, strengthen legislatures, and revamp social security systems. The mandate emphasized "shared prosperity" through its support for reform of health and education; for improving the poor's access to decision making and increasing government accountability and transparency; for micro enterprise initiatives to increase credit to the poor; and for projects that enhance marginalized groups' productivity and participation in the growth process.

More recently, U.S. leadership has again encouraged renewed emphasis on social programs. In his speech at the IDB annual meeting in March 1998, Deputy Secretary of the U.S. Treasury Lawrence Summers proposed to double IDB lending for primary and secondary education. This proposal evolved into a commitment made at the 1998 Summit of the Americas in Santiago,

Chile, of both the IDB and the World Bank to double their lending for education to $5 billion each over the next five years.

However, U.S. influence on the policy agenda of the international financial institutions is not immutable. First the absence of new capital replenishments in the World Bank and the IDB, and the difficulty the United States has had in maintaining support for concessional programs in the banks, means it no longer has the leverage on strategic and policy issues that periodic replenishment discussions once provided. In addition, there have been the difficulties in securing congressional approval for an increase in U.S. commitments to the IMF. Second, U.S. influence has from time to time been undermined by the awkward constraints imposed by specific legislative mandates. The decertification of Colombia during 1996 and 1997 under antinarcotics legislation, for example, meant the United States could not support IDB sponsored loans and grants (and on the latter the United States exercised veto power) to fund antipoverty, women's leadership, and other programs that could have contributed more effectively to mainstreaming and strengthening legitimate public institutions, while simultaneously attacking a root cause of the drug trade—widespread poverty.

In the future, effective use of these institutions will require more coherent efforts within the U.S. government: more interagency coordination among executive agencies (between U.S. Treasury, which is the U.S. government's coordinating agency for these financial institutions, and USAID, the State Department, the Commerce Department, etc.), and between the administration and Congress. Given declining financial contributions, the United States will also increasingly need to rely on collaboration—with other nonborrowers and with borrowers—in defining hemispheric priorities.

Plurilaterally—through the Engagement of Civil Society and Private Actors

U.S.–Latin America relations are nowadays more porous; they have stretched beyond governments to include the civil society and private partnerships. A main challenge facing the U.S. foreign policy establishment is to expand and deepen the existing web of private exchanges, nurturing the many nongovernmental and private initiatives of the private sector and of civil society groups in the United States and Latin America that support "sound and shared" prosperity.

Over the last twenty years, civil society organizations have played a critical role in promoting shared growth in Latin America and the Caribbean. Tens of thousands of organizations have sprouted, filling the void created by the adjustment of the markets and the changing role of the state. Working with small businesses and local governments, these organizations are engaged in the delivery of social programs throughout the region. (Through its bilateral aid program, the United States contributed to the growth of these organizations. It used its diminishing resources to support work with nongovernmental agents, thereby channeling resources directly to communities in need and avoiding leakages caused by ineffective bureaucracies.)[19]

Leadership of the U.S. private sector is also critical to affecting "sound and shared" prosperity. For example, the adoption of anti-corruption initiatives and uniform accounting standards in the hemisphere will encourage sound growth by improving decision making and the allocation of resources (simultaneously safeguarding U.S. investments) and will also encourage shared prosperity by eliminating the inequities associated with corrupt practices. These are the kinds of issues that should command increasing attention of such groups as the Council of the Americas, the Council on Foreign Relations, and the Conference Board. These private U.S. organizations have counterpart groups of business leaders in Latin America. For example, the Group of Fifty, launched in 1993, builds networks among the most accomplished executives in the region to channel practical initiatives that further economic and social progress in Latin America.

Conclusion

In conclusion, post–cold war relations with Latin America have matured from traditional military and strategic alliances into a hemispheric partnership to advance a multidimensional agenda. This agenda includes promoting the region's democratic and social stability, improving regional competitiveness, and strengthening economic performance. Success along these dimensions will not only advance the region's development but also respond to several of the most-cited U.S. foreign policy concerns—trade expansion, protecting American foreign investment, and stemming the flow of illegal immigration and drugs.

However, success in all these areas depends heavily on the capacity of countries to sustain and deepen market reforms—and that in turn depends on their ability to reduce poverty and inequality. Policies that help balance the forces of globalization with social equity and thereby broaden the base of beneficiaries of market reform are critical if reform efforts are to be sustained. Critical among these policies is improving the level and distribution of education in the region. Education reform, however, like other second generation reforms, is politically complicated and technically demanding. Through its small but focused bilateral aid programs, and through its influence in the multilateral banks, the United States has provided useful backing for what has become a hemispheric commitment to improve education. Sustaining the momentum for education reform will require continued U.S. support, based on enlightened self-interest: education is key to the shared prosperity in the region that benefits the United States.

Put another way, the new hemispheric agenda requires new instruments. The shift from aid to trade necessitates further opening of U.S. markets if trade liberalization in Latin America is to benefit the poor. With the dwindling of aid and the region's increasing integration in global markets, the United States must participate even more effectively in the multilateral organizations. The multilateral development banks, in particular, have become a critical channel for U.S. political and financial influence. Finally, as hemispheric relations grow more diffused, and the number of civil society and private actors expands, the challenge for the United States lies in cultivating private exchanges and initiatives to promote sound and shared growth in the region.

Notes

[1]These countries include: Argentina—77 percent, Chile—72 percent, Peru—69 percent, and Colombia—67 percent; figures are gross enrollment rates. *UNESCO Statistical Yearbook*, various years.

[2]The shares of income of the richest 10 percent in these countries in 1950 were as follows: France—36.2 percent, Germany—36 percent, U.K.—33.2 percent, U.S.—28.9 percent, Canada—27.4 percent. Brenner et al. (1991). Of the Latin American countries, the current share of income of the richest 10 percent is as follows: Brazil—47.9 percent, Chile—46.1 percent, Venezuela—42.7 percent, Colombia—46.9 percent, Mexico—39.2 percent, Ecuador—35.6 percent. World Bank (1998).

[3]A comparison of per capita income in Brazil and the Philippines illustrates this point. In 1995 Brazil's per capita income (in international dollars) was almost twice that of the Philippines, but per capita income of the poorest 40 percent of the population was still lower (about four-fifths) that of the Philippines. Despite Brazil's greater national wealth and its proximity to the United States, in 1995 the United States exported more to the Philippines per capita than to Brazil per capita.

[4]What are America's top foreign policy concerns today? A Gallup Poll conducted mid-decade reveals that American public opinion on foreign policy reflects "pragmatic internationalism," favoring an active role by the U.S. in world affairs, but only as far as it impacts domestic problems. The two top-cited foreign policy concerns are stopping the flow of illegal drugs into the U.S. and protecting jobs of American workers. Ranking fourth is controlling and reducing illegal immigration; sixth is reducing the U.S. trade deficit with foreign countries; and ninth is protecting the interests of American businesses abroad. Support for more humanitarian goals (such as defending human rights, protecting weaker nations against aggressors, and helping to improve the standard of living of less developed countries) has decreased significantly, dropping to its lowest level in two decades. Reilly (1995).

[5]IDB (1997), p. 50.

[6]Birdsall and Londoño (1998), p. 12.

[7]According to the International Labor Organization, Argentina is one of the worst performers with unemployment increasing from 7.5 percent in 1990 to 17 percent in 1996. Other unemployment rates for the region recorded in 1996 are Brazil—6 percent, Chile—7 percent, Mexico—6 percent, Peru—9 percent, Uruguay—13 percent, and Venezuela—12 percent.

[8]Lustig and Deutsch (1998), p. 3.

[9]The shortfall in health is smaller compared to other regions. Average life expectancy is about two years below the expected, given income (Figure 1b). This result is perhaps due to a smaller gender gap in education than elsewhere, the positive effect of mothers' education on infant mortality, and relatively more spending and innovation in the health sector in Latin America.

[10]Our measure of inequality is the coefficient of variation, the mean-adjusted standard deviation of schooling (years of education estimated using Barro-Lee's frequency distribution for the population twenty-five years and over within categories of education, i.e., no schooling, incomplete primary schooling, completed primary schooling, incomplete secondary schooling, completed secondary school-

ing, incomplete higher schooling, and completed higher schooling). An increase in the coefficient of variation indicates an increase in the inequality of education.

[11]Birdsall and Londoño (1997).

[12]Birdsall, Bruns, and Sabot (1996) provide quantified comparisons of the effects on education spending per child of differences in economic growth and demographic changes between the two regions.

[13]However, the poorest countries in terms of per capita income do not have access to world capital markets and will not in the foreseeable future. Concessional lending to these countries is all the more necessary.

[14]The European Union has agreed to negotiate a reciprocal agreement with Mercosur (Argentina, Brazil, Paraguay, Uruguay, and Chile).

[15]The *Latinobarometro* (1996) public opinion poll of seventeen Latin American countries reflects considerable anxiety about employment stability and poverty as well as concern for social policy. Eighty-five percent of the Latin Americans surveyed felt that poverty had increased over the prior five-year period. Sixty-four percent believed the quality of education had declined or stayed the same, 55 percent viewed this pattern in health, and 64 percent felt similarly with respect to access to housing. In South America and Mexico, employment and education were viewed as the highest priority problems, while in Central America employment and inflation took priority. In South America and Central America, 68 percent and 77 percent, respectively, responded that they were worried or very worried about losing their job.

[16]Lora and Barrera (1997) analyzed thirteen countries during the 1985–95 period, and found that the adoption of trade liberalization policies was associated significantly with faster growth of the real incomes of the poorest 60 percent of the population and with the decline of the real revenues of the wealthiest 20 percent. However, these findings conflict with those of previous studies. The effects of trade liberalization on total income distribution are complex and influenced by many factors, including the countries' relative factor endowments, global technology changes, and recomposition of world trade patterns.

[17] The 1996 farm bill maintained most U.S. export support programs though it lowered funding levels to comply with the World Trade Organization's agricultural agreements.

[18]The consensus was articulated in the landmark 1994 Summit of the Americas.

[19]USAID's New Partnership Initiative launched in 1995 builds on ongoing agency programs and reform efforts, fostering synergies among the business community, local governments, and civic organizations. The program exemplifies how U.S. aid can multiply development initiatives in the region by encouraging exchanges and cooperation at the grassroots level.

5

United States–Latin American Relations at the Century's Turn: Managing the "Intermestic" Agenda

ABRAHAM F. LOWENTHAL

Exactly 100 years ago, at the turn of the nineteenth century to the twentieth, the United States became a significant international power by projecting its influence southward, first in the circum-Caribbean region and then eventually throughout all of South America.

From that time on, relations with the countries of Latin America and the Caribbean have been a significant aspect of defining

ABRAHAM F. LOWENTHAL is the founding president of the Pacific Council on International Policy, a Los Angeles based international leadership forum focusing on the international trends and relationships of greatest importance for the western United States. A widely published authority on Latin American and inter-American affairs, Dr. Lowenthal is also a professor of international relations at the University of Southern California and vice president and deputy national director of the Council on Foreign Relations. Dr. Lowenthal gratefully acknowledges helpful comments on an earlier draft by Frank Bean, Albert Fishlow, Peter Hakim, Jane Jaquette, Christopher Mitchell, Ambler Moss, Robert Pastor, Andres Rozental, George Shenk, Michael Shifter, Gregory Treverton, Viron P. Vaky, and Bernardo Vega as well as research assistance by Bernarda Duarte, Catherine Holt-Cedeño, and Pedro Villegas, and manuscript preparation by Emma J. Woodford.

the U.S. place in the world. By the mid-twentieth century, the
United States had become the preeminent influence throughout
the Western Hemisphere: economically, politically, culturally, and
militarily. A hegemonic relationship with Latin America became a
cornerstone of U.S. foreign policy: mostly unchallenged and therefore presumed, but vigorously defended whenever it was (or
seemed to U.S. policy makers to be) called into question.[1]

As the twentieth century ends, relations between the United
States and Latin America have entered a new era. Some of the
prime U.S. interests in regard to Latin America have been
achieved or have receded, the borders between Latin America and
the United States have blurred, the agenda of salient issues in
U.S.–Latin American relations has been largely transformed,
many of the key actors shaping U.S. policies are different from
those most influential in the past, and new U.S. policy approaches
should consequently evolve.

In the years to come, the United States will need to focus more
attention on a range of issues—immigration, narcotics, the environment, public health, and border management—which flow
directly from the unique and growing degree of interpenetration
between the United States and its nearest neighbors, especially
Mexico and the countries of Central America and the Caribbean.

These issues are neither classic security concerns nor are they
primarily economic, commercial, or financial in nature—although
they do have both security and economic dimensions. They com-
bine international and domestic facets and actors in new ways, and
are therefore problematic for governmental processes that were
originally designed to separate domestic and foreign policy considerations. As Bayless Manning pointed out in *Foreign Affairs* as early
as January 1977, such "intermestic" issues pose complex challenges
for American foreign policy.

"Intermestic" issues are of increasing concern to the American
public, which puts them at or near the top of its priority list; yet
because of their international aspects they cannot be dealt with
successfully by the United States alone. Significant tensions arise
because vociferous domestic demands that decisive steps be taken
on such concerns as narcotics, illegal immigration, and environmental pollution often conflict with what it takes to secure the

international cooperation needed to confront problems that transcend borders.

One of the greatest challenges for the United States today and for the foreseeable future is to devise, adopt, and implement approaches that can successfully engage Latin American governments and nongovernmental actors in helping to manage continuing problems that are at the heart of contemporary inter-American relations but that cannot be successfully addressed by unilateral U.S. policies. The substance, quality, and texture of much of U.S.–Latin American relations in the early twenty-first century will be largely shaped by whether effective and internationally cooperative policies can be fashioned and implemented to deal with these "intermestic" questions, and whether such policies can be sustained—not only in the United States but elsewhere in the Americas, particularly in the countries closest to the United States.

Traditional U.S. Interests in the Americas

From the Spanish American War and the construction of the Panama Canal a century ago until very recent times, Latin America's main significance to the United States was conceived in terms of military security, political solidarity, and economic advantage.

For many years, indeed, Latin America, and especially the Caribbean Basin, was central to the forward defense strategy of the United States. The Panama Canal itself, the Sea Lines of Communications (SLOCs) criss-crossing the Caribbean, and the military and naval facilities protecting access to the canal were all considered important security assets. Strategic materials imported from Latin America were valuable for U.S. military purposes, especially during World War II and the Korean conflict. Pan-American unity, i.e., regional support of U.S. diplomatic leadership, was a fundamental tenet of U.S. foreign policy, as a virtual Latin American bloc reliably backed U.S. positions in the world arena: after World War I, during and after World War II, and in the United Nations during the late 1940s, the 1950s, and the early 1960s. For many years, Latin America was also the main focal point for U.S. foreign private investment and the major source for many commodities central to the U.S. economy and lifestyle: petroleum, iron, copper, bauxite, and tin, as well as coffee, cocoa, sugar, and tropical fruits.

To advance and protect these three interests, and for broader geopolitical reasons, U.S. policy makers throughout the decades of this century sought to exclude potentially competing (and especially overtly hostile) extrahemispheric influence from the Americas. That was the primary aim of the repeated U.S. military interventions in the Caribbean Basin from 1898 through the early 1920s, of "dollar diplomacy" in the late 1920s, and then of Franklin D. Roosevelt's Good Neighbor Policy. From World War II through the 1980s, too, a major objective of successive U.S. administrations was to assure continued U.S. political and economic dominance in the Western Hemisphere, and particularly in the Caribbean Basin. This was the central goal of the Eisenhower administration's clandestine overthrow of Guatemala's Arbenz government; of John F. Kennedy's Alliance for Progress, as well as the Bay of Pigs invasion of Cuba and the subsequent commercial boycott of that island; of Lyndon B. Johnson's Dominican invasion; of Richard Nixon's Mature Partnership (and of clandestine U.S. intervention against Salvador Allende in Chile); of Henry Kissinger's "New Dialogue"; and of Ronald Reagan's Caribbean Basin Initiative, his invasion of Grenada, and his undeclared Contra war in Nicaragua.

During the thirty years from the early 1960s through the early 1990s, however, Latin America's objective importance to the United States on these traditional dimensions steadily declined.[2] Changes in technology first and then the waning of the cold war transformed defense calculations, and Latin America became much less relevant to U.S. strategic concerns. Even before the cold war ended, there was no credible scenario by which the military security of the United States could be directly threatened in the Americas. The network of military and naval facilities in the Caribbean lost its priority, therefore; indeed, not even the Panama Canal is as significant as it used to be, for U.S. Navy task forces are organized around aircraft carriers that are too large to transit the canal, as are the supertankers that bring petroleum to our shores. It is noteworthy that the largest remaining U.S. naval base in the Caribbean—the Guantanamo Bay facility in Cuba—became important again in the 1990s not because of military considerations but as a holding spot for Haitian "boat people" seeking entry into the United States.

Latin America's previous quasi-automatic diplomatic solidarity with the United States ended in the 1970s, as many Latin American nations came to act independently and in their own interests, often perceived more in economic than in security terms, and more in concert with other developing countries of "the South" than with the "Colossus of the North." Diversification of international ties has been a catchword of Latin American diplomacy for many years. When Latin American countries align with the United States today, it is mainly because of specific and concrete shared interests, not from a general presumption of Pan-American unity or of natural convergence of interest.

Latin America's relative economic importance to the United States also ebbed from 1960 through the 1980s, as the shares of U.S. trade with Latin America and of U.S. foreign private investment in the countries of Latin America and the Caribbean—as fractions of total U.S. foreign trade and foreign investment— declined sharply, with the explosion of U.S. investments and commerce in Europe and Asia. Whereas Latin America had accounted for more than 40 percent of U.S. foreign direct investment in 1950, for instance, this figure had dropped to 13 percent by the mid-1980s.

Latin America's New Relevance to the United States

Because of the relative decline in Latin America's significance for the United States in familiar security, political, and economic terms, it was an open question as the 1990s began whether Latin America would "fall off the map" of U.S. government concerns, especially as the cold war's end removed the element of worldwide competition for influence with the Soviet Union that for forty years had made every contested region seem important, at least for the top policy-making circles in the United States.

After the cold war's end, those who had most strenuously argued during the 1980s that Latin America—and especially Central America and the Caribbean—remained significant for U.S.

security began to suggest, on the contrary, that the Caribbean Basin and Latin America as a whole would be of diminished interest to the United States, now that the Soviet threat was no longer relevant. The logic of disengagement was reinforced, in this view, by U.S. budgetary pressure; by skepticism in Washington, New York, and elsewhere about Latin America's economic prospects; by doubts that the U.S. private sector would want to expand its presence in the area, with so many other opportunities in Asia and in both Western and Central-Eastern Europe; and by generally prevailing negative public attitudes in the United States about Latin America and the Caribbean. It was widely contended that Latin America would become ever more marginal in world affairs.

In fact, however, Latin America, or more accurately, the northern part of the region, has become more salient for the United States in the 1990s. Considerably increased U.S. attention has been paid to Mexico, to Central America and the Caribbean, and to a lesser degree to South America. Relations with the countries of the Western Hemisphere, especially with Mexico and the Caribbean Basin nations, have once again become a featured aspect of the U.S. world role. Latin America certainly does not command the highest priority from U.S. foreign policy makers, but it has not been badly neglected and indeed probably receives more sustained attention from both policy makers and the attentive public now than in previous decades. Instead of dropping off Washington's map, Latin Americans have helped redraw it.

Latin America's greater importance to the United States during the 1990s owes partly to the major twin trends emphasized in other chapters of this book: the simultaneous turns in the region toward democratic governance and free market economies. Latin America's progress in achieving electoral democracy in virtually every country—and in beginning to consolidate some of the habits and institutions of democratic governance in many—has greatly improved the region's prospects for partnerships with the United States, both at the state-to-state level and among corporations and other nongovernmental actors. Shared political values and institutions have been strongly reinforced by the paradigm shift in Latin American approaches to economics, the state's economic functions, and the role of the private sector. Convergence about the appeal of democratic politics and free markets throughout the Western Hemisphere (except in Cuba) has unquestionably enhanced the possibilities for inter-American cooperation. The vision of a Free Trade Area of the Americas, a cornerstone of declared U.S. policy in the 1990s, would not be possible, indeed, but for this convergence, however incomplete and fragile it may still be.

For much of Latin America, the most significant reason for renewed importance in American foreign policy has been economic. Latin America has become the fastest growing export market for U.S. goods and services, with U.S. exports growing twice as fast to Latin America as to the rest of the world. Latin America is the one market where U.S. goods and companies have consistently retained a competitive advantage. In 1997 the United States exported more to Brazil than to China, more to Argentina than to Russia, more to Chile than to India, and twice as much to Central America and the Caribbean as to Eastern Europe. If projected trends continue, U.S. exports to Latin America will be higher in 2010 than to Japan and the European Union together.

U.S. merchandise exports to Latin America and the Caribbean have grown overall from $34.5 billion in 1987 to $134.5 billion in 1997, and from 13.7 percent of all U.S. exports in 1987 to nearly 20 percent in 1997, but the overall figure masks the extraordinary importance of Mexico as a market. In Mexico alone, U.S. exports have jumped from $32 billion in 1991 to $71 billion in 1997; total U.S. exports to Mexico, the Caribbean, and Central America amounted to nearly $88 billion.

Latin America is also increasingly significant to the United States as a major and relatively secure energy supplier. Some 33 percent of the petroleum imported into the United States in 1997 came from Latin America and the Caribbean, up from 27 percent in 1990. A combination of geopolitical calculations, new discoveries and technologies, and rising Latin American willingness to privatize (or at least allow a greater role for foreign investors in) the energy sector will probably continue to drive this share up in the next few years.

U.S. foreign direct investment is likewise expanding in other sectors—agriculture, environmental technology, manufacturing, telecommunications, mining, many services, and tourism. It is drawn to Latin America by its significant markets, political and financial stability, relatively favorable human and physical infrastructure, and growing opportunities for privatization. As was the case in the first half of the century, Latin America is attractive for the U.S. business community.

Economic issues—centered on trade, finance, and investment—have long been at the heart of the relationships between the United States and Latin America, especially with the larger countries in the region, and they will remain important. Whenever broad national security concerns decline, it is concrete private sector interests that have largely defined the agenda of bilateral and regional relations and shaped their character.

With the globalization of economic interactions, however, an ever-larger share of the relevant economic decisions owes to the workings of markets—that is, to decisions by private actors—rather than to national government policy. Unlike an earlier era when expropriations and nationalizations were frequent, the U.S. government role in inter-American economic relations is quite limited. Latin America will not often rise high on the agenda of U.S. foreign policy because of economic issues.

The "Intermestic" Agenda

The main reason many Latin American countries have recently gained enhanced prominence in the making of U.S. foreign policy concerns less pleasant ways that Latin America affects the United States: as the principal source of surging immigration into the United States, legal and illegal; and as the widely perceived root of other problems facing the United States, including the narcotics trade, environmental deterioration, and epidemic threats to public health. These are today the key reasons Latin America matters to the broad U.S. public, and to many of those most active in demanding specific policies.

When voters in U.S. exit polls after presidential elections and in other public opinion surveys in recent years have been asked how important foreign policy issues are to them, most downplay the significance of foreign policy or international considerations. But when asked to list their own highe;t priority concerns, the same Americans have consistently identified "curbing illegal immigration," "stopping the drug trade," and "protecting the U.S. economy" as three of their top priorities. Although they do not identify these as "foreign policy" problems, they understand that America's nearest neighbors are at the heart of these issues. Pat Buchanan's 1996 presidential campaign speeches, for example, mentioned Mexico more frequently than any other foreign country, for Mexico is central to all three problems. Ross Perot, too, focused his most virulent attacks on Mexico and the Caribbean Basin countries, portraying them as sources of immigrants, drugs, and disease, and the places to which American multinational firms are exporting jobs. The AFL-CIO, anti-immigration lobbies, and environmental groups share this preoccupation with Mexico, Central America, and the Caribbean.

A quandary, however, is that the policy approaches most attractive to the U.S. public for responding to these "intermestic" issues may interfere with obtaining the sustained Latin American cooperation needed to address the underlying problems. This tendency is exacerbated by the highly fragmented process through which the United States makes and implements policy, allowing diverse actors to affect issues in different arenas, in uncoordinated and often contradictory ways. The challenge of managing the intermestic agenda is not only substantive and political, but procedural and bureaucratic.

Narcotics: Dealing with Demand and Supply

Efforts to cope with dangerous drugs in the United States illustrate how policies fashioned to deal with domestic facets of an "intermestic" concern may thwart responding effectively to its international components and thus undermine the prospects for successfully confronting the problem.

Some 12.8 million Americans regularly (i.e., once a month or more) consume prohibited narcotics, about 600,000 of them at least weekly, in an addictive fashion. The consequences for U.S. public health, economic productivity, family structures, social cohesion, and individual competence and welfare arising from this consumption are highly adverse. The financial costs to American society brought about by drugs have amounted to an estimated $300 billion already during the 1990s; the costs to individual lives and the social fabric are truly incalculable. All these problems are reinforced and compounded by the corruption and violence that are attributed at least in part to the criminalization of the narcotics trade, and to the incentives that substantial demand therefore creates for clandestine activity. No serious observer doubts the destructive impacts of narcotics consumption in the United States.

Nor is there any doubt that Latin American growers, producers, and traffickers are central to the narcotics trade. Peru is the world's largest producer of coca (the raw material for cocaine), and Bolivia is the second largest coca producer. Colombia is the world's largest refiner and producer of cocaine and is a main source of heroin; some 80 percent of the cocaine and 30 percent of the heroin entering the United States today comes from Colombia. Cocaine is currently Latin America's second largest export.

Brazil, the Dominican Republic, Ecuador, Jamaica, Mexico, Panama, Paraguay, and other countries are also part of the trafficking chain. By far the main link today is Mexico; some 70 percent of the cocaine and 20–30 percent of the heroin entering the United States in the 1990s is plausibly estimated to have come through Mexico. The extent to which Mexican law enforcement agencies, including the antinarcotics units themselves, the Mexican military, some Mexican business and financial executives, and even senior Mexican political leaders or their families have been involved in the drug trade has become painfully evident in recent years.

That dangerous drugs are largely imported from Latin America makes it understandable that Latin Americans are widely blamed for the U.S. drug trade. The tendency to blame the foreign suppliers is by no means new; from the nineteenth and early twentieth centuries—when laws prohibiting the possession and use of opium, heroin, and cocaine were first introduced—drugs have often been treated in the United States and other high-consumption countries as a problem of foreign origin, to be combated by eradication, law enforcement, and interdiction in the territory of drug-producing and trafficking countries.

Substantial experience over many decades has made it clear, however, that the consumption of dangerous drugs in the United States cannot be curtailed effectively by measures taken in Latin America or in other foreign countries. Study after study has shown that interdiction does not significantly reduce the flow of narcotics; it mainly displaces production from one place to another for a time and/or causes shifts (often only temporary) in the preferred route for international transit. Imports of dangerous drugs do not decline appreciably, no matter how ingenious and vigorous the interdiction efforts. Even if considerably greater interference with the flow were possible, the economics of the drug trade—and the increasing availability of domestically grown drugs and of synthetic substitutes—assure that the cost of narcotics to consumers would not rise appreciably.

"The supply-side theory that has driven American drug policy for almost a century is fatally flawed," as former State Department official Mathea Falco and many other qualified analysts have pointed out.[3] The historic view that the U.S. drug problem is primarily a result of foreign exports is harder to sustain than earlier, in fact, because domestic production of illegal drugs, including vast quantities of marijuana, accounts for an ever-increasing share of U.S. consumption.

Yet still today, as for many decades before, the recurrent pattern has been for U.S. public officials to respond to actual or latent public concern about narcotics by announcing strenuous programs to combat the drug trade at its foreign sources. Time and again, the U.S. government has turned to supply focused and internationally based antidrug campaigns in order to assuage aroused U.S. public opinion. That was the background of President Richard M. Nixon's "Operation Intercept," a high-profile effort to force Mexico's government to curb marijuana and opium production; of that administration's well-known pressures against Turkey and its "French Connection" drug traffickers; and of the same administration's creation of a Cabinet Committee for International Narcotics Control.

Similar motives underlay the high-profile proclamations by the Reagan and then the Bush administration of an international "war on drugs," to be fought primarily in Latin America. Drug control was a salient issue in the 1988 presidential election campaign, as polls then showed it was a major concern for voters. The Bush administration established the office of National Drug Control Policy and appointed the nation's first "drug czar," William Bennett. President Bush also committed himself to "bring to justice" Panamanian strongman Manuel Noriega, who was portrayed as a linchpin in the narcotics trade; this promise eventually led to the U.S. invasion of Panama in December 1989, and to the capture, trial, and imprisonment of Noriega. That the drug trade was unaffected by removing Noriega from power—indeed the drug traffic through Panama actually increased—caused no obvious rethinking of U.S. policies or concepts.

Beginning during the Bush administration and especially during the Clinton years, the sophistication of U.S. antinarcotics programs has improved somewhat. More attention has been directed to and budgets have been modestly increased for programs aimed at reducing demand, providing treatment, and offering rehabilitation, although two-thirds of total U.S. government spending continues to be devoted to interdiction and enforcement.

U.S. officials came to recognize that unrelievedly negative and punitive policies do not work, and introduced conditional economic assistance to countries in order to diminish the economic dislocations caused by supply reduction efforts. They also came to understand that attempts to reduce the international supply and to curb the trade in drugs need to be multipronged, dealing not only with eradicating crops and disrupting the traffic, but also with precursor chemicals and the production process, money laundering operations, criminal justice reform, arms trafficking, corruption, and the strengthening of local governments against both insurgent challenges and the narcotics networks.

Apparently persuaded that the drug trade is driven much more by domestic demand than by foreign supply, the Clinton administration began early on to shift the orientation of U.S. antinarcotics policy from interdiction, crop eradication, and law enforcement toward domestic educational and treatment programs. But it, too, learned that domestic political imperatives require confronting—or appearing to confront—what is largely an internal and highly intractable problem with prompt, vigorous, and visible activities against foreign enemies.

The epitome of the U.S. effort to project the antinarcotics efforts against foreign (and primarily Latin American) countries—and thus to demonstrate vividly to the U.S. public that the government is protecting their interests—is the annual certification process in which the U.S. government evaluates whether and how foreign governments are working to curtail the drug trade. Each year the administration must report to Congress (by March 1st) on whether foreign governments have been cooperating actively and sincerely in the "war on drugs" and therefore merit "recertification"; if not, whether they should instead be "decertified," with the imposition of sanctions, including the withdrawal of U.S. aid, trade preferences, and other benefits; or whether a temporary waiver of sanctions should be granted because of "national security" considerations. Despite its early turn toward demand reduction approaches, the Clinton administration has in recent years made the certification process more rigorous and visible, and has applied sanctions in some cases, notably against Colombia. Each year thus far it has certified Mexico, although a congressional initiative to withhold certification from Mexico, led by Senator Dianne Feinstein of California, came close to passing in 1998, losing only by a margin of 51–45.

The annual certification process provides a handy way for U.S. political leaders to highlight their concern about the narcotics trade for domestic political consumption, but neither "decertification" nor the threat of decertification has had any lasting positive impact on the efforts of target countries to counter the drug trade. On the contrary, there is good reason to believe that the process is not only ineffective but to some extent counterproductive, in that it distracts the energies of antinarcotics personnel in trafficking countries toward virtually meaningless but readily quantifiable indicators (such as tons of cocaine seized or acres of coca destroyed), rather than keeping it focused on the most important target: the organizational capacity of the drug cartels themselves.

The unilateral certification procedure mandated by the 1986 Anti-Drug Abuse Act is worse than ineffective and counterproductive; it is damaging. The certification review is gratuitously patronizing and insulting to Latin American governments; it is asymmetrical in that no one evaluates U.S. performance; it provides a convenient argument to local demagogues eager to portray U.S. imposition as the real menace rather than to allow a focus on drug trafficking; and it undercuts the political basis for sustained and effective inter-American cooperation. The certification process predictably leads to stylized rituals of quasi-compliance and quasi-condemnation, and to sterile arguments about supply versus demand as the major drivers of the drug trade. Rather than nurture cooperation, certification typically pits the governments of the United States and Latin America against each other.

As Mexican researcher Jorge Chabat points out, the certification process has led to a "game of simulation in which the main goal is not to stop the traffic of illicit drugs into the United States but to convince the American public that the Mexican government is doing its best," and therefore to "downplay Mexican failures in the combat of drug trafficking and to stress Mexican achievements."[4] Thus antinarcotics policy is twice distorted by the imperatives of domestic American politics—first to exaggerate the requirements for Latin American action against drugs, and then to misrepresent those actions in order to placate U.S. public opinion, so that Latin American cooperation can be sought on other issues.

The case against the current U.S. certification process is compelling, and many in Washington—both in the executive and Congress—are coming to favor change. Some favor merely providing greater flexibility in applying the law: giving the president greater discretion, easing the automaticity and extent of sanctions, and providing for more nuanced "levels" of certification rather than a starkly dichotomous choice. Consensus is beginning to emerge, however, on reorienting antinarcotics policy from a unilateral U.S. approach to a multilateral inter-American framework.

Building upon the limited success of the Inter-American Drug Abuse Control Commission, two veteran U.S. analysts and former practitioners of multilateral and inter-American diplomacy, retired Ambassadors Viron P. Vaky and Luigi Einaudi, have proposed a hemisphere Inter-Governmental Narcotics Commission to manage antidrug efforts throughout the Americas. The pro-

posed commission would involve the highest official from each
country responsible for antinarcotics efforts and would meet periodically to establish broad norms and principles, draw up and
coordinate operational strategies, establish specific targets, review
detailed plans to accomplish the adopted goals, and evaluate performance in the antinarcotics arena.

The challenge, as Vaky and Einaudi recognize, is to structure an
agreed multilateral framework that can actually be effective and to
convince both the U.S. and Latin American governments to
employ it. This can only be done if the United States is genuinely
prepared to entrust goal setting, planning, and performance evaluation to collective efforts on which it retains a substantial voice,
and if Latin American governments are willing to cede some
power and perhaps some sovereignty to an international body with
technical assistance capacity and enforcement authority.

Efforts to diminish the consumption and destructiveness of
drugs need to emphasize both the reduction of demand and the
mitigation of harm. Studies show that school promotion and other
educational programs can reduce drug use among young
teenagers, and that sustained treatment programs can substantially reduce the tendency to resume use. Complementary efforts
to diminish the harm caused by drugs—such as by providing clean
needles to addicts in order to decrease the transmission of HIV
and other diseases—can also make a positive contribution.[5] But
even if domestic efforts to curb demand and alleviate harm are
given the emphasis they deserve, it will still be vital to have international cooperation against drugs. Until and unless the transnational networks promoting the drug trade can be weakened, this
destructive traffic will continue because the revenues are so large.

The drug trade and its harmful effects both in the United States
and in Latin America cannot be successfully confronted by unilateral domestic policies, nor by "international" approaches that are
externally imposed in ways that inevitably undercut cooperation.
The damage done to United States–Mexico relations in 1998 by
"Operation Casablanca," in which U.S. law enforcement officials
violated Mexican laws in a major "sting" operation, nicely illustrates this dilemma. In their effort to pursue Mexican drug smugglers and money launderers aggressively, U.S. officials trampled on

Mexico's sovereignty and then compounded the damage by initially publicizing the operation in order to win domestic plaudits before reversing course, apologizing, and downplaying the incident.

Only sustained and intimate international cooperation—and mutually agreed, complementary policies that focus priority attention and resources on reducing domestic demand, providing treatment and rehabilitation, mitigating harm, and combating transnational networks—has any real chance to work. To achieve this kind of cooperation, U.S. policy makers will have to learn how to transcend the compelling yet self-defeating imperatives of domestic politics. It is too early to be certain that a genuinely multilateral approach can be forged and generally accepted, but it is clear that only such an approach can significantly reduce the drug trade and minimize inter-American frictions.

Immigration: The Quintessential "Intermestic" Issue

Even more than the narcotics trade, the major flows of migration from Mexico, Central America, and the Caribbean to the United States illustrate the increasing inseparability of domestic and international realities, as well as the difficulties presented when "domestic" and "foreign" policies are uncoordinated and even downright contradictory.

Like the flow of drugs, the flow of people across frontiers responds both to demand and supply considerations. Migration stems both from "push" factors in source countries—poverty, inequity, violence, repression, and unsatisfied expectations—and "pull" influences in countries of destination, particularly wage differentials and the magnet effect of the recipient labor market, which employs immigrant workers for a variety of jobs, mainly in low-skill sectors. As with drugs, too, the flow is facilitated by organized networks, legal and illegal, that broker and mediate the relationship between demand and supply: providing information, surmounting legal and other barriers, and otherwise guiding immigrants toward available jobs.

Over the course of America's history as a nation of immigrants, the opportunities for and the supply of immigrants have usually been correlated. Waves of migration have flowed and ebbed, to a large extent, in relation to the needs of the U.S. economy. When America's labor requirements have waned, the combination of market signals and periodic legislation has reduced the flow of immigration. Anti-immigrant sentiment has emerged from time to time, usually in periods of economic downturn, but it has generally receded with restrictionist measures and then with improvement in the business cycle.

This rough long-term balance between international pressures for emigration and U.S. receptivity to immigrants has been more fundamentally upset in recent years. Cycles of recurrent bust in Mexico, civil wars in Central America, repression in Cuba and Haiti, continued rapid population growth in many Central American and Caribbean nations, the broader impact of economic globalization, and the widening gap between wage levels in the United States and its Caribbean Basin neighbors—together with the influence of networks of already incorporated immigrants and families—have all combined to intensify the pressures for immigration into the United States, both documented and undocumented (or "illegal"). Similar factors account for a parallel rise in immigration from East and Southeast Asia.

The total number of immigrants entering the United States rose sharply during the 1970s, 1980s, and 1990s, and has now reached levels unprecedented since early in the twentieth century. More legal immigrants entered the United States from 1971 to 1990 than in the previous fifty years, and the rates of undocumented immigration and visa-overstays have also surged. Immigration from Mexico, Central America, and the Caribbean has been especially large—the first two flows gravitating toward California, Texas, other southwestern states, and Illinois, the last mainly toward southern Florida, New Jersey, and a number of Atlantic seaboard cities including Boston, New York, Baltimore, and Washington.

Latin American and Caribbean migration to the United States during the past thirty years has included substantial numbers of all four types of entrants: legal immigrants, coming to the United States with full documentation to permit residence here; refugees and asylees, also here legally but under different statutory provisions and often without prior documentation; undocumented or "illegal" migrants, entering the United States without valid documentation and without a "well-founded fear of persecution" in their home countries that could confer refugee status; and "nonimmigrant entrants," primarily persons who are overstaying their visas, valid only for a temporary visit. Although most discussion in the United States today focuses on the third category, these persons actually comprise only about 10 percent of the foreign born persons living in the United States today.

Taken together, the number of Latin American and Caribbean-origin persons who have entered the United States since 1970 and are currently residing in this country amount to some 10 million people. The overwhelming majority of these immigrants, some 55 percent, are from Mexico, but there are also significant numbers of immigrants from El Salvador, Nicaragua, Guatemala, Honduras, Cuba, the Dominican Republic, Haiti, Jamaica, and other Caribbean Basin countries.

Resistance to the continuing expansion of Latin American and Caribbean migration to the United States, especially to those entering without proper documentation, has been climbing in recent years. Stopping "illegal immigration" has become one of the American public's top concerns, especially in those parts of the country that feel themselves most directly affected by immigration: southern California and southern Florida. Local and state legislative initiatives, public opinion polls, "talk radio" programs, letters to the editor, anti-immigrant lobbying efforts, and other evidence all point to rising anti-immigrant and highly restrictionist sentiment, often tinged with racism. Political leaders have reinforced the exclusionary impulse, as was the case, for example, when California's Governor Pete Wilson used Proposition 187, a measure to deprive illegal immigrants of various social services, as a "wedge" issue to defeat Democratic candidate Kathleen Brown. With the end of the cold war, foreign policy considerations favoring immigration have virtually disappeared, and restrictionist sentiment has grown, therefore, without much counterargument from the foreign policy community.

Domestic pressures in the United States to cope with immigration have produced a series of legislative measures, notably the 1986 Immigration Control and Reform Act (IRCA) and the 1996 Illegal Immigration Reform and Immigrant Responsibility Act (IIRIRA).

IRCA was a negotiated compromise intended to reassure an aroused public that illegal immigration would be curbed and that U.S. control of the nation's borders would be restored—while also continuing to make migrant workers available to agricultural enterprises and to others dependent on immigrant labor and providing more humane treatment to those persons already in the United States. IRCA's "grand bargain" legalized the status of unauthorized workers who were already in the United States, while providing for future sanctions against employers who would knowingly employ illegal immigrants. Employer sanctions were adopted and implemented, however, without an effective verification system or significant monies allocated for enforcement, so that millions of illegal immigrants from Mexico, Central America, and the Caribbean continued to enter the United States during the late 1980s and early 1990s and to work with forged documents, while public resentment revived.

As the new wave of illegal immigrants crested, pressures mounted in the United States again for more restrictionist measures and stricter enforcement. Sentiment against immigration and immigrants intensified, with anxiety about job displacement and the cost of social services for immigrants, fear that bilingual education and other such provisions show a resistance to assimilation by Latin American and Caribbean immigrants, and broader (although mostly unarticulated) concerns about the effects of immigration on the ethnic composition of communities.

As was the case with the narcotics issue, the Clinton administration's first response to the immigration issue was relatively relaxed, with an appreciation of the underlying and long-term features of migration. The administration "had little initial interest in border enforcement matters," and in early 1993 recommended trimming the number of Border Patrol agents to save money.[6] But Clinton changed his position when it became obvious that restrictionist sentiment was rising again. The administration announced an expansion of the Border Patrol in mid-1993, highlighted border control measures from that time on, and supported and signed the 1996 Illegal Immigration Reform and Immigrant Responsibility Act, which considerably tightened U.S. immigration laws and their implementation.

As a result of IIRIRA and other recent U.S. legislation, it became harder for immigrants to enter the United States, less attractive for immigrants to reside in the country, and easier for the United States to deport undocumented immigrants:

- 5,000 new Border Patrol agents and 1,500 additional investigators for the Justice Department's Immigration and Naturalization Service (INS) have been authorized, and the Border Patrol has been provided with substantial additional and improved equipment to detect and detain illegal border-crossers.
- Sixty-two miles of walls and fences made of steel, concrete, chain-link, and barbed wire have been constructed along the border with Mexico.
- More secure and effective procedures have been instituted for employers to verify the immigration status of prospective employees.
- Requirements that legal immigrants have their economic status guaranteed by U.S. citizen sponsors have been made more demanding.
- Rules and procedures have been revised to expedite deportation of illegal immigrants, and illegal immigrants who are caught in the United States are now barred from receiving an immigrant visa for three to ten years, depending on how long they have been "unlawfully present" in the United States.
- An earlier program that allowed successful applicants for U.S. visas to receive their documents within U.S. territory, rather than require them to return first to their home country, has been ended.
- Legal immigrants have been declared ineligible for various social service programs, including Supplemental Security Income (SSI), Medicaid, and Food Stamp assistance.
- A uniform policy has been adopted to return to their home nations without further review all Caribbean migrants inter-

cepted in international waters, primarily Haitians and Cubans, and a unique agreement has been reached between the United States and authoritarian Cuba to restrict Cuban migration to this country.

- Treatment of long-term residents who have developed strong social and family ties in the United States has become more stringent, with the requirement that an undocumented migrant must show that deportation would cause "exceptionally and extremely unusual" hardship to a U.S. citizen or lawful permanent resident, without any consideration of the effect of the deportation on the migrant himself or herself.
- The United States has radically escalated efforts to deport to their home countries international migrants who have committed crimes in the United States. Some 50,000 "criminal aliens" were deported in 1997, more than 75 percent of them to Mexico and most of the rest to Central American and Caribbean nations. As the Dominican Republic's ambassador to the United States has astutely observed, this measure is equivalent to having the United States pay the travel costs of returning hundreds of Moscow-trained guerrillas to their Caribbean homes at the height of the cold war!
- Experimental military technologies have been adapted for border control purposes, and the support role of the U.S. military and the National Guard in border enforcement has expanded.

All these measures have probably not actually reduced illegal immigration to any significant extent. As with narcotics interdiction efforts, these unilateral border control measures have largely displaced the flows of migration from the previous locations to others, raised the risk and difficulty of entry, and thus increased recourse to and the cost of illegal smugglers and document forgers. The flow of migration continues, criminals benefit, migrants suffer, but the appearance of vigorous action aids government authorities who respond to short-term domestic political exigencies. The border appears to be under more control, and political authorities are thus better protected against the charge that they are condoning illegal immigration.

Mounting Latin American pressures for migration to the United States, coupled with rising restrictionist and anti-immigrant sentiment and more exclusionary U.S. immigration laws and enforcement, will intensify inter-American friction over migration in the years to come. That friction is inevitable for the time being, as long as the demand for emigration, especially from Mexico and the Caribbean Basin, exceeds the receptivity of the United States to immigrants. The policy challenge is not how to eliminate this friction now, but how to manage the tensions for the time being without causing unnecessary collateral damage to other interests and inflicting inhumane treatment on the migrants themselves, until the underlying gap between demand and supply might be restored, in the medium and longer term, through a combination of changes in the U.S. labor market and economic and demographic transformations in the source countries.

No one doubts the sovereign right of the United States to fashion and apply its own laws to regulate immigration, and the inevitability of responding primarily to domestic pressures and politics in doing so. As with the certification procedure in the narcotics field, however, current U.S. immigration laws and practices undermine potential international efforts to cope with the phenomenon, while also damaging the prospects for cooperation on this and other issues.

Removing or reducing the safety valve of emigration, reducing remittances from immigrants to source countries, and repatriating criminals without careful procedures to protect the source country: all these steps undoubtedly increase the prospects for social and political instability in Mexico, Central America, and the Caribbean. The predictable consequence of this instability is to intensify pressures for immigration and at the same time slow the economic development that might provide expanded employment opportunities (and thus reduced pressures for emigration) in these countries.

Callous treatment of immigrants not only contradicts core U.S. values and traditions but stokes anti-American resentment in neighboring countries, and makes it more difficult to build cooperative approaches on the management of migration flows and on other issues, including antinarcotics programs. Again, domestic measures designed to deal with the immediate local impact of a transnational phenomenon interfere with the external policies needed to cope with the important international aspects of the problem, further exacerbating the problem in consequence.

The United States could more effectively pursue its own interests in the humane and politically acceptable management of international migration if it were able to adopt and consistently apply bilateral and multilateral approaches that enlist the sustained cooperation of source countries. Considerable progress along those lines has been made in recent years with Mexico: with the establishment of the Joint Border Liaison Mechanism, the Border Port Control, and the Working Group on Migration and Consular Affairs of the U.S.-Mexico Binational Commission, and with the adoption of the Memorandum of Understanding on Consular Protection of Mexican and U.S. Nationals, as well as through the research carried out by ten scholars from each country through the Mexico-U.S. Binational Study on Migration. Such efforts hold the promise of much more effective programs to manage migration by concentrating in a strategic and integrated way on demand and supply, and on networks on both sides of the border. But this promise is undermined when unilateral U.S. measures are undertaken that are seen by Mexico or other Caribbean Basin governments as punitive and demeaning. When U.S. immigrant bashing occurs, the source country governments, responding to their own domestic politics, must devote more energy, resources, and visible engagement to protecting their nationals and to attacking (and trying to change) U.S. policies, rather than to considering possible cooperative efforts to reduce or at least manage migration flows.

In the case of Mexico as well as Central America and the Caribbean, a preferable approach to the management of migration would be to coordinate and integrate measures within the United States and within the sending countries to point in the same direction: to improve labor standards and reduce wage differentials, curb repression and protect human rights, improve public understanding of the causes and consequences of migration and of the process and rhythm of assimilation, and try to restore over time a rough equilibrium between the demand and supply of immigrants.

At the very least, such bilateral and regional approaches would work out procedures to assure that criminals are not unleashed on vulnerable societies without procedures for their repatriation under secure conditions; that migrants are treated in accordance with law on both sides of the border and have their human rights adequately protected; that undocumented immigrants are not subject to repression upon their return to source countries; and that other forms of exchange between the United States and its neighbors are not stifled or stymied because of border control programs.

Beyond these advances, it may well be possible at this stage to elicit important cooperation from Mexico and perhaps other source countries for measures to discourage excessive and unregulated migration in exchange for programs to permit temporary work or "sojourner" status in the United States. Such proposals merit careful examination as an alternative to the current trend toward destructive and yet ineffective immigration restrictions.

In the long run, intense frictions over immigration cannot be resolved by restrictive legislation or punitive social policies. The best prospect for reducing or removing these frictions would arise out of prospective demographic and economic changes in the source countries—which could bring population, resources, and employment opportunities in those countries into better balance. For this to happen, economic development strategies based on increasingly open trade and investment regimes with the United States are central requisites.

But these regimes, in turn, will be much harder to adopt and sustain if the United States unilaterally restricts immigration in response to domestic pressures. Again, a well-crafted U.S. policy for the future, taking into account the full range of U.S. interests in relations with its closest neighbors, and in particular its longer-term interests, requires that U.S. officials transcend immediate political exigencies. As with narcotics policy, there may be no neat, total, and permanent resolution of the problem. If the United States would focus more on international cooperation as a necessary aspect of effective policy, it could improve the prospects for more attractive trade-offs, could manage the problems more effectively, and could avoid unnecessary damage to collateral interests and objectives.

Managing the "Intermestic" Agenda

Narcotics and immigration policies are the most salient and contentious examples of "intermestic" problems—arising from causes in several countries and requiring, for an effective response, a combination of domestic and international policies and actors, working in concert. These policy domains also best illustrate the inherent tensions between domestic political imperatives and international policy requisites for dealing adequately with transnational problems that cannot be resolved in one country alone, even in one so large and powerful as the United States.

But there are other such issues, and they are bound to comprise an important part of the inter-American agenda in the years to come, particularly in U.S. relations with Mexico, Central America, and the Caribbean. Polluted water or contaminated air on one side of the U.S.-Mexico border inevitably affects conditions on the other side, and measures to mitigate the damage often require international cooperation. Forest fires arising from negligent agricultural practices and excessive population pressures in Mexico or Central America produce unpleasant and dangerous conditions in the United States that create a U.S. stake in more equitable growth patterns to the south. Troubling increases in the incidence of tuberculosis and other infectious diseases in southern California and elsewhere in the United States cannot be curbed without cooperative international public health programs, involving testing and treatment in the source countries. In all these and other such instances, there is a natural tendency to blame the problem on foreign causes and to adopt punitive and restrictive measures to protect the United States against an unwanted international flow, but such responses undercut the possibility for the sustained and intimate cooperation over many years that would be required to confront effectively a difficult transnational problem.

Increased trade, tourism, investment, and cultural, political, and demographic exchange between the United States and its

closest neighbors will not preclude intense, complex, and sometimes destructive international tensions in the region; indeed,
increased interpenetration produces and exacerbates such tensions. Nor will enhanced democratic governance in Mexico and
the Caribbean Basin countries necessarily reduce inter-American
conflict; on the contrary, it may well produce symmetrical political
pressures to pin the blame for tough problems on the United
States. The impulse to assert sovereignty and to pin responsibility
for dealing with a tough problem on the other side of the border is
reciprocal and interactive. A troubling counterproductive dynamic
is all too likely to develop in the years to come precisely in the most
intertwined and interdependent of U.S. relations, those with its
closest neighbors.

Only effective bilateral and multilateral policies can manage the
conflicts that intensified proximity will foster. Securing these policies will require managing domestic political pressures so as to
make it possible to elicit international cooperation.

The first step toward designing, adopting, and implementing
effective policies is to recognize the requisite for international
cooperation as well as the recurrent temptation to embrace unilateral and punitive approaches, and to give priority to assuring that
the American people and Congress understand this contradiction.
This chapter is intended to make a modest contribution in that
regard.

Second, conscious attention should be focused on how to adapt
the governmental, legislation, and bureaucratic processes by which
policies on "intermestic" issues are formulated, adopted, and
implemented. These adaptations are needed to take into account
the extraordinary interpenetration of the United States and its
nearest neighbors and to consider the intricate interweaving of different issues that are all affected by the accelerating functional
integration that is blurring borders in the Caribbean Basin region.

Third, policy makers and the attentive public in the United
States and its close neighbors in Mexico, Central America, and the
Caribbean need to put today's issues and problems into perspective by reflecting on how U.S. relations with the region have
changed over the past century—from the Spanish-American War
of 1898—and how they might evolve in the next century.

It is high time to recognize that the United States has become an overwhelming and continuing influence in its border region and that, by the same token, the vast and growing Caribbean and Mexican diasporas in the United States have irreversibly changed the shape and character of U.S. relations with these close neighbors.

Airlines and the telephone companies treat Mexico, Central America, and the Caribbean for most purposes as part of the domestic U.S. market, not as "international." Within a matter of years, it is quite possible that the "major leagues" of U.S. baseball will include franchises in Monterrey, Santo Domingo, and Havana, eligible to play in the "World Series" up to now limited to North American teams. It is hard to define the frontier between "Latin America" and "Anglo America" in the 1990s, but it is certainly north of San Diego in the U.S. West and of Miami in the East.

In the twenty-first century, it will be increasingly difficult to talk sensibly about U.S.–Latin American relations in general and aggregate terms. U.S. relations with South America are already changing, reverting in some ways to the pattern of the 1920s when the United States was only one of several external influences, but also taking on new shape with the emergence of strong regional integration in South America and significant South American relationships with Europe and Asia. As Chile's Ambassador to Brazil, Heraldo Muñoz, has observed, South Americans and the United States "can live with a degree of mutual indifference."

No such indifference is possible, in either direction, between the United States and its closest neighbors in Mexico, Central America, and the Caribbean. Very few predictions can be made with confidence about international relations in a period of turbulence and transition, but it is safe to say that the challenges of managing the "intermestic agenda" produced by the U.S.–Caribbean Basin relationship will be significant in U.S. policy for years to come.

Notes

[1] I have written extensively elsewhere about this relationship, particularly in Lowenthal (1976) and (1990), especially chapter 2. See also Smith (1996).

[2] The intensive Washington debates on Central America during the 1980s

derived, in my judgment, mainly from the gap between the Reagan administration's subjective appraisal of the region's supposed significance to U.S. security and its modest actual importance. It was not so much "national security" as "national *in*security," a psychopolitical impulse that produced this gap. See Lowenthal (1990), chapter 3.

[3]Falco (1995).

[4]Jorge Chabat, "Drug Trafficking in US-Mexican Relations: the Politics of Simulation." Paper presented at the International Conference organized by the International Studies Association and the Mexican Association of International Studies, Manzanillo, Mexico (December 11–13, 1997).

[5]On "harm reduction" approaches, see Nadelmann (1998). As if to illustrate this essay's thesis, President Clinton found himself (in April 1998) rejecting a program for exchange of needles because of domestic political pressures just when he was in Santiago, Chile, at the Western Hemisphere Summit, trying to enlist Latin American leaders in multilateral efforts against drugs.

[6]See Andreas (1998).

6

Political Evolution
in the Hemisphere

JORGE I. DOMÍNGUEZ
SUSAN KAUFMAN PURCELL

Democracy in Latin America
and U.S. Interests

During the past decade, Latin America has become a region characterized almost entirely by elected civilian governments. The one
glaring exception is Cuba, and Washington has lost no opportunity to highlight its failure to become a member of the hemisphere's democratic club. The importance that the United States
gives to democratic development in Latin America is more than
mere rhetoric. In recent years, when democracy has been threat-

JORGE I. DOMÍNGUEZ is the director of the Center for International
Affairs and the Clarence Dillon professor of international affairs at Harvard
University. He has written and edited several volumes concerning politics and
governance in Latin America and the Caribbean and has been an editor and
advisor for several television series, including "Battle for El Salvador," which
won a Peabody Award. Dr. Domínguez is a member of the editorial boards
for *Mexican Studies, Cuban Studies* (coeditor), *Political Science Quarterly,* and *Revisa
de Ciencias Sociales;* a contributing editor of *Foreign Policy;* and a member of the
Inter-American Dialogue and the Council on Foreign Relations.

ened by the possibility of a military coup, Washington has worked hard, both publicly and privately, both alone and together with its Latin neighbors, to thwart the military plotters. Paraguay in 1997 and Venezuela in 1989 and 1992 are perhaps the best known examples. The United States has also welcomed the accelerating transition to competitive, democratic politics in Mexico in recent years.

One does not have to be a specialist in Latin American history, however, to know that the United States has not always or consistently favored democrats over autocrats in the region. There are many examples of cases in which Washington gave not only tacit but also active support to military efforts to overthrow democratically elected governments. The most notorious recent example is U.S. support for the military coup against Salvador Allende in Chile in the early 1970s. Washington was less overt in its strong desire to see Joao Goulart's government replaced by the Brazilian military in the early 1960s.

But the reality is even more complicated than the above examples might suggest. The U.S. government has also supported dictators in the region, only to turn against them when they were under siege and back instead those trying to replace the autocracy with an elected democratic regime. Furthermore, Washington has worked hard to support democrats in one Latin American country while simultaneously maintaining its alliance with nondemocratic rulers in neighboring countries. This was especially true during the cold war. Since the Soviet collapse, however, the United States has consistently supported democratic regimes over authoritarian ones.

SUSAN KAUFMAN PURCELL is vice president of the Americas Society and the Council of the Americas. From 1981–88 she was a senior fellow and director of the Latin American Project at the Council on Foreign Relations. At that time she also was a member of the State Department's Policy Planning Staff, with responsibility for Latin America and the Caribbean. She is a director of Valero Energy Corporation, The Argentina Fund, and the Scudder Global High Income Fund and sits on the boards of the National Endowment for Democracy and Freedom House. Dr. Purcell is a member of the editorial boards of *Journal of Democracy* and *Hemisfile*.

These shifts and turns on the part of Washington have led some observers to charge that U.S. policy toward the hemisphere has been inconsistent, contradictory, and even immoral. Perhaps this is so, at least in certain selected cases. On the other hand, an argument can be made that there is no great virtue in consistency for consistency's sake. U.S. policy toward Latin America has in fact been consistent in that it has always put the interests of the United States before those of Latin America. Often, Washington has believed—sometimes correctly and sometimes not—that what was good for the United States was also good for Latin America. This usually translated into political and economic systems that were friendly to the United States and to U.S. capital. Sometimes these interests were best attained by supporting authoritarian regimes and at other times, by supporting democratic ones. It usually depended on what the available political options were at the time in the specific Latin American countries.

The issue of whether or not Latin American regimes were perceived as friendly to the United States was viewed not only in a hemispheric context, but more important, in a global one. This was an important consideration particularly during the cold war years, when the United States was explicitly engaged in a global competition with the Soviet Union. Any Soviet inroads in Latin America, which Washington (and others) viewed as the U.S. "backyard," were interpreted as tipping the global balance of power toward the Soviets at the expense of the United States.

In order to prevent the Soviets from making inroads in the hemisphere, a top U.S. priority was to avoid allowing individuals who were seen as too friendly to the Soviets or too evenhanded toward the Soviets and the United States to come to power. Anti-American Latin leaders were also considered suspect, since they might ultimately decide that the enemy of their enemy should be their friend—a mindset that would favor Soviet expansion. It was not always possible, however, to predict accurately how an elected or nonelected Latin American leader would behave once in office. This explains why U.S. policy at times focused on the removal of troublesome rulers rather than the prevention of their accession to power.

In addition, sometimes the perceived threat to U.S. interests was neither ideological nor intentional. Instead, it was the result of incompetent leadership and/or weak political institutions in Latin America. Both factors often led to political instability, which was viewed by Washington as providing opportunities for Soviet mischief making. U.S. policy makers saw Latin America as providing numerous opportunities for the Soviets to create trouble because of the widespread poverty, illiteracy, and despair that characterized much of the population.

U.S. policy toward Brazil in the early 1960s and Chile in the early 1970s can be understood in terms of these concerns. The government of Joao Goulart, who succeeded to the presidency when the elected president resigned, was seen as anti-American and too favorably disposed to the Soviet Union. Goulart's efforts at reform were seen as potentially threatening to U.S. economic interests and ultimately destabilizing within Brazil. The Brazilian military's view was not much different, and the fact that Washington was seen as sympathetic to their concerns and plans for a coup was an important factor in spurring them to action and in allowing them to quickly consolidate their control over the country and win international support.

The Chilean case was similar, although the country was considerably smaller and less important geopolitically than Brazil. But because Latin America was viewed in global rather than purely hemispheric terms, no country was too small to become the object of Washington's concerns. As the Cuban missile crisis had showed only a decade earlier, a small island country of only 10 million people armed with Soviet missiles could be more threatening to U.S. interests than a large country hostile to the United States that lacked such missiles. Like the Goulart government, the Allende government was seen by U.S. policy makers as threatening U.S. economic interests, as too friendly toward the Cubans and Soviets, and as creating political instability as a result of its actions. An important difference between the two cases, however, is the greater role that the United States played in destabilizing the Allende regime and pressing the Chilean military to intervene. The explanation may have more to do with the contrast between the Johnson and Nixon administrations in Washington than with the global situation or developments on the ground in Chile.

Although the United States favored right-wing military regimes over left-wing democratic governments in the cases of Brazil and Chile, this does not mean that Washington always preferred military regimes to left-wing elected governments. The biggest threat to U.S. interests during the cold war was perceived to be Communist dictatorships (i.e., left-wing military regimes). The key examples are the Sandinista government in Nicaragua and the Castro regime in Cuba. When faced with such governments, U.S. policy became stridently and actively prodemocratic. The reason was that elections were regarded as the key tool for removing the dictators from power. In the case of Nicaragua, the Sandinistas believed they were too popular to lose an election. Fidel Castro has never been that naïve.

Finally, Washington has not hesitated in removing its support from friendly authoritarian regimes once they could no longer guarantee political stability. The case of Fulgencio Batista in Cuba is one example. The Pinochet regime in Chile is another. Dictatorships that became strongly opposed by the populations that they governed were regarded by Washington as liabilities, since if they collapsed due to popular pressures, their successor would undoubtedly be hostile to the United States and possibly cause the United States more problems than the demise of the friendly dictatorship.

The fact that the United States has not steadfastly befriended and supported democratic governments in Latin America did not necessarily mean that all other things being equal, democratic regimes were not preferable. The problem was that other things were rarely equal. Latin America was not the United States, or even Western Europe. It was a developing area, with weak political institutions and insurmountable economic and social problems. In most cases, Washington saw itself confronted with no good alternatives. This led the United States to choose the least bad alternative. During the cold war—or other periods in which U.S. interests in the hemisphere could be threatened by hostile foreign powers—the best alternative was a friendly government that could guarantee political stability. Sometimes such governments were both democratic and socially progressive in the context of their times. Examples include the Betancourt government in Venezuela, the Figueres government in Costa Rica, and the first Frei government in Chile. At other times they were conservative military regimes such as those of Pinochet and the successive military regimes that governed Brazil between 1964 and 1985.

The collapse of the Soviet Union and the resulting end to the cold war did not alter the way in which the United States defined its interests in Latin America. It did, however, allow Washington to be somewhat less concerned about, and more tolerant of, potential political instability in the region. This was because there was no longer a hostile superpower poised to take advantage of such instability at the expense of U.S. national interests. Nor could governments formerly allied with the Soviet Union, such as Castro's Cuba, stir up much trouble in the region in the absence of the multibillion dollar a year Soviet subsidy. In addition, the Soviet collapse meant that left-wing democratic regimes, if they came to power in Latin America, would not affect the U.S. global position in ways that they had during the cold war. In fact, with the United States as the only global superpower, they had much to gain by being friendly to the United States and nothing significant to gain by being hostile to Washington.

Stated differently, the end of the cold war enabled the United States to take more risks in terms of its policy toward Latin America than had been true when Washington was engaged in a global competition with a hostile superpower. The main risk that seemed worth taking was to press for the successful completion of a transition to democratic government that had begun in Latin America during the 1980s.

As a successful, wealthy, and powerful democracy, the United States has tended to believe that its form of government is the best that has been devised to date. Washington has also believed that democratic countries make good allies and help sustain peace, since democracies rarely go to war with each other. In addition, institutionalized democracies have also been regarded as the most stable forms of government because they are legitimate in the eyes of the governed and accountable to them. What better way to ensure a friendly, stable Latin America than to take advantage of the opportunity afforded by the end of the cold war to support democratic transitions in the remaining undemocratic countries and help institutionalize the still fragile democracies in those countries that already had elected governments?

Changes within Latin America that had occurred throughout the cold war years also made the new prodemocracy policy more feasible. The region had become more urban and educated. New technology gave its people access to information about developments in other parts of the world, as well as within their own borders. Policy failures by nondemocratic governments during the 1970s and 1980s also had led Latin Americans to begin demanding more democratic and accountable rulers. Finally, the collapse of communism deprived statist economic strategies of legitimacy, opening the way to the adoption of market economies that, at least in the case of the Western democracies, were seen as congruent or even supportive of democratic politics. This new appreciation of democracy and market economies even led to an unprecedented willingness on the part of Latin democracies to work together to support each other's elected governments and prevent undemocratic governments from coming to power.

Perhaps the best example of how the new international environment, combined with the new realities in Latin America, affected U.S. policy is the Mexican case. During the cold war the United States did not pressure Mexico to democratize its *sui generis* one-party authoritarian political system. When the system came under threat because of failed economic policies, Washington supported the efforts of several Mexican presidents to make the transition to a more open and market oriented economy. Only after the Soviet threat had disappeared, and Mexicans themselves began demanding a more democratic and accountable government, did Washington publicly support such a transition. The change in policy was perhaps best symbolized by President Clinton's official meetings with the leaders of the main opposition parties during his May 1997 visit to the country.

It seems likely that for the foreseeable future the United States will continue to support democratic governments in Latin America and oppose efforts to overturn them, particularly if the majority of Latin voters feel the same way. There is, of course, the possibility that repeated disappointment and failure on the part of such governments to deliver on their promises could lead to political instability and even breakdown. In such cases, the Latin American militaries, backed by significant groups within their societies, might see themselves as having no alternative but to take power once again. Ideally, however, that stage will not have to be reached, and the United States will not have to deal with that kind of situation. Instead, the Latins, with the support of the United States, will use their ability to hold their governments accountable in order to replace badly performing leaders with more competent ones who will take the necessary steps to improve the functioning of their democratic governments.

The Relationship between Democracy and Open Markets

Never before in Latin America's history have so many countries featured constitutional governments, elected in free and competitive elections under effective universal suffrage, that choose to pursue market economy policies. In the early twentieth century, many Latin American governments pursued open economy policies, but rulers were chosen either by a narrow oligarchy or by the military. In mid-twentieth century, many Latin American governments were chosen democratically but pursued statist economic policies that sought to de-link their economies from the world market to the extent possible. Thus the combination of free politics and free markets in the 1990s is genuinely unprecedented.

The Long (and Misguided) Life of Democratic Pessimism

Perhaps for this reason, scholars, policy makers, and many ordinary citizens have found it difficult to imagine that democracy and open markets could co-exist, much less thrive jointly. In the 1970s there was a pervasive, and seemingly well-grounded, pessimism about the capacity of democracies in Latin America to implement sound economic policies to foster economic growth. The prevailing view at that time was that democratically elected governments were unlikely to adopt sensible economic policies. There seemed to be, some argued, an elective affinity between orthodox economics and bureaucratic-authoritarian regimes, on the one hand, and between economic malperformance and the demagogic populism of civilian politicians, on the other.

In the late 1980s and early 1990s, democratic rule returned to Latin America and made its bold appearance in Eastern Europe. Then, the democratic pessimists argued that democracy in the political realm works against economic reforms. Populist demagogues will prevent or undermine open market policies. Economic reforms, alternatively, could advance under democratic conditions in certain cases but, if so, they would be politically destabilizing; rent-seeking business firms and privileged labor union bosses would work to overthrow the democratically elected economic reformers. The least pessimistic of the democratic pessimists allowed that democracies might enact economic reforms and still survive provided strong executives (presidents or prime ministers) forced their peoples to be free.

The historical record does not bear out many of the arguments of the democratic pessimists. Latin America's authoritarian regimes proved to be as inept at managing the economy as democratic populists had been. (There is no significant statistical relationship in Latin America during the 1970s or 1980s between political regime type and economic performance.) The catastrophic collapse of the region's economy in 1982–83 was principally the responsibility of the authoritarian governments that had governed most Latin American countries in the late 1970s.

Consider the allegedly sterling economic performance of General Augusto Pinochet's dictatorship in Chile (1973–90). His government deserves appropriate credit for launching several valuable structural economic reforms. And yet its record of performance falls well short of economic wizardry. According to the U.N. Economic Commission for Latin America, Pinochet's Chile had the dubious distinction of experiencing in 1982 the worst one-year drop of gross domestic product per capita (−14.5 percent) of any country in the Americas. The arrogance and mistakes of

Pinochet's economic team are key explanations for the severity of that collapse. Moreover, according to the Inter-American Development Bank, Chile's average annual growth rate of gross domestic product per capita (in 1988 dollars) from 1981 to 1990 was just 1 percent—a miracle, yes, in public relations.

Democratic pessimists, nevertheless, did have an important insight. Democratic governments in Latin America did not have a good record of sound, sustained, sensible macroeconomic policies and performance. Constitutional governments in Brazil in the early 1960s (Goulart presidency), in Chile in the early 1970s (Allende presidency), and in Argentina in the mid-1970s (Peron presidency), among others, were characterized by stunningly irresponsible economic policies that impoverished their countries, brought untold hardship to millions, and contributed to the breakdown of democratic politics. And yet, even in these same countries, the historical record also suggested that some democratic governments could perform much better at managing economic policies; examples would include Brazil in the late 1950s (Kubitschek presidency), Argentina in the mid-1960s (Illia presidency), and Chile in the mid- and late 1960s (Frei presidency). One key question, therefore, was whether democrats could learn and change their economic preferences and policies. Another key question is whether democrats could win the support of many of those who, at some moment, had supported authoritarian rule.

The Critical Junctures for Change

Latin America's great depression of the 1980s did wonders for the prospects of democracy and markets. The severity and duration of this economic crisis forced many to rethink fundamental assumptions about the statist import-substituting framework for economic policies that had prevailed in the region for decades. When the crisis broke, authoritarian governments still ruled most countries; in the then-recently democratizing countries, much of the blame also fell on discredited authoritarians. The economic crisis itself contributed to further open the political systems.

This economic crisis did not produce instant learning, however. The constitutional governments of José Sarney in Brazil and Raúl

Alfonsín in Argentina resisted making fundamental changes and proved incapable of addressing the economic crisis successfully. Their double failure persuaded other politicians in their countries and, by example, elsewhere in Latin America that further changes had to be implemented.

At the moment of economic crisis, there was available an international pool of theoretical and empirical ideas that emphasized the utility of markets. These ideas had become dominant in the governments of the industrial countries in the 1970s and 1980s; they were nested in the international financial institutions, in private foundations, and in universities. They were learned by young technopols in the making—politically adept and involved technically qualified people—and brought back home for application. In the 1990s the presidents of Brazil and Mexico and the finance ministers of a great many Latin American governments have earned social science doctorates. Most importantly, reformist technopols had spent much time in the opposition; some had been political exiles.

This crisis alone did not "cause" the opening of politics, but it facilitated it. It permitted technically expert opposition leaders to criticize authoritarian technocrats on their own terms. Opposition technopols, in addition, derived legitimacy from the international community to challenge the government and, in so doing, built their own constituencies at home.

Beginning in the 1970s, another international pool of ideas became available. It asserted the centrality of democracy as the way to govern and the importance of respect for human rights in the relationship between state and society. The worldwide federations of Christian Democratic, Social Democratic, and Liberal parties, prominent in Western Europe, contributed mightily to this international change. Especially pertinent for Latin America was Spain's experience under President Felipe González and his Social Democratic government. Spain's Socialists demonstrated that market oriented policies fostered the consolidation of democracy and, just as importantly, that voters would reward politicians who dropped past statist commitments and adopted promarket policies. And they did so speaking Spanish.

In the United States, human rights and democratic concerns

first became salient in the Congress and then during Jimmy Carter's presidency. Though nearly discarded during Ronald Reagan's first term, the centrality of democracy as an organizing principle for U.S. foreign policy gathered support during Reagan's second term and especially during the Bush and Clinton presidencies.

The international community began to demand democracy in politics and competence in economics just as a new generation of Latin American elites was at last capable and willing to supply them. In this way, the governments of the major industrial democracies, including the U.S. government, the international financial institutions, and the major private foundations, made a powerful contribution to Latin America's simultaneous double transition: democratization and marketization. The principal explanation for the particulars of each of these changes is found within each country, but the synchronized hemispheric sweep of the change can only be understood as part of a common international process. Latin America's transformation is a dramatic example of the power of ideas and the effectiveness of international action to facilitate, foster, and support changes within each country.

The Logic of Democracy and Markets

Market reforms (especially deregulation, privatization, and the termination of business subsidies) can serve the goals of democratic politics. Statist economic arrangements often permit and foster close connections between economic and political elites, reducing the prospects for wider participation and fair contestation. Statist economics privileges business groups whose profits depend on political connections and not necessarily on efficiency or quality. Market reforms can break the ties between political and economic elites, reduce the opportunities for corruption and rent-seeking behavior, and create a level playing field for economic actors. Insertion into international markets including free trade agreements provides external actors with the leverage needed to defend constitutional government, should it come under attack.

Freer markets permit less room for arbitrary state action such as those that gripped much of Latin America from the mid-1960s to the late 1980s. Markets do not ensure civil society against an authoritarian state, but markets can be one important check on the abuse of state power. Markets may not disperse power enough, and in Latin America's small economies market power is often highly concentrated, but markets disperse power more than if it were centralized in the hands of state decision makers.

Democracy can help consolidate a market economy. In countries where levels of societal contestation and political instability have been very high and organized opposition forces have been strong, democracy can reduce many transaction costs. There may be fewer disruptions from labor strikes or insurgencies if the would-be supporters of these strategies can find more cost-effective alternatives to advance their interests within democratic politics. In addition, democratic regimes can involve the political opposition in support of a market economy more effectively than can authoritarian regimes.

Most importantly, a democratic political system committed to a market economy, and capable of delivering on that commitment, is the more effective and stable long-term political response to the problems posed by the rational expectations of economic actors. Rational economic actors look for rules and institutions that endure even as presidents, ministers, and economic cabinets change. Authoritarian regimes can provide certain assurances to economic actors for some time, but democratic regimes can also provide long-run assurances provided government and opposition are committed to the same broad framework of a market economy. In this sense, the opposition gives the most effective long-term guarantees about the continuity of a market economy; when the opposition supports the basic principles and rules of a market economy, then economic actors rationally can expect that a change of government leaders will not imply the overthrow of a market economy. And only democratic political systems embody the compromises and commitments that may freely bind government and opposition to the same framework of a market economy.

In democratic political systems, moreover, elections provide routinized means for sweeping away failed policies and politicians and starting afresh. Authoritarian regimes cannot get rid of mistaken policies or wrong-headed leaders so readily. In the logic of democracy, leaders must elicit the consent of the governed and are thus more likely to consolidate efficient economic reforms for the long run, setting and signaling clear and stable political and economic policy rules that help to shape the rational expectations of economic actors. That has been the long-term experience of Western Europe, North America, and Japan, and in the 1990s it became at long last Latin America's experience as well.

No democratic regime has ever survived in the absence of a market economy. The more controversial part of this analysis may be, therefore, that democracy, especially in Latin America, can be good for markets. To this story we turn next.

Internalizing Capitalist Policies and Democratic Practices

In many Latin American countries, democratic institutions and procedures in the 1990s worked to set the long-term rules that enable rational economic actors to believe that the open market economy is here to stay. To be sure, democratic politics works through civil contestation. Conflicts may take a long time to be settled. The settlement is often a compromise in which each side must yield to some extent. And yet, the harder the struggle and the longer the conflict, the more credible the bargained outcome often is. In none of the cases discussed below was the process simple. In many instances, politicians had to give up on many of their cherished hopes. But once an agreement was reached, time and again it helped to set and then begin to consolidate the foundations for Latin America's comprehensive economic turnaround in the 1990s.

Chile

By the late 1990s Chile featured the most clearly consolidated open market economy. The birth of that consolidation can be set precisely. In March 1989 Chile's broad based democratic opposition coalition, the Democratic Concertation (constituted principally of the Christian Democratic party, the Socialist party, and the Party for Democracy), adopted a detailed social and economic program for government. After spirited and contentious debate, the coalition agreed to support the broad framework of a market economy and to pursue policies consistent with that framework. Once in power, the Democratic Concertation coalition indeed delivered. Economic actors could count on the long-term endurance of open market economy policies precisely because all the major political parties endorsed it. Democracy's capacity to fulfill the rational expectations of economic actors was superior to that of the Pinochet dictatorship.

Equally important was the commitment of Chile's new democratic government from the very outset to seek a consensus on economic policy that was often larger than its share of votes in Congress. For example, the first significant measure of the new democratic government was to increase taxes, with the revenues earmarked for social spending in order to begin to address the legacy of the dictatorship's neglect of social issues. The new government negotiated the key details of the tax package with the center-right opposition. The measure was enacted through a congressional super-majority. In this instance, it was the center-right party, National Renovation, that successfully addressed the problem of rational expectations: Chileans from the right and the left were ready to invest in the health and education of their people.

Argentina

Argentina worked hard in the twentieth century to achieve underdevelopment. Its economic history since the 1930s is a textbook case of persistent policy incompetence and economic decline. Argentina turned around in the 1990s, and its story illustrates as well the utility of democracy for the transition toward a more open market economy.

In May 1989 Carlos Menem was elected president of Argentina, returning the Peronist party to power for the first time since the 1976 military coup. In contrast to his party's long and deep statist economic preferences, Menem endorsed orthodox macroeconomic policies and a turn toward more open markets but, faithful to the Peronist tradition, sought to assert the power of his presidency to enact these changes. Menem commanded markets to be free by decree—and he failed. In his first two years in office, he issued three times more presidential decrees with the force of law than all Argentine presidents combined since the adoption of the constitution in the mid-nineteenth century. Economic recession and yet another bout of hyperinflation forced a reconsideration. In early 1991 Menem appointed Domingo Cavallo as economy minister.

Cavallo's key insight was to understand that Argentina's central macroeconomic problems could only be addressed through politics and that the procedures of democracy were especially apt for this task. Argentines had no reason to believe the word of the president, for no president's word had deserved to be trusted in their lifetimes. Argentines had confidently come to believe that the government would never tame inflation. Thus Menem's mania for decrees proved counterproductive. And, as Menem's fourth economy minister in less than two years, Argentines at first had little reason to believe Cavallo either whose earlier brief service as Central Bank president under military rule had been a fiasco.

Menem's and Cavallo's new anti-inflation policy required, therefore, a self-binding strategy. The 1991 "convertibility law" established the free convertibility of the national currency into dollars. The exchange rate with the dollar would be fixed and unchanged. The central bank was prohibited from printing paper money to cover budget deficits unless new currency issues were backed by gold or foreign reserves. Most importantly, this policy was adopted not through a decree but by an act of Congress; henceforth, only the Congress could authorize a change in the value of the currency or the issuance of paper money under other rules. The purpose of the law was to bind the president, the economy minister, the Congress, and through the Congress, the Peronist party to the anti-inflation policy. The law was an immediate, stunning, and enduring success. It has become the anchor of Argentina's impressive macroeconomic performance in the 1990s.

Only through a democratic procedure could Argentina's economy finally turn around. Argentina's executive and legislative branches have jointly enacted most of the significant measures to promote an open market economy (including detailed approval of privatization decisions), thereby contributing to make the new rules credible for the long term.

Several subsequent democratic steps helped to consolidate Argentina's new open market economy. First, in preparation for the 1995 presidential election, the leading opposition presidential candidate, José Octavio Bordón (FREPASO), endorsed the fundamentals of the new economic framework. In that way, economic actors could begin to consider that market rules would endure even if Menem were defeated for re-election. Second, in July 1996 Menem replaced Cavallo as economy minister but the fundamental orientation of economic policy continued. That personnel change sent the clear signal that the new framework was a policy of the government, not just of one person. Third, in preparation for the October 1997 nationwide congressional elections, a new opposition alliance was formed between the country's second and third largest parties, the Radical party and FREPASO. The alliance formally endorsed the new economic framework, this time not just as the personal decision of the leading opposition candidate but as a program to which the parties were committed. Specifically, the alliance pledged continuation of the convertibility law and the policies of privatization and deregulation.

It was, in short, not the president's authority to enact decrees, nor the talent and boldness of his economy minister, nor even the entire governing team that could ensure the consolidation of Argentina's shift to an open market economy. Consolidation began only when the opposition endorsed the change in framework and when the policy survived the departure of its key architect. Only democracy can commit the future.

El Salvador

In the early 1980s no one would have forecast that by the late 1990s El Salvador's brutal civil war would have ended, that fair and competitive elections would have become the norm, that no military coup attempt would have succeeded again, and that those who had pledged to kill each other would sit side by side as members of Congress. Peace came to El Salvador because the lesson of Thomas Hobbes's *Leviathan* was right once again: after many years of devastating battle, of a life "nasty, brutish," citizens searched for order and found it through a complex and far-reaching political contract. Peace, not surprisingly, became the founding stone of prosperity. According to the United Nations Economic Commission for Latin America, El Salvador was Central America's top economic performer in the 1990s.

Democratic procedures helped to build the peace. El Salvador's democratic left played a crucial role in constructing the bases for a peace settlement prior to the formal agreement. For example, in the 1980s Rubén Zamora had been allied with the revolutionary insurgency and been its international civilian spokesman. Eventually, his party, the Democratic Convergence, chose to participate in the 1989 and 1991 national elections. After the latter, the ruling conservative party (ARENA) and the Democratic Convergence reached an agreement to organize the legislature, voting for each other's respective candidates. Thus the democratic left reassured the military and conservative elites that it could be trusted to be law abiding and to govern, and it signaled to the insurgents that much could be gained through elections.

Democratic procedures have also increased the likelihood that economic growth would endure. In May 1995 President Armando Calderón Sol's ARENA government was compelled by economic exigencies to raise the value added tax. Deserted by his normal allies in parliament who feared the political repercussions of the vastly unpopular increase, Calderón Sol made an agreement with the new Democratic party, led by the leading former revolutionary commander, Joaquín Villalobos, to get the tax increase enacted through Congress. This decision turned out to be very costly politically for Villalobos and his party, however.

In June 1997 a new opposition majority in El Salvador's Legislative Assembly revoked the legal framework that would govern the privatization of the state owned telephone company. At the very moment of this legal derogation, however, the opposition took the initiative to propose detailed negotiations with the government; indeed, the opposition had objected precisely to the government's insistence in implementing the privatization of the telephone company through a decree and with little political consultation. The negotiations succeeded. In July 1997 a super-majority in the Legislative Assembly approved the privatization of the telephone company under procedures that made it more likely that there would be greater room for competition and more effective regulation.

El Salvador is at an earlier stage than Chile or Argentina in learning how to use democratic procedures to consolidate a market economy, but Salvadoran politicians from the right and the left are slowly learning, too, that both democracy and markets are enhanced by making each support the other, and that in the long run only a democratic opposition can ensure the future of market oriented economic reforms.

Brazil

Dr. Fernando Henrique Cardoso was Brazil's best internationally known social scientist for decades. He was also a man of the left and a political exile during the military government. Cardoso intellectually observed, and personally suffered, the arbitrariness of Brazil's oversized state under military rule. He also learned firsthand about the volatility, indiscipline, and unreliability of Brazil's political parties. As a member of Congress, finance minister, and eventually president of Brazil, he set for himself the goal of democratizing Brazil. That required shrinking the bloated state, making it subject to the laws, and re-inventing Brazil's parties and parliaments to make democratic procedures work.

Cardoso has acted in the persistent belief that laws enacted by Congress are by far the superior means to re-order Brazil's economy in time for better performance in the twenty-first century. To be sure, the process of economic reform through Congress is maddeningly slow, in part because the president's party is a congressional minority and in part because coalition and party discipline are sufficiently feeble that each vote must be negotiated afresh. But acting through Congress gives a greater measure of assurance than a mere presidential decree would that today's economic rules will endure tomorrow.

By the late 1990s Brazil's Congress had approved key proposals on privatization of the petroleum and telecommunications sectors. The fixed-line telephone sector became open to private capital. And private capital can enter as well a petroleum sector that had long been monopolized by a single state enterprise. Important privatizations have also occurred in the iron ore, electricity, and railroad sectors, among others. The Congress has enacted some administrative reforms and slowly and haltingly has made progress to enact meaningful social security reforms. In each instance, a multiparty coalition was required to adopt the change; that very fact of multipartisanship, in turn, makes it more likely that today's policies will be supported by many parties tomorrow. Laws are superior to decrees, and coalition governments and supermajorities are often superior to one-party simple majorities in increasing the likelihood that new rules will be credible and long term.

In late 1997 the Southeast Asian financial crisis that had broken out in the second half of the year threatened to overwhelm Brazil; the Brazilian stock market tumbled badly. In November the Cardoso government announced a combination of tax increases, payroll cuts, and other spending reductions intended to slash the budget deficit. By this time, international investors, too, had begun to learn the lesson of democracy and markets: they praised the measures but held back to assess whether Congress would support them. The Congress did; the crisis eased. Democratic procedures played an important role in this successful outcome.

Brazil's economy in the 1990s did not perform as well as those of Chile, Argentina, or El Salvador, but Brazil's economic restructuring and prospects have been advanced through democratic procedures and make it more likely that its economic growth rate will improve in due course.

Nicaragua

Nicaragua was one of Latin America's economic basket cases in the last quarter of the twentieth century. Cuba and Nicaragua were the only two Spanish American countries whose gross domestic product per capita fell substantially during the first half of the 1990s. The legacy of civil and international war made it virtually impossible for Nicaraguans to address their country's fundamental economic problems. Their national legislature barely functioned.

One of the most enduringly divisive issues was the dispute over property seized by the Sandinista government (1979–90). Success in sorting out property disputes eluded the 1990–96 government of President Violeta Chamorro. That was one important reason for the poor economic performance: Nicaragua had no credible property rules.

Arnoldo Alemán took office as president of Nicaragua in January 1997 trumpeting that he would step on toes, recover properties "usurped" by the revolutionaries, and bring order to property relations. His stance was reminiscent of Argentine President Carlos Menem's belief that the president alone could right economic wrongs. Alemán failed in his quest until he turned toward democratic compromise. In November 1997 a legislative super-majority constituted of Alemán's Liberal party and the Sandinista Front for National Liberation enacted a new property law to settle property disputes and open a new chapter in the country's political and economic history. The law was just a beginning; much detailed conflict resolution must follow it. But Nicaragua's story demonstrates yet again the utility of democratic procedures to consolidate political and economic peace and re-open the possibility of economic growth.

Objections to the Argument

Some might object that, in some important respects, democratic procedures in Latin America are a sham at worst, superficial at best, and that the core of the difficulty is attributable precisely to a shotgun wedding between democracy and the market.

Democracy requires, theorists would insist, that majority preferences in economic policy, as expressed in elections, should translate into government policy. And yet there has often been a yawning gap between campaign election discourse on economic issues and eventual government policy. This gap was most marked in the 1982 election of Salvador Jorge Blanco in the Dominican Republic, the 1989 election of Carlos Menem in Argentina, and the 1990 election of Alberto Fujimori in Peru. The gap was also considerable in the 1985 election of Víctor Paz Estenssoro in Bolivia, the 1989 election of Carlos Andrés Pérez in Venezuela, and the 1989 election of Michael Manley in Jamaica. In each case, once elected, the winner proved to be much more economically orthodox and pro–open markets than campaign discourse had suggested. Many voters, understandably, thought that politicians had lied. The connection between the preferences of voters and the actions of elected officials had been severed at democracy's peril. But the mendacity of politicians could also injure the credibility of these politicians more readily: if they had lied to the voters, why would they not lie to investors?

Voters had subsequent chances to pass judgment on the liars and the relative merits of the programs eventually adopted. In the Dominican Republic and Venezuela, the voters punished the liar's party in the next presidential elections. In Argentina and Peru, voters approved a change in the constitution to permit the incumbent president's immediate re-election, and then re-elected each. And in Jamaica the liar's party was also rewarded with the electoral ratification of its incumbency. In these second elections after the politicians sinned, voters discerned differently in various countries according to the efficacy of results. Democracy malfunctions when politicians lie. But democracy is self-correcting: it allows the voters to render judgments iteratively. So too in the case of markets: investors could judge the results and, in most cases, they joined in the judgment of the voters.

In many other cases, campaign programs all along have been closer to the actual programs of government. This has been the case in all Chilean elections since the restoration of democracy and in El Salvador since the late 1980s. The connection between promises and policies was also quite close in the 1994 elections in Brazil and in Mexico.

Three broad trends, in brief, were evident in the relationship between economy and elections in Latin America in the 1980s and 1990s. First, in the midst of economic crisis in the 1980s, voters tended to vote against the incumbent party in virtually every country where competitive elections were held (Colombia was the principal exception). Second, in a number of these elections, key politicians lied, but voters retained the opportunity to pass judgment on them or their parties at the next election. Third, by the mid-1990s "sincere" campaigning had become more common. Incumbents had little choice but to run on their record. More importantly, challengers in many countries—including countries as different as Brazil and El Salvador—chose to contest power on the basis of a transparent program. Blatant electoral deception—troubling and damnable as it is—may have turned out to be just a regrettable transitional phenomenon.

Another line of concern is that democracies will only endure so long as there is economic prosperity and, relatedly, that democracies will return to statist, populist habits in the face of economic setbacks. The 1990s provide at least one modest test of this proposition. In December 1994 a financial panic hit Mexico. To some degree, it affected the entire region, and it hurt Mexico, Argentina, and Uruguay quite badly. And yet no Latin American government was overthrown by the armed forces in 1995, nor did any democratic government backtrack on its commitment to a market economy framework. Most impressively, Argentine voters re-elected Carlos Menem despite a deep recession with very high unemployment. Statism and populism, these voters understood, were not the answer to a business cycle downswing, even a severe one. And neither Menem, nor his principal opponent José Octavio Bordón, advocated adoption of statist or populist policies.

There are other grounds to object that the connection between democracy and the market is not so benign. Many of the devices designed to maintain fiscal discipline barely meet the test of democracy. Closed and technical styles of decision making reinforce the unresponsiveness of the state to societal demands. At times democratically elected presidents rule by decree, deliberately bypassing the legislature. This has been the case in virtually every country discussed in this chapter. The turn toward a market opening has coincided with spectacular cases of corruption that led to the impeachments of incumbent presidents in Brazil and Venezuela. Concern about corruption looms large in nearly every country. During the early stages of the privatization of state enterprises, for example, there are many opportunities for government officials to favor certain business groups. And the court systems are always slow, often inept, and in many instances corrupt. All of this, and more, is true. In every instance, however, the performance of authoritarian regimes was either no better or, in fact, worse.

One enduring cost of democratic politics for the efficient and transparent operation of the economy is pork barrel expenses. These no doubt remain high. Pork barrel expenditures are part of President Alberto Fujimori's strategy in Peru to build his popularity among the poor and in rural areas in order to withstand opposition to his rule. Pork barrel deals still grease the wheels of the Brazilian Congress, as it lurches forward to enact important reforms that will in due course reduce the scope of pork barrel. In Mexico, President Ernesto Zedillo pacified nearly-rebellious state governors from his own party by placing the principal revenue sharing schemes in the hands of state governments. In the Dominican Republic, former President Joaquín Balaguer built his career as a very successful electoral politician on pork barrel goodies. These costs are difficult to purge from democratic politics, and most Latin American countries have yet to do so—nor are the prospects encouraging for success in this regard.

Moreover, there remain tragic instances of systematic political and economic malpractice where the ills of Latin America's democratic past remain very much alive. Ecuador is a case in point. No successful presidential candidate since the return of civilian rule in 1979 has been both a supporter of sound market oriented macroeconomic policies *and* "sincere" about it during the presidential campaign. Each successful Ecuadoran presidential candidate during the past two decades has been deceitful during the campaign, albeit to varying degrees. Ecuadoran political parties remain both fragmented and undisciplined. Coalitions are formed for transient tactical advantage; they are not governing coalitions of the type that has worked so effectively at various times in Chile, Bolivia, or

Colombia, for example. Presidents have lacked congressional majorities and, consequently, have relied on decrees. Congress notoriously retaliated by impeaching the most hyperactive president, Abdalá Bucaram, in 1997. Most parties are clientelistic and rents-providing in their approach to politics; most of these parties are regionally based and lack a national scope. And yet, whereas Ecuador might have been the "poster boy" for Latin American populist democracies decades ago, in the late 1990s it is noteworthy because it has become an exception. No other Ibero-American country is so badly governed.

Democracy is no panacea to cure all of Latin America's political and economic ills. But democracy in Latin America in the 1990s—given the region's history and context—is serving far better the needs of its people than ever before or than alternative political regimes could. Democratic politics is more likely to represent the preferences of citizens, to construct the structures and rules that will address credibly the rational expectations of economic actors, and to enact the wise rules that make us free.

Checking Corruption

The transition to democratic regimes in Latin America seems to have coincided with growing corruption. At least that is the impression one gets from reading and watching the Latin American media as well as the foreign media. Yet appearances are deceiving. Corruption has a long history in Latin America. It only *seems* to have become more pervasive of late precisely because Latin America's new democracies have freed up the media to report about it.

In fact, an argument can be made that, despite the growing reports of corruption, the countries are becoming less corrupt. This is in part the result of fewer opportunities for graft. When the Latin economies were more statist, people were more dependent on getting permission from their government to engage in all sorts of activities that in free market economies required no permission or only a reasonable number of permits. Until the recent economic opening in the region, government bureaucrats had the power to make or break individuals and businesses by virtue of their decisions regarding import and export permits, the ad hoc setting of duties, the granting of licenses, and the like. In order to "facilitate" the bureaucracy's decision making or ensure that the government acted favorably on one's petition, supplemental, under-the-table payment was often required and demanded. Now that many countries have done away with most if not all of the formerly required licenses and permits, the opportunities for such extortion have been severely reduced.

The reduction of government subsidies for the media also has been instrumental in creating a freer, more muckraking press. Latin American newspapers in particular have discovered that there is a market for newspapers that shed light on the behavior of government, the private sector, and the like. A good example is the recent success of the newspaper *Reforma* in Mexico City. Despite the government's early attempts to bankrupt it by encouraging the government controlled union to interfere with the distribution of the paper, the combination of a dedicated staff and a public that was tired of government and private sector corruption enabled the paper to survive.

The other development that favored increased press freedom was technological advance that made it easier for people in Latin America to get their information from sources not subject to government control. The fax machine, the computer, and cable television have all been instrumental in keeping Latin Americans informed about what is happening in their own countries.

Although the transition to democracy in Latin America was therefore helpful in allowing corrupt behavior to be made public, other factors played an important role as well. Democracy in a country with a very statist economy will probably be less corrupt than such an economy in a more closed political system, but it will still be corrupt since people will be too dependent on government favors and approval. The combination of a democratic regime with a market economy is probably the best in keeping government corruption in check, since people are freer to pursue their interests without having to pay off scores of individuals at each

turn. Even better is a democratic political system, a market economy, and the existence of diversified sources of information that
are not easily controlled by a small group of people. Latin America
is closer to this model today than ever before in its history.

At the same time, Latin American democracies are far from
being institutionalized. In addition, they exist in societies in which
the majority of citizens still receive very little education and are
poor. As a result, many Latin Americans are not well equipped to
protect and defend their interests, let alone their government, from
groups intent on harming both. One need only think of the powerful, well organized, and wealthy drug cartels in order to appreciate the magnitude of the problem facing those government
officials intent on bringing them to justice.

In addition to the scarcity and maldistribution of resources in
Latin America, which make it difficult to hold governments and
powerful private citizens accountable for corrupt or illegal behavior, there is the problem of malfunctioning, or nonfunctioning,
legal systems. Unfortunately, the fact that legal systems in Latin
America are modeled on Roman law, which gives authorities relatively great discretion in applying the law, has tended to work
against the institutionalization of the rule of law in these societies.
Too much discretion is the functional equivalent of a statist economy. It provides too many opportunities for buying the kinds of
legal decisions and outcomes desired. It also allows the continuation of unequal treatment of citizens having unequal power as well
as economic resources. In a culture that has not been traditionally
egalitarian to begin with, as is the case with most Latin cultures,
the high degree of legal discretion serves to create cumulative
inequalities.

The situation is not hopeless for Latin America's new democracies, however, in part because of a changing international environment. For some time now, U.S. businesspeople have been
complaining about the Corrupt Foreign Practices law, which for-
bids them from bribing or paying off corrupt officials in foreign
countries in which they are trying to do business. It is not that U.S.
businesses want to be corrupt. Rather, they have felt at a compara-
tive disadvantage vis a vis their competitors. Germany is a particu-

larly egregious example. There, the government allows its private sector to deduct the costs of foreign bribes for tax purposes. Instead of rescinding the Foreign Corrupt Practices Act, however, Washington decided to try to raise other countries to the U.S. standard. It is beginning to look as if the United States might succeed. If so, foreign investors in Latin America would be able to take a collective stand against corrupt Latin officials. Since Latin America's new market economies require foreign capital and technology, the results could be impressive.

Another reform that is needed in order to reduce corruption in Latin America's new democracies is the creation of a civil service in which positions are filled by an impersonal examination. At the present time, political appointees fill Latin American bureaucracies for the most part. One need only read a book such as Gore Vidal's *1876* in order to see that the United States, prior to implementing civil service reform, looked like the stereotype of a corrupt Latin American government.

There are those who believe that corruption in Latin America has little to do with forms of government or economic systems and more to do with culture and values. Undoubtedly, some cultures are more tolerant of corruption than others. In fact, what is considered corrupt in one society is considered natural and acceptable in another. On the other hand, cultures can and do change. As people in Latin America have become better informed about other cultures, and as the high costs of corruption have become better understood, they have begun to demand more honest behavior on the part of their leaders, both in the public and private sectors. The economic austerity programs that governments throughout the region have had to implement as part of their restructuring efforts no doubt encouraged their change of heart. When economies are growing and people's economic situations are improving absolutely, if not relatively, they are willing to overlook high-level corruption. When people are being asked to tighten their belts, however, at a time when the individuals asking them to do so are getting richer and richer as the result of special privileges and illegal behavior, they become angry and protest.

Democracy, therefore, is not a panacea for corruption. What it can and does do is provide a competitive environment in which

those who are out of power have an incentive to seek out and pub-
licize corrupt behavior on the part of the government. To help
ensure that democracy reduces the prevalence of corrupt behavior
and practices, however, other changes are also necessary. These
include movement toward a less discretionary legal system and the
creation of a civil service. Foreign anticorruption pressures are also
useful, and the reduction of the state's role in the economy is
essential. Latin America's transition to democracy is occurring in a
context in which at least some of these factors exist, which is
encouraging.

Recommendations for Institutionalizing Democracy

The current wave of new democracies is not the first for Latin
America. Several countries in the region had their first experience
with democracy in the late nineteenth century. More recently,
democracy took hold again during the 1950s into the early 1960s, a
period that one author described as "the twilight of the tyrants."
The fact that the tyrants returned should give us pause before pro-
claiming that this time democracy is here to stay in Latin America.

It is already clear that threats to Latin America's democracies
exist. They are inherent in the region's new democratic institutions, which need to be strengthened. They also emanate from the
economic policies that are being implemented and the social structures on which they are being imposed. To a lesser extent, problems emanating from the international sphere can also be
identified.

Any efforts to strengthen Latin America's democracies must
therefore focus on all these areas. It is not enough merely to
improve the functioning of the political institutions. Although in
theory dissatisfied citizens have the option in a democracy of voting out incumbents who are not performing satisfactorily, the reality is somewhat more complicated. It is difficult to hold elected
officials accountable if you are poorly educated, lack the means to
get to the polls, and must spend all your energies trying to feed
yourself and your family, to cite just some of the problems facing

Latin America's voters. The institutionalization of democracy in the hemisphere, therefore, must deal with all these challenges.

U.S. policy cannot solve the problems of poverty and inequality in Latin America, which predate the very existence of the United States. Furthermore, there is no consensus on how to do so. Washington can, however, attack these problems indirectly by pursuing policies that contribute to the success of Latin America's market economies. Although successful market economies are no guarantee of democratic stability, they certainly play an important role in facilitating democratic institutionalization.

Perhaps the most useful contribution that the U.S. government can make, therefore, is to pursue policies that keep its own economy growing and its interest rates low. A growing U.S. economy provides an important market for Latin American exports and generates employment in the exporting countries. This is particularly so for Mexico, Central America, the Caribbean, and most of the Andean countries, which have a large proportion of their trade with the United States. Although countries such as Brazil and Argentina sell a smaller percentage of their total exports to the United States, these exports constitute an important source of foreign earnings in absolute terms and also create jobs.

Furthermore, trade and investment are closely linked. Maintaining a close trade relationship between the United States and Latin America will help ensure that U.S. investors stay interested and involved in the region. Technology transfer, of great benefit to Latin America and the Caribbean, also is positively correlated with trade and investment.

Finally, given the still relatively high levels of public and private sector foreign debt in Latin America, a sharp rise in U.S. interest rates would reduce the region's rate of economic growth and, by extension, the resources available for social programs. Higher U.S. interest rates would also severely reduce the inflow of foreign capital to the region and threaten the financial, economic, and political stability of a number of Latin American governments.

In the political sphere, the first order of business is to ensure that elections are free and fair so that the vast majority of the population will easily accept their results as legitimate. Latin America has already made significant progress in this area, particularly in those countries that are highly urbanized. It is harder to tamper with votes in well-observed urban voting booths. The rural area is another matter entirely. Voting booths are few and far between, relatively speaking, and voters are less educated, poorer, and more able to be manipulated. Nevertheless, heightened public awareness and concern over the problem have begun to produce solutions. International and domestic observers, quick or parallel vote counts, and the presence of the media in rural precincts all have helped make the rural vote a more accurate reflection of voters' real preferences.

Other reforms are still needed, and much could be gained by copying changes adopted by Mexico during the 1990s. These include the issuance of tamper-proof voting credentials, complete with color photos and a computerized chip containing a copy of the voter's fingerprint. Representatives of all major parties are encouraged to serve as poll watchers. International observers are invited to do the same. The government provides a subsidy to all major parties so that they will have funds to purchase advertising time on radio and television in particular. The most important reform, however, was the creation of an independent electoral institution at the federal level. Its members are selected not by the executive but by Congress, and they are empowered with solving electoral disputes, performing a quick count of votes throughout the country, and otherwise ensuring compliance with the democratic rules of the game.

The United States government, together with other democracies and international institutions such as the United Nations and the Organization of American States, worked closely with the Mexican government and with nongovernmental organizations in designing and helping to finance these reforms. This model should now be applied to other Latin American electoral systems that need improvement. Recent literature on democracy has tended to downplay the importance of "electoral" democracy, which is characterized by free, but not necessarily fair, elections. They consider it far removed from real or "liberal" democracy. Despite its imperfections, however, so-called electoral democracy is an absolutely necessary first step on the road to a liberal democracy. The strengthening of electoral democracy in Latin America should therefore remain a high priority for Washington.

The other key area ripe for reform is the judiciary. Until there is the rule of law in Latin America, democracy will not become entrenched. Judicial reform is perhaps the most intractable political challenge facing the region. Perhaps the first change that needs to be made involves the selection of judges. They are now mainly appointed by incumbent governments, without any legislative input and with no reference to their legal qualifications. New rules are needed to give the legislature the power to confirm such appointments, and minimum standards for nominating judges must be set. Paying judges competitive salaries would also help reduce the incidence of bribery, but it is no guarantee. A complete review is needed of existing regulations in order to make them more specific, less contradictory, and less susceptible to discretionary decisions.

The U.S. government is already working in these areas, as well as Latin American government officials and individuals in the U.S. and Latin American private sectors. U.S. experts in relevant areas are being sent to Latin America, although more can and should be done to bring Latin American lawyers, judges, and the like to the United States to increase their familiarity with successful judicial reforms that have been undertaken here.

On the other hand, perhaps the most important contribution that Washington can make to strengthen the rule of law in Latin America is once again an indirect one. By continuing to pursue policies at home that support and fortify market economies in the region, Washington will help ensure the growth of demands from U.S. and other investors for more predictable and enforceable laws and regulations to protect their Latin American investments. Already we have seen some response by Latin American governments in the form of new laws that for example protect intellectual property. On the international level, the United States has taken the lead in pressing for international anticorruption conventions and agreements to make it more difficult for foreign companies to invest in countries that have illegally seized private properties owned by foreigners. Such international leadership puts additional pressure on Latin American and other emerging market economies to modernize their legal systems if they wish to continue receiving foreign capital and direct foreign investments.

Although the rule of law is widely recognized as important for the successful institutionalization of democracy, less discussed is the relationship between the rule of law and the creation of more just, equitable societies. In societies without functioning judicial systems, or where the rule of law is applied with great discretion, the rich will always win and the poor will always lose. The establishment of well functioning legal and judicial systems in and of themselves will not put an end to inequality; it will, however, give people who have been abused and mistreated an additional tool that they can use to begin to correct the situation.

Latin American legislatures also need improvement. Many of their members are new to the job. They usually are understaffed and lack the most minimal tools, such as computers, to aid them in their work. In some countries, such as Mexico, they are prohibited from being immediately re-elected. This means that a core group of experienced legislators cannot be created, which tips the balance of power toward the executive. It also means that the ties between members of Congress and their districts are very weak. Allowing re-election of congressional representatives would undoubtedly help correct these problems.

U.S. policy in this area should focus more on establishing and nurturing links between the U.S. Congress and its Latin American counterparts. In some cases, such as that of Mexico, such ties have existed for some time. They have not been an important part of the U.S.-Mexico bilateral relationship because the Mexican legislature was not really independent of the executive. That situation changed after the July 1997 midterm elections, when the president's party lost control of the Chamber of Deputies. As a result, both the Mexican representation on the commission, as well as the role that the commission will play, will now change. In fact, the growing importance of legislatures in Latin America should be taken as a new opportunity for the U.S. Congress to seek a more established, regular relationship with its hemispheric counterparts.

Now that the hemisphere's presidents have institutionalized periodic summit meetings, Washington should explore the possibility of setting up comparable summits to be attended by legislative leaders. These could be complemented by periodic meetings among legislative staffers to exchange information and ideas regarding ways of increasing the effectiveness and efficiency of Latin America's legislatures.

An inefficient, overgrown, and highly politicized bureaucracy has long characterized the executive branch of Latin American governments as well as other branches of government. Such widespread presidential discretion in filling government positions, particularly in countries where good paying jobs are scarce and where government remains a major employer, undermines democratic values and the legitimacy of elected governments. Civil service reform is badly needed, therefore, throughout the hemisphere. As mentioned earlier, such reform would also help reduce corruption.

Washington is already having an indirect and positive impact in this area as a result of its support of conditional lending to Latin America by the International Monetary Fund and other international financial institutions. A reduction in the size of the public sector is often a condition for continued Latin American borrowing from such institutions. Other U.S. policies that support market economies in the region constitute another indirect way of dealing with the problem of overblown government bureaucracies. This is because bloated government payrolls are often the result of an absence of job opportunities in the private sector. If the Latin American economies continue to grow, governments will cease to represent the only employment opportunities for many of Latin America's white-collar workers.

Much work also needs to be done to educate eligible voters regarding the mere mechanics of voting, as well as to better inform them of their rights. Issues also need to be better explained to them. Both USAID and the congressionally funded National Endowment for Democracy have committed substantial sums of money to prodemocracy programs in Latin America. In a sense, the problem is part of a larger social problem. Although it is not absolutely necessary to be highly educated in order to be able to defend your interests through your vote, it certainly helps. Education reform should therefore be a high priority throughout Latin America, with the initial focus on providing a basic education in the fundamentals.

The United States has already begun to give more attention to the problem of education reform in Latin America. In part, this was the result of the Clinton administration's need to come up with a new issue after it was unable to get Congress to approve the fast-track authority needed to expand free trade in the hemisphere. The solution to the problem of education reform is not necessarily to spend more money but to allocate it and spend it more effectively. In fact, there is a growing awareness that much of the money that is already allocated to education is being wasted or inefficiently used. Clearly the existence of computers and other new technology should open up new opportunities for creative policy making in this area. By giving educational reform a higher priority than in the past, Washington is helping to mobilize institutions such as the Inter-American Development Bank and the Organization of American States, which have expertise and resources that are relevant to the problem.

A final issue that U.S. policy must deal with is so-called reform fatigue. Despite years of austerity and sacrifice, large numbers of Latin Americans have experienced no significant improvement in their living standards, and some have even seen their standard of living decline. There is also a widespread and still growing sense that democracy is accentuating the economic inequities that already were great prior to the implementation of the economic reforms. Stated differently, Latin American democracy needs to adopt measures to give greater numbers of voters a larger share of the rewards of a market economy. The dramatic decline in inflation has helped, as has the introduction of private pension funds, with each contributor controlling his or her own account. But more direct reforms are also needed, such as more progressive tax systems and additional progress in ensuring compliance with tax laws. Other experiments such as profit sharing or the granting of stock options should also be considered.

Some of the fallout from reform fatigue is already evident in the electoral arena in the form of growing support for populist strongmen. One example is Hugo Chávez, the Venezuelan military man who launched an unsuccessful coup against President Carlos Andrés Pérez in 1992 and who is now running for president on a platform that includes disbanding the Venezuelan Congress. Large numbers of Paraguayan voters also supported the candidacy of former coup leader Lino Oviedo for president, until he was jailed.

U.S. policy must obviously continue to distinguish between failed coup leaders who leave the military to compete for power in the electoral arena and military men who take power by force. The former are no threat to U.S. interests as long as they accept the democratic rules of the game. The latter do threaten U.S. interests in a democratic Latin America. For this reason, Washington must continue to oppose military takeovers and work with other governments in the region to discourage or thwart them. The U.S. should also continue to insist that only democratic governments will be eligible to join a Free Trade Area of the Americas. U.S. votes in international financial institutions in favor of loans to any particular Latin American country should also remain conditioned on its having an elected civilian government. These kinds of policies are much more effective than threats to cut off the already minimal amounts of aid that the United States still provides to the region.

Finally, despite the new budget surplus in the United States, it seems doubtful that Congress will be willing to increase its aid funds to Latin America. The region is wealthy compared with other developing areas. And in light of the recent Asian crisis, it seems reasonable to assume that Washington's attention will be diverted to that region. Perhaps this is for the better. Perhaps one of the best ways to strengthen Latin American democracies and U.S. relations with them is for private groups in the United States and Latin America to work together more. One of the problems with Latin American democracy in the past was that it was usually limited to the national level, with state and local governments remaining under the control of small groups or strong leaders who ruled them as fiefdoms. Much of the pressures for both democratization and government accountability over the past decade has, in fact, come from local nongovernmental institutions that have been supported by counterparts in the United States. This model of "foreign aid" seems better suited to the new economic and political realities of the hemisphere than the old model of governments helping governments.

7

Trouble Ahead?
Prospects for U.S. Relations
with Latin America

PETER H. SMITH

Aspirit of heady optimism pervaded U.S.–Latin American relations throughout the early 1990s. Either out of volition or necessity, Latin American leaders implemented economic reforms in keeping with the dictates of the Washington consensus. Rejecting utopian formulas of both left and right, citizens and activists embraced the virtues of democratic politics. And throughout the region, there emerged a positive and pragmatic view of the United States. No longer hampered by the distortions of the cold war, it was thought the United States and Latin America could pursue

PETER H. SMITH is professor of political science, Simón Bolivar professor of Latin American Studies, director of the Center of Iberian and Latin American Studies, and director of Latin American Studies at the University of California, San Diego. His publications include more than a dozen books and sixty book chapters and journal articles. His most recent book is *Talons of the Eagle: Dynamics of U.S.–Latin American Relations*. Dr. Smith has served as a consultant to the Ford Foundation and other institutions and as codirector of the bilateral Commission on the Future of United States–Mexican Relations and of the Inter-American Commission on Drug Policy.

their natural coincidence of interests. Prospects for hemispheric collaboration were better than they had ever been.

Responding to these opportunities, the United States (tentatively under George Bush, more decisively under Bill Clinton) established "free trade" as the centerpiece of inter-American policy. U.S. strategy has promoted not only the reduction of trade barriers but also an entire package of economic reforms (for investments, privatization, reduction of state roles, environmental protection, etc.). Application of these policies throughout Latin America would presumably enhance efficiency and lead to economic growth, strengthen forces for democratic change, and consolidate close relationships with the United States. Beginning with NAFTA and then with the Free Trade Area of the Americas, FTAs would bind together "market democracies" throughout the hemisphere. Good things would go together.

Things are not quite working out that way. This chapter attempts to say why. To be sure, there has been significant progress during the 1990s within Latin America and in the relatively harmonious tone of inter-American diplomacy (photo ops with the U.S. president are highly prized commodities). But beneath this veneer of good will, there exists a good deal of tension and uncertainty in U.S.–Latin American relations. What might this mean for the future? And for U.S. policy?

To address such questions, I focus on three concerns: policymaking processes in the United States, current trends within Latin America, and the content of the inter-American agenda. I conclude with broad suggestions for U.S. policy.

The U.S. Policy Process

A fundamental obstacle to smooth and cooperative U.S.–Latin American relations derives from the policy-making process in Washington. During the cold war, the formation and implementation of U.S. foreign policy rested in the hands of a relatively cohesive elite, the so-called foreign policy establishment. Resulting measures were not always farsighted or effective, but the anti-

Communist strategy of "containment" yielded a great deal of consistency.[1] That is no longer the case.

One symptom (or cause) of this situation is the amount of attention devoted to Latin America. It was predicted by many, and hoped by some, that the region would become a truly high priority for the United States during the 1990s. As Robert A. Pastor, an experienced and top-flight analyst, wrote in *Foreign Policy* in 1992, the end of the cold war "offers powerful reasons for moving the Americas from the periphery of U.S. policy toward the center." Yet the region remains—as during the cold war—a mid-level priority. It is more important to Washington than South Asia or Africa, for instance, but a good deal less important than Europe (Western and Central/Eastern), East Asia, and the Middle East. With the possible exception of Mexico, always a special case, there is little sense of urgency about the region.

Partly as a result, U.S. policy suffers from bureaucratic balkanization. This has long been true, but the trend has become exceptionally pronounced since the end of the cold war. Different agencies have different policies: Treasury has one policy for Latin America, Commerce another, State has another, INS another, DEA still another, and so on. There is little discernible effort to reconcile these policies. The State Department and/or the White House might be expected to perform this role, but thus far they have not.

Even more conspicuous has been the growing importance of domestic politics and electoral concerns. Issues that now dominate inter-American relations—trade, investment, drugs, migration— touch on matters of local concern (for which reason they are sometimes called "intermestic"). State and local leaders take vocal stands on matters relating to Latin America, and they tend to be heeded in proportion to their political weight. Hence the passage of Propositions 187 and 209 in California.

In addition, Congress plays a central part in policy formation on key issues for the hemisphere (as shown by IRCA in 1986, the Anti-Drug Abuse Act of 1988, the ratification of NAFTA in 1993, and the Helms-Burton bill of 1996). Rather than evaluate foreign policy issues on their merits, legislators tend to respond to constituent groups in order to enhance prospects for their own re-election; frequently, too, they engage in "log-rolling" deals on issues that bear no substantive connection to each other. And to the extent that the interests of individual Congress members diverge from those of the administration, there is bound to be discord and confusion.

Inconsistent Policy

Predictably enough, this dynamic leads to inconsistent outputs. One glaring contradiction stands in relation to Mexico: the United States embraces economic integration through NAFTA on the one hand, and constructs walls along the border on the other. (Some would even assert that Washington has taken steps to militarize the border, a claim that was dramatized by the tragic death of a Texas teenager in May 1997.) The resulting contradiction has emerged on three levels. One is symbolic (and hence political): the construction of a wall along the U.S.-Mexican border seems utterly inconsistent with the spirit of a newfound economic partnership. A second is procedural and institutional: although NAFTA made no provision for labor migration, the U.S. emphasis on unilateral assertion undermines the principles of cooperation and consultation enshrined in the free trade agreement. The third is substantive: experience around the world has shown that economic integration tends to foster social integration. Freer trade encourages transnational investment—which generally stimulates cultural interaction and, ultimately, labor migration.[2] By taking anti-immigration measures, the Clinton administration is tacitly attempting to restrict and curtail the social consequences of the economic policy that it has so strongly endorsed. You cannot have it both ways.

There are numerous other policy contradictions. But the most conspicuous instance, and the one with perhaps the most far-reaching consequences, comes from the November 1997 refusal of Congress to grant fast-track authority to the Clinton administration. Throughout the 1990s, as noted above, the U.S. government made free trade the keystone of its policy toward Latin America. Ever since the Miami Summit of December 1994, in particular, the Clinton administration has avidly promoted a Free Trade Area of the Americas. Suddenly an alliance of organized labor, environmental groups, and disgruntled Democrats—plus some conservative Republicans who insisted on assurances that no U.S. foreign aid would go to organizations performing or promoting abortions, an utterly extraneous issue—dismantled the administration's approach to Latin America.[3] There is no policy to take its place.

This denouement has provoked a strong reaction in Latin America. As one Peruvian columnist acidly noted in *Expreso*, November 16, 1997:

> The repercussions of this legislative humiliation are potentially devastating. The immediate and practical effect will be that it will be impossible for U.S. officials to broach complex initiatives of major importance. In the absence of a continued U.S. drive, the Free Trade Area of the Americas (FTAA) has been condemned to what it has been so far: a bombastic rhetorical exercise rich in expressions of good will, but lacking concrete results. Chile's dream of joining NAFTA has likewise been cut short, and the same can be said about APEC trade opening talks.

Without fast-track, most observers agree, there will not be FTAA or any other formal integration scheme involving the United States.

Granted, reaction has varied across the continent. Not everyone is anxious to join a hemispheric scheme under the tutelage of the United States. Chile, twice tempted (and spurned), now appears more intent on diversifying its trade partnerships than on joining NAFTA. And Brazil, always reluctant to recognize U.S. pre-eminence, has attempted to affirm its position as a continental power: already the dominant country within Mercosur, Brazil officially launched in April 1994 its proposal for a South American Free Trade Area, or SAFTA. Its proclaimed goal was to create a free trade zone for "substantially all trade" within the continent (in GATT speak) over the ten-year period from 1995 to 2005. In addition, SAFTA would confirm Brazil's historic claim to continental leadership on a par with the United States. Not surprisingly, there was reported to be much relief in Brasília over the failure of fast-track in the United States.

Weakness in the U.S. position became clearly evident during the Summit of the Americas in Santiago, Chile, in April 1998.

Although President Clinton assured his fellow heads of state that "our commitment to the Free Trade Area of the Americas will be in the fast lane of our concerns," the U.S. delegates were unable to press these issues with force and credibility. "There will be a lot of smiling and back-slapping this weekend," as one Latin American finance minister confided, "but the reality is that we are growing frustrated and more and more skeptical that the United States is really committed to free trade."[4]

To be sure, the summit resulted in a unanimous pledge to make "concrete progress" toward creation of an FTAA by the end of the century and to adopt an intensive schedule for negotiating sessions. Leaders of the hemisphere decided to set up a multilateral process for evaluating progress against illicit drug trafficking, and they agreed to hold inter-American summits "periodically"—with the next gathering to be hosted by Canada. Perhaps most important, they also adopted an ambitious plan (with anticipated loans of $6 billion from the World Bank and the Inter-American Development Bank) to provide universal access to elementary school education by the year 2010 and high school education to 75 percent of the region's youth by the same year. Conspicuous, however, was Washington's low-key demeanor on the question of free trade. According to José Miguel Vivanco of Human Rights Watch, the educational plan represented "the silver lining to Clinton's failure to get fast-track—a shift away from trade to human issues."

Parenthesis: Outlooks for Free Trade

As of this writing, it seems possible to imagine three general scenarios for the structure of the Western Hemisphere. One envisions prolongation of the status quo, with a three-member NAFTA as the only formal trade accord connecting Latin America to the United States—plus Mercosur as a point of gravity in South America, thus creating a kind of "asymmetric bipolarity" within the hemisphere. The failure of fast-track virtually assures the continuation of this situation for the foreseeable future. Under these circumstances countries other than Mexico will be free to pursue alternative strategies, such as subregional integration schemes and/or "plurilateral" openings to extrahemispheric trading partners. Current negotiations between the European Union and Mercosur, Chile, and Mexico are likely to intensify; the Latin American members of APEC—Mexico, Chile, and Peru—will also seek to strengthen ties in the Asia-Pacific region.

A second possibility might be called "NAFTA-plus"—that is, a scenario under which NAFTA would undergo limited expansion to include three or four other countries of Latin America. The process would begin with Chile, which was invited to begin negotiations at Miami in December 1994, and then move on to other countries. In fact, however, the list of viable candidates seems to be very short—and congressional disenchantment with NAFTA makes this a dubious prospect.

A third general scenario envisions the achievement of an FTAA, assuming that the White House eventually obtains fast-track authority. Via links with the United States, all countries of Latin America would have access to capital and markets of the advanced industrial North. Theoretically this could come about through successive accessions to NAFTA, in which case the resultant extent of hemispheric integration would be relatively deep, although this now seems unlikely. An alternative path might include some kind of FTA or other "docking" arrangement between NAFTA and Mercosur (or SAFTA). More feasible would be the promulgation of an entirely new hemispheric organization, in which case the degree of integration would be relatively shallow.

To be viable, FTAA will have to include and accommodate Brazil, which has taken a firm and singular stand on negotiating strategies. While U.S. delegations have (in general) wanted to accelerate agreements, Brazil has called for caution and care; whereas Washington has proclaimed that FTAA should go well beyond global WTO standards, Brazil has insisted that it should merely meet WTO guidelines; while U.S. representatives have argued that discussions should take place between individual countries, a position that greatly favors the United States, Brazil has argued in favor of participation by groups, such as Mercosur or SAFTA; and though Washington has wanted to achieve market openings (through reduction of tariffs and nontariff barriers) early in the FTAA negotiations, Brazil has sought to postpone consideration of such matters. Beneath these political expressions of discord are divergences in national interests and aspirations. But FTAA simply cannot function without Brazil, so it would be essential for negotiators from Washington and Brasília to find some means of reconciling these differences. In tacit recognition of this fact, the Santiago Summit stipulated that Brazil and the United States should jointly chair final stages of the FTAA process during the years 2003–2005.

For the short to medium term, however, continuation of the status quo seems by far the most realistic prospect. For many in Latin America, this comes as a great disappointment.

Latin America:
Seeds of Disenchantment

Latin America has not lived up to U.S. expectations. This remark is not intended as a criticism of Latin America or its citizens. Rather, it is a criticism of U.S. expectations and facile assumptions about the region. It is also a warning.

Economic reform has not yet produced its anticipated results. Overall rates of growth have been sluggish and uneven: less than half the countries of Latin America, and less than one-third the countries of Latin America and the Caribbean, have averaged more than 4 percent per annum throughout the 1990s. (The year 1997 showed the best performance in a quarter of a century, with an average growth rate of 5.3 percent, but there are no guarantees this will continue.) The external debt has in the meantime climbed to $650 billion, a substantially higher level than in 1982.

Inequalities have sharpened. Working people have continued to suffer the brunt of restructuring: in Mexico and Argentina the average wage is about 30 percent below 1980 levels; in Peru the average worker makes just over a third of what he or she made in 1980. About 200 million people in Latin America survive at poverty levels. The richest quintile in Latin America now receives 19 times the income of the poorest 20 percent. Benefits have yet to trickle down.

This situation could have serious political repercussions. "After almost a decade of reform," Sebastian Edwards wrote in *Foreign Affairs* (March/April 1997):

the region has little to show in improved economic performance and
social conditions. Poverty has not been reduced. Growth has been modest at best. In many countries wages have stagnated and job creation has
been sluggish. The reining in of inflation has been one of the few com-
mendable accomplishments.

Without visible signs of improvement, Edwards continues, "political support for Latin American reformist governments will erode."
Since the United States is so closely identified with the "Washington consensus" that promoted neoliberal economic reform, this
would have profound and negative implications for U.S.–Latin
American relations.

Politics has a dark side as well. Corruption continues unabated
in some countries, but the problems are deeper than that. More
pervasive has been the emergence of what Fareed Zakaria in
Foreign Affairs (November/December 1997) has called "illiberal
democracy," regimes that respect free (if not always fair) elections
but do not respect constitutional guarantees. According to one
respected scholar, nearly half the countries of Latin America had
in 1993 "levels of human rights abuse that are incompatible with
the consolidation of [liberal] democracy." Similarly, a December
1997 report from Freedom House rates eight nations of Latin
America as "free," ten (including Brazil and Mexico) as "partly
free," and one—Cuba—as "not free." Democracy still has a long
way to go.

One must exercise care about cause and effect. It is not entirely
clear how much of the inequality and poverty now present in Latin
America is the result of economic reforms promoted by the United
States and/or the international community at large over the last
fifteen to twenty years. And with some partial exceptions, it seems
unlikely that the United States bears responsibility for the emergence of illiberal democracies.[5] What can be said, however, is that
U.S. policy has not managed to prevent these undesirable developments.

Disenchantment has already begun to appear. There are ample
signs of resistance to regional economic integration. In itself, the
Chiapas uprising of January 1994 is probably not a good example;
more revealing, perhaps, is the extent of sympathy it aroused
throughout Mexican society. Elsewhere, too, small and medium

businesspeople and agriculturalists have begun to raise their voices. It seems entirely too early to presume that nationalism has vanished from the Latin American landscape.

This observation gives rise to a hypothesis: the greater the democratization in Latin America, the more complex and conflicted will become the relationship with the United States. To date Washington has been able to work and deal with executive leaders in highly presidentialist systems. As opposition parties, legislative bodies, nongovernmental organizations, and grassroots movements become more and more involved in policy debates throughout Latin America, the more difficult it will be for Latin American governments to speak with a single voice; and the more that impoverished and disadvantaged segments of Latin American society gain effective political voice, the more they will challenge neoliberal economic policies and prevailing conventional wisdom. Ironically, the more that the Latin American policy process comes to resemble that of the United States, the more contentious will be the region's dealings with the United States.

The Broader Agenda:
Not-Quite-Convergent Interests

A third general problem relates to national interests. Early in the 1990s it was fashionable to speak of an unprecedented "convergence" of Latin America's interests with those of the United States. This has been largely (not completely) true with respect to free trade. In connection with other key items on the inter-American agenda, Latin American interests diverge significantly from U.S. preferences.

Issue #1: Drug Trafficking

Illicit drugs pose a major problem for U.S. society. Approximately 12.8 million Americans consume illegal substances on a current basis (that is, within the past thirty days). This represents a decline from the 1979 high of 25 million but an increase over the 1992 low, and it still constitutes nearly 6 percent of the household population aged twelve or older. There are about 9.8 million current users of marijuana, by far the nation's favorite drug, and about 1.5 million current users of cocaine. Especially intractable has been "frequent" usage of cocaine; the number of those who consume on a weekly basis (and thus are addicted) has remained close to 600,000 since the mid-1980s. There has been a recent rise in the population of heroin addicts (also around 600,000) and, over the past five years, a substantial increase in experimentation with illicit drugs by American teenagers. The implication is inescapable: nearly fifteen years after Ronald Reagan first declared a "war on drugs," consumer demand remains steady and strong. And as the Office of National Drug Control Strategy reported in 1997: "Illegal drugs continue to be readily available almost anywhere in the United States. If measured solely in terms of price and purity, cocaine, heroin, and marijuana prove to be more available than they were a decade ago when the number of cocaine and marijuana users was much higher."

In response, the United States has made determined efforts to suppress the production and transit of illicit drugs throughout the hemisphere. According to this logic, a reduction in supply from Latin America will push up the retail price of drugs in the United States—and this in turn will lead to a reduction in demand. Without supply there can be no demand; it is as simple as that. Washington has therefore adopted two basic approaches: elimination of sources of supply by destroying crops and laboratory facilities, and interdiction of shipments bound for the U.S. market. As the federal allocation for antidrug efforts has sharply expanded, from $2.7 billion in FY 1985 to a requested $16.0 billion for FY 1998, the commitment to supply reduction has remained remarkably firm, claiming just about two-thirds of the total budget.

Another instrument of U.S. policy is the annual process of "certification," mandated by Congress as an amendment to the Foreign Assistance Act of 1986. According to the statute, governments that fail to cooperate with U.S. antidrug strategy will lose foreign assistance and face U.S. opposition in multilateral lending organizations. In 1996 and 1997 Colombia was denied certification; in 1998 it received a national interest waiver. And every year, the evaluation of Mexico leads to high drama: in 1998 the Clinton administration decided to certify Mexico against opposition from a

significant number of lawmakers. Although the rituals of certification provoke recurrent controversy, the administration continues
to support the process: "While denial of certification carries
important foreign assistance sanctions as well as a mandatory U.S.
vote against multilateral banks lending money to such countries,"
according to the White House, "the major sanction is public
opprobrium at failing the standard. This process has proved
increasingly effective. It has fostered the development of realistic
performance benchmarks and increased cooperation in important
countries."[6]

The persistence of drug trafficking—together with the content
of U.S. policy—leads to serious friction. U.S. politicians regularly
succumb to the temptation to charge Latin American countries
(usually Mexico, Colombia, or Peru) with responsibility for drug
related problems in American society; in reply, Latins point their
fingers at U.S. demand. Moreover, Latin American countries face
different challenges from those in the United States. They do not
have serious problems with consumption. Instead their problems
stem from the power of cartels, from waves of narco-violence, and
from the subversion of state authority (through corruption and
other means). As described by María Celia Toro for the case of
Mexico, the most pressing concerns are fundamentally political.
One has been "to prevent drug traffickers from directly confronting state authority," to obstruct the formation of "states
within the state," and to diminish the threat of narco-terrorism. A
second goal, "equally important," has been "to prevent U.S. policy
and judicial authorities from acting as a surrogate justice system in
Mexico."[7] In other words, U.S. policy itself poses a significant danger to Mexican national interests.[8]

Issue #2: Undocumented Migration

Just as illicit drugs have continued to make their way into the
United States, so have undocumented migrants. Despite expan-
sions in U.S. quotas for legal immigration from the 1960s through
the 1980s, people continue to enter the country without official
authorization, in violation of U.S. law. Responsible demographers
estimated the total stock of "illegal aliens" to be between 2.5–4

million in the early 1990s, with Mexico accounting for 55–60 percent of the total. A more recent study puts the stock of illegal Mexicans around 2.3–3.4 million as of 1996.

Periodically, the United States has taken measures to stanch this flow. The Immigration Reform and Control Act of 1986 contained three principal provisions: (a) it would impose economic sanctions against U.S. employers who "knowingly employ, recruit, or refer for a fee" undocumented workers; (b) it offered permanent amnesty to undocumented workers who could prove continuous residence in the United States since January 1982; and (c) it granted partial amnesty for undocumented workers in the agricultural sector. Ultimately, IRCA represented a compromise between those political forces opposing unauthorized migration (from organized labor to racist reactionaries), those who benefited from its existence (mostly employers), and Latino leaders expressing concern about the potential aggravation of ethnic prejudice.

The law has achieved mixed results. The employer sanctions portion has shown itself to be toothless. It remains possible for employers to comply with the law—and still hire undocumented workers, who could make use of counterfeit documents. In contrast, the amnesty portion of IRCA turned out to be highly effective. Approximately 1.7 million applications were submitted under the "pre-1982" program and 1.3 million under the SAW program. More than 90 percent of the pre-1982 applicants had their status adjusted from temporary to permanent resident. Agricultural workers approved for temporary residence automatically received permanent resident status. As a result, nearly 3 million people acquired legal status in the United States.

Since then, the United States has redoubled efforts to deter illegal immigration. A tough stand on this issue has in fact become a hallmark of the Clinton administration, which took office in the midst of a crisis over an influx of rafters from Haiti. The administration increased the INS budget from $1.4 billion in FY 1992 to $2.6 billion for FY 1996. It sharply expanded the size of the Border Patrol. And it launched concentrated efforts at key crossing points: in 1993 the administration proclaimed Operation Hold-the-Line in El Paso, Texas (formerly known as Operation Blockade), in 1994 it launched Operation Gatekeeper in San Diego, and in 1997 it initiated Operation Rio Grande in McAllen, Texas. An INS strategic plan calls for a long-term, phased effort to extend such concentrated enforcement operations across the entire southwestern border. As Attorney General Janet Reno declared at the inauguration of Gatekeeper: "We *are* securing our nation's borders, we are aggressively enforcing our nation's borders, and we are doing it *now.* We will not rest until the flow of illegal immigrants across our nation's border has abated."

It remains unclear whether such efforts could ever be effective—or whether they will simply encourage would-be entrants to seek new modes of access. For instance, data on INS apprehensions of illegal aliens along the U.S.-Mexican border from January 1990 through August 1995 reveal substantial continuity in overall levels of migration and in seasonal cycles.[9] The first semester of 1995 showed a marked increase, on the order of 30 percent, apparently in response to the peso crisis of December 1994 and the ensuing recession, but there did not appear a mass exodus. On balance, it appears that migration from Mexico and the Caribbean obeys fairly consistent economic and social dynamics, and is relatively resistant to law enforcement efforts or to short-term pressure.

And it will continue to generate friction and misunderstanding. Labor exporting countries are likely to tolerate, if not favor, these outward flows: annual remittances to Mexico alone now amount to an estimated $4.5 billion, and the northward flow of workers provides the country with a social safety valve. These governments also seek to protect their citizens from abuse, mistreatment, and harassment within the United States. Undocumented migration tends to create bad feelings on all sides, and stepped-up measures to deter the flows tend only to exacerbate these problems.

Issue #3: Environmental Protection

Everyone ought to care about the environment. Since people all over the world live on the same planet and share the same resources, we have common interests: we gain from environmental protection; we lose from degradation. This presumption of solidarity underlies much current discussion of the issue.

Of direct relevance to the inter-American agenda is the threat of "global warming," which occurs as the earth's atmosphere traps more and more gases—mainly carbon dioxide from fossil fuels (coal, oil, natural gas, methane, and a few other gases). Creating a "greenhouse effect," the resultant canopy of gas causes the atmosphere to radiate additional heat back to the surface of the earth. Experts predict that gas accumulations could, in consequence, produce an increase in the global mean temperature of three to eight degrees Fahrenheit during the twenty-first century, a fundamental climate change that could raise sea levels by as much as two feet. This would lead to coastal flooding that, in turn, would cause enormous damage to the United States and other countries; it could totally engulf some small low-lying island states, causing them literally to disappear from the map; and it could endanger natural ecosystems and threaten agriculture.

The most voluminous source of greenhouse gas emissions is the industrialized world; the United States alone is responsible for 23 percent of the total. Another significant source is deforestation, principally in developing countries, which contributes approximately 14 percent of the overall effect. On average, 17 million hectares of tropical forests (an area equivalent to Virginia plus West Virginia) disappeared every year between 1981 and 1990. Deforestation has resulted from shifting cultivation by subsistence farmers and use of wood for fuel and, more importantly, from the inroads of commercial logging, cattle ranching, road construction, and permanent agriculture and colonization schemes. Despoliation of forests is widespread in Latin America, which accounts for 40 percent of world carbon emissions from this process, and particularly flagrant in Brazil. Of special concern to the international community has been the Amazon River Basin, host to the world's largest tropical rain forest.

Environmental issues have provoked substantial controversy and, particularly, differences in outlook between the industrialized countries of the "North" and the developing countries of the "South." This conflict has affected President Clinton's efforts to persuade developing countries to accept mandatory limits on greenhouse emissions. This U.S. plan represents a compromise between the position of the European Union, which has called for strict reductions by 2010 by industrialized nations (but not by developing countries), and a weaker proposal put forth by Japan. As Clinton admitted during his October 1997 tour of South America, "I expect to probably be criticized by all sides." And while the United States would take the lead, he said, "Emissions from the developing world are expected to grow dramatically. Forty years from now, they will exceed those of developed countries. . . . Since the issue is how to stabilize and reduce greenhouse gases in the entire atmosphere, this is clearly a global problem in which we all must do our share."

The developing world has resisted. Although President Menem of Argentina embraced the Clinton plan, President Cardoso of Brazil—a key country in this enterprise—stopped short of accepting mandatory limits. Quite clearly, the view of most of Latin America is that the United States and other rich nations have been the principal cause of the problem, so they should provide the solution: polluters ought to pay, and the wealthy should assist those in need. At least with regard to the environment, common interests do not lead directly to collective action.

Implications for U.S. Policy

This analysis leads to the inescapable conclusion that U.S. relations with Latin America are heading for difficult times. A disorganized U.S. policy process is producing incoherent (often contradictory) policy measures; developments in Latin America are provoking disenchantment and less willingness to comply with Washington's wishes; and on several key issues, Latin American preferences do not coincide with those of the United States. All these trends are becoming more apparent over time. The harmony that marked the early 1990s may not make it past the turn of the century.

What should the United States do? My suggestions fall in two categories: general orientations, and specific policy measures.

General Postures

1. Pay More Attention to the Region. This is not to say that Washington should wave a magic wand and suddenly make Latin America "more important" than Eastern Europe or the Middle East. It is to assert, instead, that the U.S. government should devote more sustained and high-level attention to the region than is now the case.[10] Inattention squanders opportunities.

In particular, the White House—and the president—should spend more time and energy on hemispheric affairs. It was noticed everywhere that President Clinton failed to make even one visit to Latin America during his first term. In his second term he embarked on three separate trips—Mexico in May 1997, South America in October 1997, and Santiago in April 1998—but these still seem to be intermittent, sporadic episodes.

What is required is more continuous attention. This does not merely mean more travel to the region or presidential participation in ever-more-grandiose summits. Instead, the president can effectively promote the hemispheric agenda by concentrating on Congress, educating the American public, and clarifying policy guidelines. Given the (very considerable) impact of domestic U.S. politics on inter-American relations, there is much to be done here at home.

Nor does this exhortation call for creation of a new institutional mechanism or an interagency "czar" for Latin American affairs. (The post of special advisor on Latin American Affairs, recently vacated by Thomas "Mack" McClarty, was never intended for this role.) On the contrary, my point is that the president—and only the president—has the capacity to bring sustained and high-level attention to hemispheric affairs. The mechanisms are in place; what remains is to make full use of them.

2. Coordinate Policy Output. Contradictory policies produce confusion and ill-will. The U.S. government, especially the executive branch, should intensify efforts to achieve consistent policy.

There are limits to what can be done. The White House cannot give orders to Congress (especially when both houses are controlled by the opposing party). Nor can the federal government control every action taken at the state and local level. But the White House could accelerate its efforts on key issues, such as fast-track authority. And it could certainly demand consistency among

different agencies within the executive branch. There is little justi-
fication for lack of coordination among these agencies. One way
to promote consistency would be to explicitly grant such authority
to a single entity. One logical candidate would be the Department
of State, which does not seem to have that mandate now; another
would be the White House itself, either through the National Security Council and/or through the post of special assistant to the
president.

3. Anticipate Disagreement and Uncertainty. There is no reason to expect
that Latin America should happily follow the U.S. lead on all
major issues, or that Latin America's development will conform to
U.S. expectations. We should anticipate contention.

We should even welcome it. Continued democratization in
Latin America is likely to increase dissonance and disagreement
over inter-American affairs. The United States should strongly
support transitions to democracy throughout the region. Almost
by definition, however, democratization involves instability. And as
pluralization (or at least decentralization) proceeds apace, it will
create more space for disagreement. In consequence, the inter-
American relationship is likely to become more difficult to manage, more resistant to control, more subject to unpredictability.
The voices of Latin American nationalism, more or less silent in
the early 1990s, are almost certain to make themselves heard. Having long promoted the cause of political stability throughout the
region, Washington must now become responsive to forces and
factors for change.

Specific Measures

1. Stick with FTAA. Over the long term FTAA probably offers the
best available hope for sustained development in Latin America,
since it would guarantee access to the global economy for all countries of the region. FTAA is liable to impose costs as well as benefits, of course, and numerous uncertainties remain, but it could
serve as an important "building block" for a liberal economic

order in the twenty-first century world.[11] U.S. abandonment of the FTAA goal, after years of exaggerated expectation, would have devastating consequences on inter-American relations.

The Clinton administration should therefore renew its efforts to gain fast-track authority from Congress at the earliest possible moment. It should neither seek nor accept a limited fast-track authority that would permit negotiations with the WTO, for instance, but not for FTAA. Such a restriction would be interpreted as a direct slap in the face of Latin America.

If fast-track can be obtained, the administration should use it with care. By this I mean that the United States should recognize and respect legitimate interests and apprehensions on the part of Latin America. There are two distinct models for FTAA: a deep integration agreement with labor provisions and environmental stipulations, one that might well require a "social fund" (as NAFTA does not) in order to be successful; or a relatively shallow agreement that calls only for the steady reduction of tariffs and NTBs. This kind of "FTA Lite" might not meet every goal but it would be preferable to U.S. imposition of a deep integration scheme against continental opposition. Nor is there any reason for these negotiations to impede current discussions between countries (and blocs) in Latin America and the EU and/or the Asia-Pacific region. For the United States, as well as for Latin America, there is much to be gained from diversification and expansion of economic ties: if things go well, everyone can benefit; if they do not, the United States (and/or FTAA) does not bear the blame.

2. Beware Silver Bullets. In the absence of fast-track authority, the administration should avoid the temptation to forge a hemispheric consensus around some other issue merely for the sake of asserting American leadership. (This warning is particularly relevant in this new era of pan-American summitry.) Aside from free trade, the most pressing issues—drug trafficking, migration, even environmental protection—yield divergent interests for Latin America and the United States. There is no basis for a genuine consensus, so there is no point in trying to impose one.

3. Revise Migration Policy. The United States has loudly asserted its sovereign right to make and enforce its own laws. That is not in dispute. The question is how best to manage (or control) migration from Latin America to the United States. Evidence and *a priori* logic suggest that this requires bilateral and multilateral cooperation and consultation at the highest levels of government. As a beginning, three subjects could provide bases for negotiation: (a) creation of a guest worker program, (b) apprehension and repatriation of smugglers or *coyotes*, and (c) promotion of economic development and job creation in traditional sending areas (perhaps through tax incentives for investments or other opportunities that might be made available through NAFTA or FTAA). In addition, the U.S. federal government should rigorously apply employer sanctions in the United States. There is nothing to be gained from pressuring Latin American governments to prevent their citizens from leaving the country, as U.S. politicians sometimes demand, since that would constitute flagrant infringement of a fundamental human right.

4. Reconcile Immigration Policy with Trade Policy. In spirit, the United States should undertake to make its immigration policy compatible with the spirit as well as the letter of NAFTA (and, eventually, FTAA). Operations Hold-the-Line, Gatekeeper, and Rio Grande do not meet this test. This does not mean that it is illegitimate or inappropriate for the United States to enforce its own laws; it means that immigration and trade policy are currently at cross-purposes. Washington should make serious efforts to resolve this inconsistency at distinct levels—political, institutional, and substantive. Otherwise there remains the danger that anti-immigrant sentiment and policy in the United States will undermine the promise and purpose of NAFTA.

5. Change Policy toward Cuba. With the passing of the cold war, there remains no reasonable basis for U.S. efforts to isolate Cuba and exclude it from the hemispheric community. Cuba is no longer a threat to anyone (except, some would say, the citizens of Cuba). Current U.S. policy antagonizes our friends in Europe and Latin

America, reduces opportunities for us to influence the course of political change within Cuba, reinforces nationalist suspicions among the Cuban populace, justifies hard-line reactions by the Castro regime—and robs the U.S. business community of investment opportunities. There are daunting political obstacles within the United States, but President Clinton could articulate clear views on the matter and publicly express the hope that relations would be normalized in time to bring Cuba into the FTAA negotiating process well before the year 2005.

6. *Revamp Drug Control Policies.* Legalization is not the only alternative to current policy on drugs. As many experts have argued, the U.S. government should restructure its priorities so as to give primary emphasis to the reduction of demand, rather than curtailment of supply. Extensive research has yielded two major findings: (a) interdiction of shipments and eradication of crops have negligible impacts on the availability of illicit drugs in the U.S. market, and (b) preventive and therapeutic efforts can effectively reduce the level of demand. With regard to Latin America, the primary emphasis should be on maintaining governability, rather than waging war on producers and/or smugglers. Recognizing that U.S. market demand is the driving force behind supply, Washington should seek genuine cooperation from Latin American authorities. One positive step in this direction would be to rescind the legislative provision for certification.

7. *Develop a Coherent Environmental Strategy.* Instead of taking up environmental issues one at a time—as in the focus on carbons emissions—the administration should forge an integrated strategy linking U.S. concerns to national interests in Latin America (and other parts of the developing world). In fact countries throughout the hemisphere face serious environmental problems—air pollution in major metropolises, water contamination in cities and towns, desertification in many parts of the countryside, threats to biodiversity and other natural resources. Leaders want to meet these challenges. In effect, the United States should offer *quid pro quo* bargains—resources to help meet pressing and practical problems within the region in exchange for support on U.S. policies

designed to address worldwide problems (such as global warming). Package deals of this nature could be good for Latin America, good for the United States, and good for the world as a whole. Without such bargains, though, Latin America is likely to resist pressure and blandishments from Washington.

Some of these recommendations would be difficult to implement. None of them can guarantee success. But taken together, they would significantly enhance the prospects for an inter-American relationship that would be harmonious over the long term and serve the genuine interests of both Latin America and the United States.

Notes

[1]On this see Smith (1996), chapters 5–8. To be sure, there were variations in tactics and measures from the late 1940s to the late 1980s, but the guiding principles for U.S. policy remained consistent throughout the entire cold war.

[2]It is often argued that economic integration should eventually diminish wage differentials between partner countries and thus reduce the incentive for labor migration. That may be true in principle but it is not apparent in practice, since economic integration also creates noneconomic incentives for continued migration. Also, any significant reduction in wage gaps between the United States and Latin America (especially Mexico and the circum-Caribbean) will take decades if not generations.

[3]It is my impression that, even without the abortion issue, fast-track would have failed to gain congressional support. See David E. Sanger, "Image vs. Analysis: Clinton's Pitch for Trade Authority Rang False among Economy's Losers," *New York Times,* November 16, 1997.

[4]Calvin Sims, "Latin America Fears Stagnation in Trade Talks with U.S.," *New York Times,* April 19, 1998.

[5]Largely in countries (such as Mexico and Peru) where U.S. antidrug strategies have tolerated and sometimes even encouraged human rights abuses.

[6]As of this writing it is impossible to evaluate the proposal to create a "multilateral" mechanism to evaluate antidrug efforts, as agreed at the Santiago Summit of the Americas in April 1998. Whatever happens, it is difficult for me to imagine that the U.S. Congress will relinquish its sovereign right to pass judgment on the performance of other nations throughout the world.

[7]Toro (1995), p. 2.

[8]"More than any other nation," William O. Walker III (1992) has said, "Mexico has been the object of coercive diplomacy by the United States." For analysis of a recent crisis in U.S.-Mexican relations see Tim Golden, "U.S. Drug Sting Riles Mexico, Imperiling Future Cooperation," *New York Times,* June 11, 1998.

[9]INS data supplied by Charles W. Haynes and Gordon Hanson, both of the University of Texas at Austin. It must be said, of course, that the number of arrests provides a less-than-perfect guide to the number of illegal entries. Apprehension statistics refer to the frequency of *events* (arrests) rather than number of

people; they make no allowance for multiple detentions; they make no adjustment for voluntary returns to Mexico; and they respond to the intensity and magnitude of enforcement by the U.S. Border Patrol (the correlation between agent-hours and apprehensions over the 68-month span from January 1990 through August 1995 is +.299).

[10]As trade and investment have expanded, by contrast, the U.S. private sector has come to devote a good deal of its attention (and assets) to Latin America. This stands in sharp relief against governmental lassitude.

[11]For an opposing view see Gordon (1998), pp. 13–16. Gordon's concern that FTAA would "undermine" the global trade regime and provoke defensive reactions in Asia overlooks the possibility that FTAA could help achieve an inclusive international system by (a) incorporating all countries of the hemisphere, and (b) provoking other nations and blocs to liberalize their policies; he also neglects the political aspects of FTAA and integration schemes in general.

8

The Foreign Policy
Challenge for the United States

ALBERT FISHLOW

Introduction

Latin America has made great strides over the last decade and a half. This is not to deny, at the same time, that the years since 1982 have been difficult ones. Indeed it is exactly that basic contrast that virtually defines the present situation. Previous chapters have made clear that the region is close to a turning point. Within the economy as well as in politics, but to a lesser degree in social terms, significant reforms have occurred. The region is poised either to move forward in a different and substantial way, or to fall back to misguided efforts to reconstruct the past.

Much of that outcome depends upon internal initiatives and actions. Moreover, the United States, as a government, now plays a much reduced role in policies affecting the region. But an extended layer of nongovernmental interaction is of central importance to the outcome. Whether one is speaking of the economic, political, or social realms, there is therefore scope for the evolution of a new and different relationship between countries of the hemisphere and the United States.

In the next sections, I wish to develop this basic conclusion. I start in the first instance by emphasizing the immense, but yet inadequate, changes that have occurred in Latin America over this recent period. Then I wish to pose the ways in which the United States can play a decisive, but self-interested, part in the outcome. I conclude by focusing upon the two kinds of hemisphere one may have in the year 2020.

Great Change, Continuing Needs

Over the last decade, virtually all of the region has made a great change in the economic model it now follows. To be brief and blunt, capitalism has triumphed. Countries have altered their prior commitment to, and belief in, a state managed development strategy.

At the macroeconomic level, there has been a new commitment to price stability, made possible only by dependence upon much reduced governmental deficits. Monetary policy in recent years has played a regulatory role rather than the inflationary one it has made possible for almost the entire post–World War II period. Real interest rates are at record levels; but so too is the continuing price stability that has been recently achieved by Argentina, Chile, Brazil, Peru, Bolivia, etc. Venezuela has been the last to yield, but it has recently done so as well. Colombia remains with its continuing adjustment to inflation, but at rates below 20 percent.

In addition, at the microeconomic level, one has seen a remarkable commitment to privatization throughout the area. That process has obviously been important in providing resources in the short term to finance governmental expenditures, but its significance goes beyond. What really counts is the continuing productivity change that new managerial guidance can provide. Not only domestic but foreign enterprises as well have entered throughout the vast range of areas that had been nationalized: telecommunications; electricity generation and distribution; production of mineral products, including petroleum, transportation, and the metals sector. Where one earlier had some 2000 nationalized enterprises in Mexico, now there persists only petroleum, petrochemicals, and power. And over future years even that participation may become smaller. Brazil is currently undergoing a process of sale of some

$60 billion in nationalized activity. Argentina has completed the process.

Equally, in dealing with the outside world, a new policy has taken root. High levels of protection, through tariffs, quotas, and other means, have yielded to much lower barriers. Average tariff levels have moved from the three-digit level to less than 20 percent. Imports, primarily from the United States, have grown by leaps and bounds over the last few years. Countries have vigorously stimulated their exports as well, rising in the 1990s to record levels of regular growth at more than 10 percent a year. Exchange rate policy has become much more prudent, even while reliance upon foreign investment for levels of advanced technology has expanded.

These profound economic changes have taken time for their beneficial consequences to be felt. Much more than modest amendment has occurred. And yet, on the other side, one has simultaneously witnessed an increase in the level of income distribution inequality. Latin America already has started from the greatest inequality in the world in the modern period; instead of regular improvement, the new capitalist model has brought increased unemployment and deterioration in the shares of income received by the poor. In addition, only where there have been regular large gains in income over the last decade, as in Chile, has there been significant reduction in poverty. In other cases, the number of poor has actually increased.

This contrast is profound. If, on the one side, Latin American countries have made a commitment to profound change, they are still plagued by the continuation, and even worsening, of past inequality. Moreover, it will not get better easily. One reason is that the countries of the region suffer—like the United States—from a deficiency of domestic saving. And there is an understandable tendency for the private sector to be resistant to large-scale changes making for greater social equality. This situation, which only Chile has seemingly overcome, and very little due to the altered scheme of social security in which the country innovated, confronts all of the others at the moment.

In the political sphere a related contradiction can be found. All of the countries in the region, Cuba excepted, now are following overtly democratic policies. This is in marked contrast to the case fifteen years ago, when many were still coming to the end of their extended rule by the local military, or in others, where single political parties still dominated both the executive as well as the legislature.

To be sure, the degree of effective rule is far from uniform. In Colombia, much of the country is ruled by insurgent forces related to the drug trade. In Venezuela, the leading candidate for the presidency, at this point at least, is from the military. In Ecuador, strong regionalism prevailed in the recent presidential election. Democracy in the region, while it has made an impressive recovery, is still not in an entirely dominant position.

More fundamentally, one has seen constitutions repeatedly amended to allow for presidents to run for re-election. No candidate who has tried has been rebuffed. The cases of Argentina, Peru, and Brazil come readily to mind. What remains to be seen is how frequently these deviations are allowed. Menem and Fujimori are apt to test the rules again. Legislatures remain weak as compared to the executive. In many countries, there are political parties in such number to make virtually impossible organized reforms. Judicial capability remains significantly underdeveloped, a source of corruption and denial of equality before the law.

The reality is a political system that has not yet coalesced. There are frequently unstable coalitions, exempt from commitment to substantive issues. One has seen the difficulty of securing legislative majorities capable of continuing action. It required an international crisis before Brazil was even able to bring some of its constitutional amendments essential to economic stability to a vote. And even then, some of the amendments to the Social Security legislation were postponed until after the election in the fall of 1998.

To go along with this contrast between the economic and political realm, there is also the reality of limited social progress. Renewal of democracy has led to recognition of inherent differences in access to privilege. Equality of opportunity is proudly pronounced in the new constitutions achieved by many of the countries, but reality is far from that ideal. The difference is nowhere better seen than the area of education. Latin America finds itself trailing far behind Asia in its increased percentage of the young enrolled in school. It is still far from full education up to the sixth grade level: in many of the countries attendance is high, but that owes itself to the high degree of repetition of school years. There is still insufficient attention to universal access to secondary training. And when public universities apply high standards of qualification for attendance, it is students who have been to private secondary education who are most highly represented. The share of total expenditure at the university level, moreover, is extraordinarily high, amounting to close to a majority of resources in some cases.

What is true of this area is replicated in other areas of social responsibility: health outlays, pension payments, housing assistance, etc. A system has evolved that corresponds to the reality of its highly unequal income distribution. The present rural poor are unlikely to move ahead. They are older and handicapped in terms of access to the benefits of education and training. But the sheer fact of substantial migration has created virtually everywhere a new urban group that can claim access to these social inputs so vital to private economic success.

In all of these areas, then, there is a vigorous contest between the promises of a bright new future and the reality of the continuity of past limitations. Latin America has much changed in recognizing the need for smaller government, but has not yet advanced very far in having those new structures responsive to the needs for the future. More difficult still is the inherent contradiction between simultaneous needs: higher savings, but less inequality; greater gains in productivity, but still opportunities for expanded employment; fiscal discipline, but greater funds for mass education and health; etc.

Latin America, despite the great advances of the recent past, thus faces the need for what has been called a second order of reforms. This new set of requirements is inherently more difficult, not only because of the contradictions just emphasized, but because of their scope. Improving the electoral processes, providing expansion in the educational system, dealing with profound income and regional inequalities—all the while seeking to implant capitalism in a durable fashion—is hardly a straightforward process. And, above all, it is fundamentally a domestic responsibility.

The Role of the United States

In this process, the United States can do relatively little. We are far from the most important source of external resources, as we were in the 1960s when the Alliance for Progress was conceived. Public moneys now disposable are trivial relative to the flow of private capital to the region. The net funds available from the World Bank and Inter-American Development Bank, while larger, are still quite modest for almost all countries in the region.

The Santiago Summit gave proof of that limitation. Four large groups of activities made up the Plan of Action adopted. Three consisted of education; preserving and strengthening democracy, justice, and human rights; and eradication of poverty and discrimination. But inherent in these requirements is a dominant domestic commitment. The United States can provide only limited assistance. That becomes clearer when one gets to the implementation of the goals. In the education area, the responsibility is left to the OAS, the IDB, the World Bank, and the Economic Commission for Latin America and the Caribbean. In the broad range of issues involved in the second category, there is more scope for overtly cooperative national action, especially when one key question is prevention and control of the drug traffic. But in eradication of poverty, emphasis switches again to a virtually exclusive domestic focus.

The fourth subject is regional economic integration. Here is the only place that a substantial commitment was required from the United States as well as the other countries of the region, including Canada. But it is also where the United States has fallen considerably short. Fast-track authorization, giving Congress a single vote on trade legislation rather than the opportunity for unlimited amendment, expired at the end of 1993, making possible a vote on NAFTA as well as the Uruguay Round, but allowing no new efforts subsequently. Despite various promises by the Clinton administration to put fast-track on the congressional agenda, it has been impossible to pass the needed legislation. This became clear late in 1997 when it was impossible to bring the subject to a final House vote. Republicans and Democrats disagree fundamentally on whether to include labor and environmental provisions. With the election of a president in 2000, it is difficult to envision early resumption of such negotiating authority. Without it, the Santiago Summit's strong words of support for freer interregional trade are a faint basis of United States hemispheric leadership.

Instead, one has seen progressively greater initiative among the South American countries, led by Brazil. Mercosur has already expanded to include Chile and Bolivia as associate members. Now negotiations are underway with the Andean Pact, due to end before 2000. Equally, in 1999 serious discussions began between the European Union and Mercosur. The stumbling block in that case is the special access of Latin American agricultural exports to Europe. Spain is playing the lead role in this process, and has become a major investor not only in the newly privatized sectors, but within the financial area as well.

Inevitably, the evolution of a Free Trade Area of the Americas becomes the critical test of U.S. policy toward the region. Policy toward Cuba will certainly change for the better once Fidel Castro passes from the scene. So too, as drug policy gives more scope to demand, as well as supply from the region, will that issue diminish as an important source of difference. Greater cooperation with regard to the environment is more likely within the region in the future as the issue is increasingly framed multilaterally.

Visions of the Future

One vision of the future is that this current impasse is but a temporarily embarrassing lapse. The United States population itself is becoming progressively more Latino, especially in the growing Southwest. California, the largest state, is to have Latinos with the largest representation in the population. This influence, cast in the direction of ever greater cooperation with Latin America, is apt to make a significant difference. Already, trade with Mexico has mounted to our third largest, after Canada and Japan. So too, trade growth with the rest of the hemisphere has been more rapid than with other regions. Inevitably, then, we will turn our concerns even farther south and complete the process begun in Miami in 1994. Foreign investment and business concerns will continuously turn southward, as it has already done in considerable volume in recent years.

There is another, and different, view. This sees a new Latin America as well as a new United States. The division occurs at the Panama Canal. NAFTA provides an integrating force that brings Mexico closer to this country, not only in trade and finance, but equally through continuing population flow. Cuba, so long absent from the discussion, will reappear, post-Castro, as an accepted leader of the Caribbean countries. It will command a large share of investment flows from the United States. The Central American countries will be included within the new grouping. Its focus, as in the past, will be the United States, both as a source for imports as well as a market for exports.

Meanwhile, South America will be much more integrated among its component states as well as more oriented to a varied world market. Trade, as well as investment flows, will be diversified among the United States, the EU, and Asia. There will be a larger set of investment flows across South American countries, as one sees now with the increasing Chilean participation. And an internal, broader market will capture exports of manufactures even while the international market will continue to favor resource oriented exports.

This vision sees the twenty-first century start more like the beginning of the twentieth than its end. Up until the Second World War, the position of the United States was sharply different than it later became. South America, save for the exports of coffee and oil, was much more oriented to Europe. British foreign investment had predominated, followed later by German commitment, rather than flows from the United States. South America was a competitor with the United States rather than a special supplier of raw materials. Recall that Argentina never entered the war, and Chile did so quite late.

Inherently, because the role of the United States as a world leader is much greater now than it had historically been, the degree of engagement with South America will be greater than it was. But the nature of the association will be distinct. To a considerable degree, the location of the "intermestic" problems will be concentrated in Mexico, the Caribbean, and Central America. That is already predominately the case with emigration flows; it is progressively occurring with the source of the drug traffic. Even the environmental issue, save for the Amazon, is substantially concentrated along the Mexican border.

Such a world will still see English as the prevalent second language, will still reflect the obvious domination of United States culture throughout the region, and will still correspond to the democratic ideals of this country. But there will be a greater influence economically of the world as a whole rather than the United States alone. That still means continuing macroeconomic stability, but allows for more national variability.

This alternative vision differs from the conventional view of hemispheric integration now so much current. But at root, it still is ultimately dependent upon Latin American ability to resolve the contradictions emphasized earlier. A slowly growing, volatile, highly unequal, and poorly governed Latin America will hardly make the grade in the next century, however it organizes its international relations. The domestic capacity to resolve these problems is what in the end will count, independently of the precise form of integration.

The United States can make a significant future contribution, not so much by direct governmental resources as it once tried to do in the 1960s, but through the continuing engagement of its private sector. Not only are the flows of resources important, but also the engagement of nongovernmental organizations. The beginning of a new millennium may be a start for new associations in our own hemisphere.

Declaration of Santiago

We, the democratically-elected Heads of State and Government of the countries of the Americas, have met in Santiago, Chile, in order to continue the dialogue and strengthen the cooperation we began in Miami in December 1994. Since that time, significant progress has been made in the formulation and execution of joint plans and programs in order to take advantage of the great opportunities before us. We reaffirm our will to continue this most important undertaking, which requires sustained national efforts and dynamic international cooperation.

The strengthening of democracy, political dialogue, economic stability, progress towards social justice, the extent to which our trade liberalization policies coincide, and the will to expedite a process of ongoing Hemispheric integration have made our relations more mature. We will redouble our efforts to continue reforms designed to improve the living conditions of the peoples of the Americas and to achieve a mutually supportive community. For this reason, we have decided that education is a key theme and is of particular importance in our deliberations. We approve that attached Plan of Action and undertake to carry out its initiatives.

Since our meeting in Miami, we have seen real economic benefits
in the Americas resulting from more open trade, transparency in
economic regulations, sound market-based economic policies, as
well as efforts by the private sector to increase its competitiveness.
Even as countries in our region have been tested by financial and
other economic pressures, and as countries in other regions have
experienced serious economic setbacks, the overall course in the
Americas has been one of faster economic growth, lower inflation,
expanded opportunities, and confidence in facing the global mar-
ketplace. A major reason for this positive record has been our
countries' steadfast and cooperative efforts to promote prosperity
through increased economic integration and more open
economies. New partnerships have been formed and existing ones
strengthened and expanded. A positive role is being played by subregional and bilateral integration and free trade agreements. We
are confident that the Free Trade Area of the Americas (FTAA)
will improve the well being of all our people, including economically disadvantaged populations within our respective countries.

Hemispheric integration is a necessary complement to national
policies aimed at overcoming lingering problems and obtaining a
higher level of development. In its broadest sense, a process of
integration based on respect for cultural identities will make it possible to shape a common, interwoven set of values and interests
that helps us in these objectives.

Globalization offers great opportunities for progress to our countries and opens up new areas of cooperation for the hemispheric
community. However, it can also heighten the differences among
countries and within our societies. With steadfast determination to
reap its benefits and to face its challenges, we will give special
attention to the most vulnerable countries and social groups in the
Hemisphere.

Education is the determining factor for the political, social, cultural, and economical development of our peoples. We undertake
to facilitate access of all inhabitants of the Americas to preschool,
primary, secondary, and higher education, and we will make learn-

ing a lifelong process. We will put science and technology at the service of education to assure growing levels of knowledge and so that educators may develop their skills to the highest level. The Plan of Action that accompanies this Declaration defines the objectives and goals we intend to achieve and the actions that will make them a reality. In order to meet our goals within the agreed timeframes, we reaffirm our commitment to invest greater resources in this important area and to encourage civil society to participate in developing education.

The decisions adopted by our Ministers of Education at the Conference held in Mérida, Mexico, last February, reflect our desire to promote specific joint initiatives designed to improve access to education, with fairness, quality, relevancy, and effectiveness. In order to consolidate and lend continuity to our decisions, we have instructed that another Conference be held in Brasilia, Brazil, in July of this year.

Today, we direct our Ministers Responsible for Trade to begin negotiations for FTAA, in accordance with the March 1998 Ministerial Declaration of San José. We reaffirm our determination to conclude the negotiation of the FTAA no later than 2005, and to make concrete progress by the end of the century. The FTAA agreement will be balanced, comprehensive, WTO-consistent and constitute a single undertaking.

We note with satisfaction the preparatory work by the Ministers Responsible for Trade over the past three years which has strengthened our trade policies, fostered understanding of our economic objectives and facilitated dialogue among all participating countries. We appreciate the significant contribution of the Inter American Development Bank (IDB), the Organization of American States (OAS), and the United Nations Economic Commission for Latin America and the Caribbean (ECLAC), acting as the Tripartite Committee.

The FTAA negotiating process will be transparent, and take into account the differences in the levels of development and size of the economies in the Americas, in order to create opportunities for the full participation by all countries. We encourage all segments of civil society to participate in and contribute to the process in a constructive manner, through our respective mechanism created in the FTAA negotiating process. We believe that economic integration, investment, and free trade are key factors for raising the standards of living, improving the working conditions of the people of the Americas and better protecting with the economic integration process in the Americas.

The region has made significant advances in both monetary and fiscal policy as well as in price stability and liberalizing our economies. The volatility of capital markets vindicates our decision to strengthen banking supervision in the Hemisphere and to establish regulations relating to disclosure and reporting of banking information.

The strength and meaning of representative democracy lie in the active participation of individuals at all levels of life. The democratic culture must encompass our entire population. We will strengthen the capabilities of regional and local governments, when appropriate, and to foster more active participation by civil society.

Respect for and promotion of human rights and the fundamental freedoms of all individuals is a primary concern of our governments. In commemorating the fiftieth anniversary of the American Declaration of the Rights and Duties of Man and the Universal Declaration of Human Rights, we agreed on the need to promote the ratification and implementation of the international agreements aimed at preserving them and to continue strengthening the pertinent national and international institutions. We agreed that a free press plays a fundamental role in this area and we affirm the importance of guaranteeing freedom of expression, information, and opinion. We commend the recent appointment of a Special Rapporteur for Freedom of Expression, within the framework of the Organization of American States.

Confident that an independent, efficient, and effective administration of justice plays a role in the process of consolidating democracy, strengthens its institutions, guarantees the equality of all its citizens, and contributes to economic development, we will enhance our policies relating to justice and encourage the reforms necessary to promote legal and judicial cooperation. To that end, we will strengthen national entities involved in the study of the administration of justice and expedite the establishment of a hemispheric center for studies on this subject.

We will combat all forms of discrimination in the Hemisphere. Equal rights and opportunities between men and women and the objectives of ensuring active participation of women in all areas of national endeavor are priority tasks. We will continue to promote the full integration of indigenous populations and other vulnerable groups into political and economic life, with due respect for the characteristics and expressions that affirm their cultural identity. We will make a special effort to guarantee the human rights of all migrants, including migrant workers and their families.

Overcoming poverty continues to be the greatest challenge confronted by our Hemisphere. We are conscious that the positive growth shown in the Americas in past years has yet to resolve the problems of inequity and social exclusion. We are determined to remove the barriers that deny the poor access to proper nutrition, social services, a healthy environment, credit, and legal title to their property. We will provide greater support to micro and small enterprises, promote core labor standards recognized by the International Labor Organization (ILO), and use new technologies to improve the health conditions of every family in the Americas, with the technical support of the Pan-American Health Organization (PAHO), achieving greater levels of equity and sustainable development.

With deep satisfaction, we note that peace, an essential value for human coexistence, is a reality in the Hemisphere. We underscore that Central America has become a zone of peace, democracy, and development and we recognize efforts to eliminate antipersonnel mines and to rehabilitate their victims. We will continue to foster confidence and security among our countries through such measures as those mentioned in the Santiago and San Salvador Declarations on Confidence-and Security-Building Measures. We encourage the pacific settlement of disputes.

We will lend new impetus to the struggle against corruption, money laundering, terrorism, weapon trafficking, and the drug problem, including illicit use, and work together to ensure that criminals do not find safe haven anywhere in the Hemisphere. We are determined to persevere in this direction.

In forging an alliance against drugs and applying the Hemispheric Anti-Drug Strategy, we welcome the start of formal negotiations at the May 4 meeting of Inter-American Drug Abuse Control Commission (CICAD) to be held in Washington within the framework of the Organization of American States (OAS), to establish an objective procedure for the multilateral evaluation of actions and cooperation to prevent and combat all aspects of the drug problem and related crimes, based on the principles of sovereignty, territorial integrity of States, shared responsibility, and with a comprehensive and balanced approach.

We will strengthen national, hemispheric, and international efforts aimed at environmental protection as a basis for sustainable development that provides human beings a healthy and productive life in harmony with nature. The Commitments undertaken at the Miami Summit and the Summit on Sustainable Development held in Santa Cruz de la Sierra, Bolivia, provide a solid basis for strengthening our actions. As parties to the United Nations Framework Convention on Climate Change, we underscore the importance of working together to further fulfillment of the agreement reached at the Conference in Kyoto, Japan, and to promote its ratification in our countries. Moreover, we will work closely to make preparations for a Conference of the Parties to be held in November of this year in Buenos Aires, Argentina.

We acknowledge that the development of energy links between our countries and the intensification of trade in the energy sector strengthen and foster the integration of the Americas. Energy integration, based on competitive and transparent activities, and in compliance with national conditions and objectives, contributes to the sustainable development of our nations and to the improvement of the quality of life of our people with minimum impact on the environment.

Recognizing the importance of, and positive role played by hemispheric institutions, particularly the Organization of American States (OAS), we instruct our Ministers to examine the strengthening and modernizing of these institutions.

We reaffirm our will to continue strengthening intra-hemispheric dialogue and cooperation within the framework of friendship and solidarity that inspires our nations.

Bibliography

Andreas, P. 1998. "The US Immigration Control Offensive: Constructing an Image of Order on the Southwest Border." In M. Suarez-Orozco (ed.). *Crossings: Mexican Immigration in Interdisciplinary Perspective*. Cambridge: Harvard University Press.

Barro, R. and J. Lee (February 1993). "International Comparisons of Educational Attainment." Paper presented at conference on "How Do National Policies Affect Long-Run Growth?" World Bank, Washington, D.C.

Birdsall, N., B. Bruns, and R. Sabot. 1996. "Education in Brazil: Playing a Bad Hand Badly." In N. Birdsall and R. Sabot (eds.). *Opportunity Foregone: Education in Brazil*. Washington, D.C.: Inter-American Development Bank.

Birdsall, N. and J. Londoño. May 1997. "Asset Inequality Matters: An Assessment of the World Bank's Approach to Poverty Reduction." *American Economic Review Papers and Proceedings*, 87(2).

Birdsall, N. and J. Londoño. 1998. "No Tradeoff: Efficient Growth via More Equal Human Capital Accumulation in Latin America." In N. Birdsall, C. Graham, and R. Sabot (eds.). *Beyond Tradeoffs: Market Reforms and Equitable Growth in Latin America*. Washington, D.C.: The Brookings Institution and Inter-American Development Bank.

Brenner, Y., H. Kaelble, and M. Thomas. 1991. *Income Distribution in Historical Perspective*. New York: Cambridge University Press.

ECLAC (Economic Commission for Latin America and the Caribbean). 1996. *Barriers to U.S.-Latin America Trade*. Washington, D.C.: ECLAC.

Falco, M. 1995. "Passing Grades: Branding Nations Won't Lessen the US Drug Problem." *Foreign Affairs*.

Gordon, B. May/June 1998. "The Natural Market Fallacy: Slim Pickings in Latin America." *Foreign Affairs*.

IDB (Inter-American Development Bank). 1997. *Economic and Social Progress in Latin America*. Washington, D.C.: IDB.

Lora, E. and F. Barrera, 1997. "A Decade of Structural Reforms in Latin America: Growth, Productivity and Investments Are Not What They Used to Be." In R. Hausman and E. Lora (eds.). *Latin America after a Decade of Reforms: What Comes Next?* Washington, D.C.: IDB.

Lowenthal, A. October 1996. "Ending the Hegemonic Presumption." *Foreign Affairs*.

————. 1990. *Partners in Conflict: The United States and Latin America in the 1990s*. Baltimore: Johns Hopkins University Press.

Lustig, N. and R. Deutsch. 1998. *The Inter-American Development Bank and Poverty Reduction: An Overview*. Revised Version. Washington, D.C.: IDB.

Nadelmann, E. January/February 1998. "Commonsense Drug Policy." *Foreign Affairs*.

Rielly, J. Spring 1995. "The Public Mood at Mid-Decade." *Foreign Affairs*.

Smith, P. 1996. *Talons of the Eagle: Dynamics of U.S.-Latin American Relations*. New York: Oxford University Press.

Toro, M. 1995. *Mexico's "War" on Drugs: Causes and Consequences*. Boulder: Lynne Rienner.

UNESCO (United Nations Educational, Scientific, and Cultural Organization). Various years. *Statistical Yearbook*. New York: Bernan Press and UNESCO Publishing.

Walker, W. 1992. "International Collaboration in Historical Perspective." In P. Smith (ed.). *Drug Policy in the Americas*. Boulder: Westview.

World Bank. 1998. *World Development Indicators*. Washington, D.C.: World Bank.

Final Report
of the
Ninety-Fourth American Assembly

At the close of their discussions, the participants in the Ninety-fourth American Assembly, on "U.S. National Interests and the Western Hemisphere," at Arden House, Harriman, New York, May 28–31, 1998, reviewed as a group the following statement. This statement represents general agreement; however, no one was asked to sign it. Furthermore, it should be understood that not everyone agreed with all of it.

Introduction

In the midst of exploding nuclear weapons in South Asia, European Monetary Union, and economic crisis in Asia, it is easy to miss a fundamental reality: no region of the world has a more direct impact on the everyday lives of U.S. citizens than does the rest of the Western Hemisphere itself.

It is the source of some of the greatest economic opportunities for the United States. Canada and Mexico, our two contiguous neighbors in NAFTA, are respectively our first and second largest trade partners. As we cross into a new century, our exports to Latin America are projected by the year 2010 to surpass those to the European Union and Japan combined. Already, we sell more to

Brazil than to China, more to Chile than to India. Venezuela is our number one energy supplier, with Canada and Mexico close behind. More than 50 percent of U.S. oil imports come from the Hemisphere.

The Hemisphere is a source of most of our recent legal immigrants. It also is a source of rancorous debates—illegal immigration and drugs. One of our most dynamic demographic developments, the rapidly expanding Hispanic population, also originates in the Hemisphere. All of these are domestic issues even more than they are international ones, and they all grow out of the proximity of our neighbors in the Hemisphere.

Seldom in history have two neighbors—Canada and the United States—enjoyed such a long period of peace and mutually beneficial trade and prosperity. But the greater challenge, if only because of its size, lies to the south, in Latin America, a region that many U.S. citizens have yet to realize is profoundly different from what it was even fifteen years ago. For that reason, The American Assembly brought together some of this nation's leading experts on the Hemisphere and on foreign policy to prepare a twenty-five-year vision for the Hemisphere, based on U.S. national interests, and to prescribe an action plan to achieve it.

This report is particularly timely. It comes a month after the Second Summit of the Americas, held in April in Santiago, Chile, in which the United States and Hemisphere governments reached a variety of unprecedented agreements pointing to a new era of cooperation and economic integration, beginning with a commitment to negotiate a Free Trade Area of the Americas (FTAA) from Alaska to Tierra del Fuego by the year 2005. But this report goes beyond that agreement. Its findings are based in part on the fact that democracy has spread and deepened as the region's citizens have committed themselves to representative government in an unprecedented fashion. Today, with the notable exception of Cuba, virtually all the countries in the Western Hemisphere rely on regular, free elections and functioning legislatures.

At the same time, market based economic principles dominate. Inflation rates have fallen to virtually record lows since the Second World War, driven by effective monetary policy and national commitment to reducing governmental expenditure and increasing revenue. International trade has expanded more rapidly in the last decade than before. The United States and Canada have benefited not only by the opening of new markets, but also by new opportunities for foreign investment. Many Latin American governments have divested themselves of ownership of railroads, airlines, public utilities, steel companies, and much of the rest of the public participation in economic life. In its place have come private control, new investment, and increasing productivity.

These changes have occurred after decades of military rule and dictatorship. They have come about after import substitution and broad public sector participation in the economy have lost widespread support. They have happened after more than a decade of deep depression and worsening income distribution that lowered the incomes of the poor and the middle class.

These new realities compel a new examination of our relationship with the Hemisphere. Despite the attention generated by an unprecedented three U.S. presidential visits to the region within the last year and the April Summit meeting, few U.S. citizens are aware of the possibilities of our relationships in our very own Hemisphere.

This report is therefore written not only for policy makers, but also for other concerned and influential citizens.

A 25-Year Vision in the U.S. National Interest

Interests

For the first time, the United States and its neighbors perceive our respective interests in the Hemisphere as largely coinciding. Economic reforms that expand markets and promote greater economic opportunity and equity tend to bring prosperity to both the United States and its neighbors throughout the Hemisphere. Transparency, accountability, and the rule of law tend to promote strong governments and stable societies. Greater economic integration, effectively implemented, benefits the interests of the United States and the rest of the Hemisphere. To achieve those goals, our hemispheric foreign policy should be grounded in free-dom—free markets, open democracies, and the unleashing of individual human potential.

The promotion of stable, prosperous, democratic governments is of utmost importance to the United States, because democracies tend to have more peaceful and cooperative relations with each other. With this cooperation, we can achieve not only our objectives of trade and investment, but also progress on other important issues that, left unattended, may erode democracy. A particularly effective tool to promote democracy is expanded trade and investment. That means completion of an FTAA by 2005. This is also important because free markets and open democratic systems are mutually reinforcing.

More than ever before, the United States must recognize that key national interest issues such as immigration, narcotics, the environment, and public health know no borders. These challenges are neither classic foreign policy concerns, nor solely domestic concerns. As a result, they require a fundamentally different policy attitude in the United States, which is to reject the unilateralism of the past, and substitute partnership for the future.

Working together with our neighbors, we should strive to

- Reduce drug consumption, production, and trafficking on a multilateral basis.
- Establish norms and incentives to ensure a healthy environment.
- Maintain reliable and sustainable sources of energy.
- Reduce illegal immigration by encouraging investment in education, health, and infrastructure development.

Vision

Our vision for twenty-five years from now, based on these interests, is a Hemisphere at peace within and among its borders, promoting policies of economic and human development, and taking the lead to advance these principles in a global context.

We envision a Hemisphere of strengthened multilateral cooperation in addition to bilateral relationships. The two are not in conflict. Strong bilateral relationships can serve to enhance effective multilateral approaches. We envision a Hemisphere of conventional arms restraint and nuclear nonproliferation where we work together as partners to help promote peaceful resolution of conflicts around the world and in the region.

We envision substantially strengthened democratic institutions and civil societies throughout the region. We envision a region of enhanced mutual understanding through increased cross-border and cross-cultural programs, and foreign-language capacity in the United States and elsewhere. We envision a region with reduced poverty, open markets, greater price and currency stability, and stronger job opportunities.

The United States should acknowledge the special intensity of its relationship with Mexico and the Caribbean Basin. The basic factors of geography and history cannot be overlooked. Here in particular, migration flows, narcotics trafficking, and cross-border pollution are of special concern and will require greater attention and more cooperative approaches. On the other hand, greater prosperity and democracy will ameliorate these problems. By helping them achieve the benefits of free trade and democracy, we help ourselves.

Economic Issues

Trade

Free trade is a guiding principle of U.S. foreign policy in the world—for a vital reason: U.S. prosperity is increasingly dependent on our exports to foreign markets and on the import of competitively priced goods and services for us as consumers. In the Hemisphere, free trade takes on even added import. Latin America is our fastest growing regional market. Without vigorous U.S. leadership on free trade we can expect a continuing proliferation of bilateral and subregional agreements that may complicate the eventual conclusion of the FTAA. In addition, a potential agreement between the European Union and Mercosur (the southern cone trade group) would put the United States at a competitive disadvantage in the largest South American market vis-à-vis its principal European competitors.

To pursue U.S. interests in the Hemisphere, the following policies and actions are imperative:

- The administration must move aggressively forward to negotiate and implement the FTAA.
- To assure congressional and public support, vigorous presidential leadership is essential. Only with strong presidential direction can we hope to engage and convince the nation of the importance of free trade to U.S. national interests in the Hemisphere and in the world, while benefiting our citizens through higher-paying jobs and lower consumer prices. Business groups, which were instrumental in the approval of NAFTA, must step up again to help form a national coalition to increase public understanding of the benefits of trade. A free trade campaign must also recognize the need to address the problems of U.S. citizens affected by globalization, and to deal constructively with issues that have arisen in the trade debate, particularly labor and the environment.
- The new Congress meeting in 1999 must give the president the necessary tools to complete the negotiations. "Fast track" legislation, facilitating the FTAA, as well as other regional and multilateral negotiations, should be introduced as H.R. 1, underlining its priority. Under fast-track authority, which every president has had since the 1970s, Congress agrees to a set of negotiating objectives and the administration commits to consulting closely with Congress throughout the negotiations. In return, Congress agrees to vote up or down on the agreement without amendment. Without fast-track authority, Latin Americans will not negotiate the FTAA, for fear that any agreement would have to be renegotiated with Congress.
- Fair labor and environmental standards, both important objectives, should be pursued vigorously and in a parallel effort, as part of our larger hemispheric strategy.

Free Market Reforms

Free market economic policies are essential to long-term prosperity and democracy in Latin America. These policies in turn create growing stable markets for U.S. goods, contributing to the prosperity of all Americans. Latin American performance in weathering the ongoing Asian crisis demonstrates that the region has come a long way in instituting free market reforms.

Still, much more needs to be done. The region remains vulnerable to domestic and external shocks. The United States can and should play a substantial role in the reform process by encouraging our neighbors in the Hemisphere to continue the privatization of state owned enterprises and the pursuit of monetary stability and fiscal responsibility. To attract and retain needed flows of foreign capital for further economic growth, almost all the countries in the region must also act on their commitments to improve the transparency of their capital markets and the independence of the central banks, encourage the adoption of international accounting standards, and solidify their banking sectors by working toward adherence to international bank regulatory standards. Continued liberalization of financial sectors contributes to the more efficient allocation of capital and thereby to sustained economic growth in the region, and the adoption of private pension plans can help develop local capital markets and conserve fiscal resources for other important social priorities.

Political Issues

The April 1998 Santiago Summit Declaration reaffirmed a regional commitment to free, fair, and competitive electoral processes as the only acceptable means for political change. It also called for a "second generation" of reforms to strengthen democratic institutions in whose success the United States has a fundamental interest. The United States should cooperate in a sustained fashion with the decisions of the countries of the region to undertake these reforms, as they are essential to deepen and sustain democracy in the region.

Strengthened Rule of Law

For example, the United States should encourage the efforts of the Latin American governments, NGOs, and business communities to guarantee for all individuals the right to due process and to protection of property rights through fair, impartial, and independent judiciaries, the right to a speedy public trial, and legal equality for men and women. These reforms are crucial to guarantee respect for fundamental human rights. They also are vital for investor confidence, fair business competition, and equitable access to justice. The U.S. government should continue to support training, technical assistance, and external financing principally through multilateral financial institutions, and emphasizing partnerships with the civil society. A priority for support is the regional judicial studies academy proposed in the Santiago Summit Declaration as well as enhanced exchanges and consultation among judges, prosecutors, and public defenders.

Anticorruption

Corruption constitutes a threat to democracy and market reforms. The Inter-American Convention Against Corruption and the OECD antibribery agreement set standards and norms that hold signatory governments accountable. Business associations, NGOs, and other parts of civil society should expand their watchdog role over government action and press for compliance with those norms. The United States should ratify these agreements, encourage other governments to do the same, and provide support to governments in the region to help with implementation. For example, the United States should provide financial and technical support to help Latin American governments develop merit based civil service with competitive salaries and establish auditing and enforcement mechanisms.

Decentralization and Strengthened Local Government

The historic and positive transformation of hierarchical, centralized political structures now under way in the region also poses a major opportunity for the countries of the Hemisphere. In 1980 only three countries elected mayors; today, virtually all provide for elected mayors and local councils and have begun to devolve resources and authority to deliver services down to the community. This fundamental democratic reform requires creating a cadre of competent local public administrators. The United States, as part of the international community, and in response to requests from countries in the region, should provide additional support for training local officials. Developing strong local governments able to deliver services more efficiently and effectively and to respond to citizen demands is important to sustaining democracy in the Hemisphere.

Conflict Resolution

The United States should, when asked, continue to play a constructive role in the resolution of internal and international disputes in the Hemisphere, working to strengthen the tools available through the Organization of American States, other multilateral organizations, and the NGO community. In the still-unresolved border dispute between Peru and Ecuador, the United States, as a guarantor, should continue supporting peaceful resolution of the outstanding issues. In Colombia, the election of a new government in 1998 offers a hopeful window of opportunity to break the cycle of violence, which in 1997 alone cost over 30,000 lives. The United States should be prepared to respond positively to Colombian requests for international support for the achievement of a negotiated resolution to internal political conflicts.

Arms Control

The United States should support Latin American efforts to establish effective, transparent arms control regimes that can avoid the introduction of sophisticated, costly, and potentially destabilizing new armaments into the region.

Social Improvement

Education

Improving education in the region is a priority if the Latin American nations are to take full advantage of the market reforms of the past decade and meet the competitive challenge of globalization. Achieving the goal reaffirmed in Santiago of universal completion of primary school by 2010 would vastly improve equal opportunity within the Hemisphere. The Hemisphere countries stated a priority for improving the quality of primary and secondary education to avoid repetition and dropouts through strengthening teacher training, adopting national standards, using technologies such as distance learning and computer linkages to improve access to knowledge, and providing greater accountability for parents and communities. The U.S. international business community, along with U.S. universities, foundations, and NGOs, should support these efforts. The U.S. government should target its support for education programs on the priorities established by the Hemisphere countries in primary and secondary education and support the commitment of the international financial institutions to double lending for education over the next three years.

Economic Opportunity for the Poor

While liberalization reduced inflation and has benefited all Latin American citizens, too many have yet to experience substantive gains in income. Despite the benefits that the poor have experienced from reduced inflation in this region, an estimated 35 percent of the population lives in poverty. Latin America is also the area that has the world's most unequal income distribution. If these poor and dispossessed do not participate more fully in the newly emerging market economies and enjoy their fruits, a political backlash could lead to disenchantment with both the region's nascent democracy and the free market. The result could be a resurrection of populist economic policies and the return of strongmen by the ballot box or otherwise. These developments would be devastating for their citizens, but also adverse to U.S. economic and political interests.

The extension of free market opportunities appears to be the best and most sustainable route out of poverty. The Hemisphere's leaders committed themselves at Santiago to reduce income inequality through measures designed to increase investment in human capital over the next decade. In addition, barriers to the access of the poor to participate in the economic life and benefits of free market reforms must be removed not only by commitment to universal primary and secondary education, but also by supporting

- Basic health services.
- Infrastructure improvements, including potable water and sanitation for individuals and accessible roads and other transportation to provide access to markets.
- The extension of credit to micro-enterprises and small farms and businesses.
- The regularizing of land titles as a means to establish capital and equity.
- Equal access to the judicial system.

Issues Linking U.S. Domestic and Foreign Policy

In the context of our evolving post–cold war foreign policy, a number of domestic concerns have assumed particular prominence. These concerns directly affect community well-being within the United States as well as relations with foreign governments, businesses, and private organizations. Lasting solutions cannot be found solely within the borders of any one country; these issues require regional and multilateral approaches.

Drugs

Drug trafficking poses a major threat to U.S. and hemispheric interests. It undermines U.S. values and threatens the viability of the new democratic institutions of the Hemisphere.

U.S. international drug policy has traditionally emphasized unilateral law enforcement and interdiction in its efforts to reduce its own domestic drug problems. This approach has not succeeded in curtailing foreign drug supplies and has often damaged hemispheric relations. In recent years, governments of Latin America have also come to recognize that drug consumption and trafficking harm their societies and public institutions. This is a critical moment for the United States to develop active, collaborative partnerships in the Hemisphere to combat drug consumption, production, and trafficking. These partnerships—including bilateral, regional, and multilateral initiatives—should reflect the common understanding that the drug problem negatively affects all countries within the Hemisphere and that all countries must bear and share responsibility to resolve it.

Central to this new approach is the abandonment of unilateral initiatives that have proved ineffective and disruptive to sustained bilateral and multilateral collaboration, including enforcement operations by U.S. agencies in Latin American countries. The United States should place more reliance on a comprehensive approach that highlights domestic programs and multilateral initiatives. All countries of the Americas should emphasize prevention programs targeting demand for drugs and programs for treatment and rehabilitation as well as interdiction and enforcement. The United States should support alternative development programs to reduce illicit drug production, judicial reform, and strengthening of viable democratic institutions. U.S. law enforcement agencies should support these efforts through training, information sharing, and liaison with Latin American counterparts.

A prominent example of the current unilateral approach to international drug control is the annual certification process, whereby the United States imposes sanctions on countries that are deemed "uncooperative" in narcotics control. While the certification process has produced some positive results, we believe that it has been, on balance, counterproductive. It has generated resentment in countries that are just as threatened by drug trafficking as the United States. This has made cooperation more difficult across a range of issues. It should be replaced by a multilateral process administered through the OAS. The goals of certification—compelling foreign cooperation in reducing drug production and drug trafficking—will be more effectively achieved through multilateral alternatives. Criteria for narcotics control cooperation would be established collaboratively and applied equally both to the United States and to other countries in the Hemisphere. Under this alternative process, individual governments could then determine what actions to take based on the OAS findings.

Immigration

Migration has joined global economic trends, sustainable development, the environment, and population growth as an important foreign policy issue. It is also an issue that is central in current political debates within this country. Latin American immigration into the United States both enriches our nation and broadens our links to Latin America. For this immigration to continue to benefit the United States, it must be legal and orderly. However, the exclusionary aspects of the 1996 Welfare Reform Act, which preclude legal immigrants from participating in social welfare programs to which they have contributed as taxpayers, should be repealed. Over the next two decades, changes in demographic trends, particularly in Mexico, may reduce the level of immigration. At the same time, U.S. policy should support economic growth and improved social conditions throughout the region to reduce the incentives to migrate.

Environment

As Latin America has moved toward democratic governments, the public is demanding increased attention to environmental concerns. This is a critical time for the United States to support Latin American efforts to address key issues: protecting biodiversity, developing and utilizing of renewable energy sources, improving water quality and supply. U.S. private and public agencies should expand transfer of relevant scientific information and technology. In addition, correcting cross-border pollution must be a shared responsibility with substantial monetary damages for transgressors. The United States should also collaborate with Latin American governments to establish a hemispheric disaster relief capacity that can respond to environmental emergencies such as the 1998 major brush/forest fires in southern Mexico and Central America.

Cuba

Cuba alone remains outside the Western democratic community. The United States should support efforts to facilitate Cuba's transitions toward democratic governments and free market economic reforms. U.S. policies should encourage increased contacts with the people of Cuba.

It is clear that the embargo has not accomplished its principal objectives. There is a need to introduce flexibility into our Cuban policy that does not undermine the ultimate goal of democracy in Cuba. Recent U.S. initiatives, including the resumption of direct flights, the easing of restrictions on humanitarian aid by the Catholic Church and others, and the U.S.–European Union accord on the Helms-Burton Law are important steps in the right direction. The United States should also move quickly to remove or reduce the remaining barriers to communication and the free flow of people and ideas by ending travel restrictions and encouraging professional and scholarly exchanges through such programs as the Fulbright Fellowships. The United States should facilitate the sale of medicine and medical supplies and equipment to Cuba. The U.S. should consider authorizing food sales through free market, nongovernmental channels, as well as expanding humanitarian assistance for the Cuban people. In addition, Congress should restore to the president the right to modify the embargo in response to positive changes in Cuba.

Final Observation

The United States is at a moment of choice. We can move forward, as this document strongly urges, to consolidate and to extend a mutually productive relationship with the rest of the Hemisphere. Or, as often in the past, we can hesitate and fail to seize the immediate opportunity.

No previous period has offered the potential rewards of the present: a chance to assure an integrated free market basis for continuing modernization and material progress; an opportunity to protect and enhance democracy within the region and to extend it to include Cuba; and a unique occasion to contribute to a world of more-available education and improved income distribution in which every American—both North and South—can flourish.

The choice is ours. And that decision will affect future generations throughout the 21st century.

Participants
The Ninety-Fourth American Assembly

MARIO L. BAEZA
Chairman and CEO
TCW/Latin American Partners
  L.L.C.
New York NY

††EVERETT ELLIS
  BRIGGS
President
Americas Society and
Council of Americas
New York NY

**EDWARD A. CASEY, JR.
Managing Director
Hills & Company
Washington DC

*JOHN H. COATSWORTH
Monroe Gutman Professor of
  Latin American Affairs
Director, David Rockefeller
  Center for Latin American
  Studies
Harvard University
Cambridge MA

**LEE CULLUM
Columnist
The Dallas Morning News
Dallas TX

MICHAEL E. CURTIN
Vice President
Bechtel Enterprises, Inc.
Washington DC

*Discussion Leader
**Rapporteur

†Delivered Formal Address
††Panelist

**RODOLFO O. DE LA GARZA
Mike Hogg Professor of Community Affairs, Department of Government &
Vice President, Tomás Rivera Policy Institute
University of Texas
Austin TX

I.M. DESTLER
Director
Center for International & Security Studies at Maryland
School of Public Affairs
College Park MD

††GUARIONE M. DIAZ
President
Cuban American National Council
Miami FL

JORGE I. DOMINGUEZ
Director
Weatherhead Center for International Affairs
Harvard University
Cambridge MA

STEPHEN J. DOYLE
Principal
The InterFlex Group
Madrid SPAIN

JOHN C. DUNCAN
Chairman
South American Gold and Copper Company, Ltd.
New York NY

GARY R. EDSON
President
ECG, Inc.
Chicago IL

**RICHARD M. ESTRADA
Associate Editor, Editorial Page
The Dallas Morning News
Dallas TX

*MATHEA FALCO
President
Drug Strategies
Washington DC

ERIC FARNSWORTH
Senior Advisor to the Counselor to the President and Special Envoy for the Americas
The White House
Washington DC

GEZA FEKETEKUTY
Director
Center for Trade & Commercial Diplomacy
Monterey Institute of International Studies
Monterey CA

ROBERT J. FILIPPONE
National Security Advisor
Office of Senator Bob Graham
United States Senate
Washington DC

†ALBERT FISHLOW
Paul A. Volcker Senior Fellow for International Economics
Council on Foreign Relations
New York NY

*Discussion Leader
**Rapporteur

†Delivered Formal Address
††Panelist

SHEPARD FORMAN
Director
Center on International
   Cooperation
New York University
New York NY

LACEY GALLAGHER
Director, Sovereign Ratings,
   Latin America
Standard & Poor's
New York NY

NELSON R. GONZALEZ
Associate Consultant
The Ulanov Partnership
New York NY

ROBERT M. HEINE
Director, International Trade
   and Investment
Dupont
Washington DC

†CARLA ANDERSON
   HILLS
Chairman and CEO
Hills & Company
Washington DC

GARY C. HUFBAUER
Director of Studies
Vice President
Maurice R. Greenberg Chair
Council on Foreign Relations
New York NY

††JAMES R. JONES
Former U.S. Ambassador to
   Mexico
New York NY

BARBARA KOTSCHWAR
Senior Trade Specialist
Organization of American
   States
Washington DC

ABRAHAM F.
   LOWENTHAL
President
Pacific Council on International
   Policy
Los Angeles CA

NORA LUSTIG
Chief
Poverty and Inequality Advisory
   Unit
Inter-American Development
   Bank
Washington DC

JENNIFER McCOY
Director-designate
Latin America and Caribbean
   Program
The Carter Center
Atlanta GA

†THOMAS F. McLARTY,
   III
Counselor to the President and
   Special Envoy for the
   Americas
The White House
Washington DC

BOB MILLER
Governor
State of Nevada
Carson City NV

*Discussion Leader
**Rapporteur

†Delivered Formal Address
††Panelist

MARTHA T. MUSE
Chairman
The Tinker Foundation Inc.
New York NY

††JOHN D. NEGROPONTE
Executive Vice President
Global Markets
The McGraw-Hill Companies
New York NY

SUSAN KAUFMAN
   PURCELL
Vice President
Americas Society
New York NY

RENATE RENNIE
President
The Tinker Foundation Inc.
New York NY

*MARK L. SCHNEIDER
Assistant Administrator
Bureau for Latin America & the
   Caribbean
U.S. Agency for International
   Development
Washington DC

**EDWARD SCHUMACHER
Managing Editor
The Wall Street Journal Americas
New York NY

DOROTHY MEADOW
   SOBOL
Assistant Vice President
Research & Market Analysis
   Group
Federal Reserve Bank of New
   York
New York NY

JEFFREY STARK
Director of Research and
   Studies
North-South Center at the
   University of Miami
Coral Gables FL

SIDNEY WEINTRAUB
William E. Simon Chair in
   Political Economy
Center for Strategic and
   International Studies
Washington DC

TIM WILKINS
Emerging Markets Reporter
Bloomberg News
New York NY

*Discussion Leader   †Delivered Formal Address
**Rapporteur   ††Panelist

About The American Assembly

The American Assembly was established by Dwight D. Eisenhower at Columbia University in 1950. It holds nonpartisan meetings and publishes authoritative books to illuminate issues of United States policy.

An affiliate of Columbia, the Assembly is a national, educational institution incorporated in the state of New York.

The Assembly seeks to provide information, stimulate discussion, and evoke independent conclusions on matters of vital public interest.

American Assembly Sessions

At least two national programs are initiated each year. Authorities are retained to write background papers presenting essential data and defining the main issues of each subject.

A group of men and women representing a broad range of experience, competence, and American leadership meet for several days to discuss the Assembly topic and consider alternatives for national policy.

All Assemblies follow the same procedure. The background papers are sent to participants in advance of the Assembly. The Assembly meets in small groups for four or five lengthy periods. All groups use the same agenda. At the close of these informal sessions participants adopt in plenary session a final report of findings and recommendations.

Regional, state, and local Assemblies are held following the national session at Arden House. Assemblies have also been held in England, Switzerland, Malaysia, Canada, the Caribbean, South America, Central America, the Philippines, and Japan. Over 160 institutions have cosponsored one or more Assemblies.

Arden House

The home of The American Assembly and the scene of the national sessions is Arden House, which was given to Columbia

University in 1950 by W. Averell Harriman. E. Roland Harriman joined his brother in contributing toward adaptation of the property for conference purposes. The buildings and surrounding land, known as the Harriman Campus of Columbia University, are fifty miles north of New York City.

Arden House is a distinguished conference center. It is self-supporting and operates throughout the year for use by organizations with educational objectives. The American Assembly is a tenant of this Columbia University facility only during Assembly sessions.

Index